Krishna's

NUMBER THEORY

for

Post Graduate Students of All Indian Universities

By

Hari Kishan
M.Phil., Ph.D.
Head, Department of Mathematics
D.N.College, Meerut
C.C.S. University, Meerut

[redacted] [redacted]

KRISHNA Prakashan Media (P) Ltd.
KRISHNA HOUSE, 11, Shivaji Road, Meerut-250 001 (U.P.), India

Krishna's

NUMBER THEORY

First Edition : 2004
Fourth Revised Edition : 2007
Fifteenth Edition : 2023
Edition : 2025

Book Code : 254–15 (A)

[redacted] : [redacted]

Published by : Sugam Rastogi & Kanupriya Rastogi
for KRISHNA Prakashan Media (P) Ltd.
11, Shivaji Road, Meerut – 250 001 (U.P.) India.
Phones : 91.121.2644766, 2642946, 4026111, 4026112 Fax : 91.121.2645855
Website : www.krishnaprakashan.com
E-mail : info@krishnaprakashan.com
Typesetting : DEBUGCC (The Computer Concern) Ghaziabad
Printed at : Shiv Offset Printers, Meerut.

Jai Shri Radhey Shyam

Dedicated to Lord Krishna

Author & Publishers

Preface to the First Edition

This book **'Number Theory'** has been written to meet the requirement of post graduate students of C.C.S. University, Meerut and other Universities. **'Number Theory'** is one of the oldest branch of Mathematics but no attempt has been made to give a Historical background of the subject. A simple and natural approach to various concepts has been adopted. The book has been written according to the latest revised syllabus.

The subject matter has been presented in such a clear and easy way that the students will have no difficulty in understanding it. The proofs of various theorems have been given in detail. Sufficient **solved examples** have been given in each chapter to illustrate the subject matter. Each chapter contains **exercise** to provide the student an opportunity to test his knowledge of the subject.

The author acknowledges his indebtness to various authors on the subject whose books have been consulted.

The author also acknowledges his indebtness to the publishers **M/s Krishna Prakashan Media (P) Ltd.**, Meerut and the printers for bringing out this book in the present nice form.

The author will feel amply rewarded if the book serves the purpose for which it is meant.

Constructive criticism and helpful suggestion for the improvement of the book will be gratefully accepted.

Preface to the Latest Edition

In this edition, the book has been revised and enlarged. New problems have been added. An attempt has been made to remove any type of mistakes of first edition.

Author will feel amply rewarded if the book serves the purpose for which it is meant. Constructive suggestion for the improvement of the book will be thankfully acknowledged.

–Hari Kishan

Syllabus

Number Theory

M.Sc. IVth Sem. (w.e.f. 2010–2011)

C.C.S. University, Meerut

The aim of the course is to give an introduction to elementary number theory, to show how certain number theoretical theorems can be applied within cryptography and to use the theory to solve simple Diophantine equations.

Contents

Division algorithm, the gcd, the Euclidean algorithm, the Diophantine equation

$$ax + by = c.$$

Fundamental theorem of arithmetic, Eratosthenes' sieve. Gold Bach conjecture. Basic properties of congruence, linear congruences. Fermat's theorem, Wilson's theorem. The functions τ and σ . Mobius inversion formula, the greatest integer function, Eular's function, Eular's theorem, Applications to cryptography. The order of an integer modulo n. Primitive roots for primes'theory of indices, Legendre's symbol and its properties, quadratic reciprocity, quadratic congruences with composite moduli. Sum of two squares, sum of more than two squares.

Detailed Contents

Chapters

CHAPTER 1 PRELIMINARIES

1.1 Introduction

Number theory is that branch of mathematics which deals with the properties of integers, more specifically the properties of positive integers. The positive integers are man's first mathematical creation. The first scientific approach to the study of integers, *i.e.*, the true origin of the theory of numbers, is attributed to the Greeks. Around 600 BC Pythagoras and his disciples made thorough study of integers. Euclid, Diophantus, Fermat, Euler, Gauss, Goldbach, Dirichlet and Ramanujan were among the main contributors of the theory of numbers. About the positive integers (natural numbers) Kronecker once remarked "God created the natural numbers and all the rest is the work of man." Number theory is an art enjoyable and pleasing to everybody. In this chapter, we shall discuss some preliminary concepts of number theory.

1.2 Well Ordering Principle

Every non-empty subset A of positive integers contains a smallest element *i.e.* A contains an element n such that $n \leqslant x \ \forall \ x \in A$.

Theorem (Archimedian Property)

For any two positive integers a and b there exists a positive integer n such that $na \geqslant b$.

Proof : We shall prove this result through contradiction. Suppose if possible there exists no positive integer n such that $na \geqslant b$. Then for any positive n we have $na < b$.

Let $A = \{b - na : n \in N\}$

Obviously A is a non-empty subset of positive integers. Therefore by well ordering property we have a smallest number say $b - n_1 a$ in A.

Now $b - (n_1 + 1)a$ also belongs to A and $b - (n_1 + 1)\,a = b - n_1 a - a$

$$< b - n_1 a.$$

Thus, $b - (n_1 + 1)a$ is a smaller number to $b - n_1 a$ in A. This contradicts the assumption that $b - n_1 a$ is the smallest element of A. Hence, there exists a positive integer n such that $na \geqslant b$.

1.3 Mathematical Induction

Theorem 1 : (Principle of Finite Induction)

Let A be a subset of positive integers N with the properties.

(*i*) $1 \in A$ and

(*ii*) whenever $m \in A \Rightarrow m + 1 \in A$

then, $$A = N.$$

Proof : Let $A \neq N$ and B be the set of all positive integers not in A *i.e.*,

$$B = \{n : n \in N, n \notin A\}$$

Since $A \neq N, B \neq \phi$. By well ordering property B must possess a least element say a. Then $a \notin A$.

Also $1 \in A$, $a > 1$. Then

$$a - 1 > 0 \text{ and } a - 1 < a \Rightarrow a - 1 \notin B$$
$$\Rightarrow a - 1 \in A$$

Now by (*ii*) $\quad (a - 1) + 1 = a \in A$

This is a contradiction. Hence, $A = N$

Second Principle of Finite Induction

Let A be a subset of positive integers N with the properties

(*i*) $1 \in A$ and

(*ii*) If m is a positive integer such that

$1, 2, \ldots. m \in A \Rightarrow (m + 1) \in A$

then $\quad A = N$

The first principle of finite induction is used more often than the second principle of finite induction but in some cases the second principle of finite induction is favoured in comparison to first.

Theorem 2 : The well ordering principle is equivalent to the principle of finite induction.

Proof : Suppose well ordering principle holds. Let A be a subset of positive integers satisfying the two conditions of principle of finite induction. Let $A \neq N$. Then $B = N - A \neq \phi$. By well ordering principle B has a least element say m. Now $m \notin A \Rightarrow m > 1 \Rightarrow 0 < m - 1 \Rightarrow m - 1 \notin B \Rightarrow m - 1 \in A$. Therefore, $m - 2, m - 3 \ldots. 2, 1$ all belongs to A. Hence, by second condition of induction $m \in A$ which is a contradiction. So $A = N$.

Conversely, suppose the principle of finite induction holds. Let A be a non-empty subset of positive integers. If $0 \in A$ then well ordering principle is obviously true. Suppose $0 \notin A$. Let $B = \{m : m \in N \text{ and } m \leqslant x \; \forall \; x \in A\}$. Obviously at least $1 \in B \Rightarrow B \neq \phi$. Also $B \neq N$ because if $k \in B$ then $k + 1 \notin B$. Therefore, second condition of principle of finite induction is violated *i.e.*, there exists an integer say m such that $m \in B$ but $m + 1 \notin B$. We shall show that m is the least element of A.

$$m \in B \Rightarrow m \leqslant x \; \forall \; x \in A. \text{ If } m \notin A \text{ then } m < x \; \forall \; x \in A$$

$$\Rightarrow m+1 \leqslant x \,\forall\, x \in A \Rightarrow m+1 \in B.$$

This is contradiction. Therefore, $m \in A$. Hence, well ordering principle holds.

Solved Examples

Example 1 : Establish the following formula by mathematical induction

$$1 + 3 + 5 + \ldots\ldots + (2n - 1) = n^2.$$

Solution : Let A be the set of all positive integers for which the given relation

$$P(n) : 1 + 3 + 5 + \ldots\ldots (2n - 1) = n^2 \qquad \ldots\ldots(1)$$

is valid.

For, $n = 1$ we have $\quad P(1) : 1 = 1^2 = 1$

which is true. This gives $1 \in A$.

Now suppose the result (1) is true for $n = m$ *i.e.*, $m \in A$ and

$$P(m) : 1 + 3 + 5 + \ldots\ldots (2m - 1) = m^2. \qquad \ldots\ldots(2)$$

Then for $n = m + 1$ we have

$$P(m+1) : 1 + 3 + 5 + \ldots\ldots (2m - 1) + (2m + 1)$$

$$= m^2 + 2m + 1 \qquad \text{[Using (2)]}$$

$$= (m + 1)^2.$$

This shows that the result (1) is true for $n = m + 1$. Thus, $m \in A \Rightarrow (m + 1) \in A$. Hence, by the principle of finite induction $A = N$ or the result (1) is true for all $n \geqslant 1$.

Example 2 : Establish the following formula by mathematical induction.

$$P(n) : 1^2 + 2^2 + 3^2 + \ldots\ldots n^2 = \frac{n(n+1)(2n+1)}{6} \text{ for } n \geqslant 1. \qquad \ldots\ldots(1)$$

Solution : Let A be the set of all positive integers for which the given relation (1) is valid.

For $n = 1$ we have

$$P(1) : 1^2 = \frac{1(1+1)(2.1+1)}{6}$$

or

$$1 = \frac{1 \times 2 \times 3}{6}$$

which is true. This gives $1 \in A$.

Now suppose the result (1) is true for $n = m$ *i.e.*, $m \in A$ and

$$P(m) : 1^2 + 2^2 + 3^2 + \ldots\ldots m^2 = \frac{m(m+1)(2m+1)}{6}. \qquad \ldots\ldots(2)$$

Then for $n = m + 1$ we have

$$P(m+1) : 1^2 + 2^2 + 3^2 + \ldots\ldots + m^2 + (m+1)^2$$

$$= \frac{m(m+1)(2m+1)}{6} + (m+1)^2 = \frac{(m+1)(2m^2 + m + 6m + 6)}{6}$$

$$= \frac{(m+1)[m+2][2m+3]}{6} = \frac{(m+1)(m+1+1)[2(m+1)+1]}{6}.$$

This shows that the given result (1) is valid for $n = m + 1$. Thus, $m \in A \Rightarrow m + 1 \in A$. Hence, by the principle of finite induction $A = N$ or the result is true for all $n \geqslant 1$.

Example 3 : Establish the following formula by mathematical induction

$$P(n) : 1(1!) + 2(2!) + 3(3!) + \ldots\ldots\ n(n!) = (n+1)! - 1,\ n \geqslant 1. \quad \ldots\ldots(1)$$

Solution : Let A be the set of all positive integers for which the given relation (1) is valid.

For $n = 1$ we have

$$P(1) : 1(1!) = 2! - 1$$

$$\Rightarrow \qquad 1 = 2 - 1$$

which is true. This gives $1 \in A$.

Now suppose the result (1) is true for $n = m$ *i.e.*, $m \in A$ and

$$1(1!) + 2(2!) + \ldots\ldots\ m(m!) = (m+1)! - 1. \quad \ldots\ldots(2)$$

Then for $n = m + 1$ we have

$$P(m+1) : 1(1!) + 2(2!) + \ldots\ldots\ m(m!) + (m+1)\,[(m+1)!]$$

$$= (m+1)! - 1 + (m+1)\,[(m+1)!]$$

$$= (m+1)!\,(m+1+1) - 1 = (m+1+1)! - 1.$$

This shows that the given result (1) is true for $n = m + 1$. Thus, $m \in A \Rightarrow m+1 \in A$. Hence, by the principle of mathematical induction $A = N$ or the result (1) is valid for all $n \geqslant 1$.

Example 4 : If a is any real number then show that

$$a^n - 1 = (a-1)\,(a^{n-1} + a^{n-2} + \ldots\ldots + 1)\ \forall\ n \geqslant 1$$

Solution : Let

$$P(n) : a^n - 1 = (a-1)(a^{n-1} + a^{n-2} + \ldots\ldots + 1). \quad \ldots\ldots(1)$$

For $n = 1$ we have

$$P(1) : a^1 - 1 = (a-1).1$$

which is true.

Now suppose $P(1), P(2), \ldots\ldots\ P(m)$ are all true *i.e.*,

$$P(m) : a^m - 1 = (a-1)\,(a^{m-1} + a^{m-2} + \ldots\ldots + 1).$$

Then $\quad P(m+1) : a^{m+1} - 1 = a^{m+1} + a^m - a^m + a - a - 1$

$$= a^m(a+1) - (a+1) - a(a^{m-1} - 1)$$

$$= (a+1)\,(a^m - 1) - a(a^{m-1} - 1)$$

$$= (a+1)\,[(a-1)\,(a^{m-1} + a^{m-2} + \ldots\ldots + 1)$$

$$- a[(a-1)\,(a^{m-2} + a^{m-3} + \ldots\ldots + 1)]$$

[By induction hypothesis]

$$= (a-1)\,[(a+1)\,(a^{m-1} + a^{m-2} + \ldots\ldots + 1)$$

$$- a\,(a^{m-2} + a^{m-3} + \ldots\ldots + 1)]$$

$$= (a-1)\,[a^m + a^{m-1} + a^{m-2} + \ldots\ldots + 1].$$

This shows that the result (1) is valid for $m + 1$. Hence, the result will be true for all positive integral values of $n \geqslant 1$.

Example 5 : Prove that for all $n \geqslant 1$, $\frac{n^5}{5}+\frac{n^3}{3}+\frac{7n}{15}$ is an integer.

Solution : Let

$P(n)$: $\frac{n^5}{5}+\frac{n^3}{3}+\frac{7n}{15}$ is an integer for all $n \geqslant 1$.

For $n = 1$, we have

$$P(1) : \frac{1^5}{5}+\frac{1^3}{3}+\frac{7.1}{15}=\frac{1}{5}+\frac{1}{3}+\frac{7}{15}$$

$$=\frac{3+5+7}{15}=1.$$

which is an integer. Therefore, the given result is true for $n = 1$.

Now suppose $P(1), P(2), \ldots\ldots., P(m)$ all are true *i.e.*,

$P(m)$: $\frac{m^5}{5}+\frac{m^3}{3}+\frac{7m}{15}$ is an integer.

Then

$$P(m+1) : \frac{(m+1)^5}{5}+\frac{(m+1)^3}{3}+\frac{7(m+1)}{15}$$

$$=\frac{m^5+5m^4+10m^3+10m^2+5m+1}{5}$$

$$+\frac{m^3+3m^2+3m+1}{3}+\frac{7m+7}{15}$$

$$=\left(\frac{m^5}{5}+\frac{m^3}{3}+\frac{7m}{15}\right)+(m^4+2m^3+3m^2+2m)+\left(\frac{1}{5}+\frac{1}{3}+\frac{7}{15}\right)$$

= an integer

[$\because$ $\frac{m^5}{5}+\frac{m^3}{3}+\frac{7m}{15}$ is an integer by induction hypothesis and $\frac{1}{5}+\frac{1}{3}+\frac{7}{15}=1$]

This shows that the given result is true for $(m+1)$. Hence the result will be true for all integral values of $n \geqslant 1$.

Example 6 : Prove that

$$\frac{1}{2.3}+\frac{1}{3.4}+\frac{1}{4.5}+\ldots.+\frac{1}{(n+1)(n+2)}=\frac{n}{2(n+2)}, \forall n \in N.$$

Solution : Let $P(n) : \frac{1}{2.3}+\frac{1}{3.4}+\frac{1}{4.5}+\ldots.+\frac{1}{(n+1)(n+2)}=\frac{n}{2(n+2)}, \forall n \in N$

For $n = 1$ we have

$$P(1) : \frac{1}{2.3}=\frac{1}{6}=\frac{1}{2(1+2)}.$$

This shows that the given result is true for $n = 1$

Now suppose $P(1), P(2), \ldots., P(m)$ all are true *i.e.*,

$$P(m) : \frac{1}{2.3}+\frac{1}{3.4}+\frac{1}{4.5}+\ldots.+\frac{1}{(m+1)(m+2)}=\frac{m}{2(m+2)}$$

Then $P(m+1): \frac{1}{2.3}+\frac{1}{3.4}+\frac{1}{4.5}+\ldots+\frac{1}{(m+1)(m+2)}+\frac{1}{(m+2)(m+3)}$

$$=\frac{m}{2(m+2)}+\frac{1}{(m+2)(m+3)}$$

$$=\frac{1}{2(m+2)}\left[m+\frac{2}{m+3}\right]$$

$$=\frac{1}{2(m+2)}\frac{[m^2+3m+2]}{(m+3)}$$

$$=\frac{(m+1)(m+2)}{2(m+2)(m+3)}=\frac{m+1}{2(m+1+2)}.$$

This shows that the result to true for $n=m+1$. Hence, by mathematical induction, the given result is true for all $n \in N$.

Example 7 : Show that $n! < \left(\frac{n+1}{2}\right)^n$ for all $n > 1$.

Solution : Let $P(n): n! < \left(\frac{n+1}{2}\right)^n \ \forall n > 1.$

Now for $n = 2$, we have

$$P(2): 2! = 2 < \left(\frac{2+1}{2}\right)^2 = \frac{9}{4}. \qquad \ldots\ldots(1)$$

This shows that the given result is true for $n = 2$.
Suppose the result is true for $n = m$ *i.e.*,

$$P(m): m! < \left(\frac{m+1}{2}\right)^m. \qquad \ldots\ldots(2)$$

Then for $n = m + 1$ we have

$$P(m+1): (m+1)! = (m+1)m!$$

$$< (m+1)\left(\frac{m+1}{2}\right)^m, \text{ [using (2)]}$$

$$=\frac{(m+1)^{m+1}}{2^m}. \qquad \ldots\ldots(3)$$

We have

$$\left(\frac{m+2}{m+1}\right)^{m+1} = \left(1+\frac{1}{m+1}\right)^{m+1} = 1+(m+1)\frac{1}{(m+1)}+\ldots > 2. \qquad \ldots\ldots(4)$$

Now from (3), we have

$$P(m+1) : (m+1)! < \frac{(m+1)^{m+1}}{2^m}$$

$$< \frac{(m+1)^{m+1}(m+2)^{m+1}}{2^{m+1}(m+1)^{m+1}} \qquad \text{[using (4)]}$$

$$= \left(\frac{m+1+1}{2}\right)^{m+1}$$

This shows that the given in equality is true for $n = m + 1$. Hence by mathematical induction the given inequalities is true for all $n > 1$.

Example 8 : Show that the sum of cubes of three consecutive natural numbers is divisible by 9.

Solution : Let $P(n)$: Sum of cubes of three consecutive natural numbers starting with n is divisible by 9.

For $n = 1$ we have

$$P(1) : 1^3 + 2^3 + 3^3 = 1 + 8 + 27 = 36$$

which is divisible by 9. Therefore, $P(1)$ is true.

Suppose $P(m)$ is true, *i.e.*, is divisible $m^3 + (m + 1)^3 + (m + 2)^3$ by 9 *i.e.*,

$$m^3 + (m+1)^3 + (m+3)^3 = 9k. \qquad ....(1)$$

We will show that $P(m + 1)$ is true *i.e.* $(m + 1)^3 + (m + 2)^3 + (m + 3)^3$ is divisible by 9.

We have

$$(m+1)^3 + (m+2)^3 + (m+3)^3$$
$$= (m+1)^3 + (m+2)^3 + m^3 + 9m^2 + 27m + 27$$
$$= m^3 + (m+1)^3 + (m+2)^3 + 9(m^2 + 3m + 3)$$
$$= 9k + 9[m^2 + 3m + 3], \quad \text{[using (1)]}$$
$$= 9(k + m^2 + 3m + 3).$$

This shows that $P(m + 1)$ is true. Hence, by mathematical induction, the result is true for all $n \in N$.

Example 9 : Show that every even power of each odd number greater than 1 when divided by 8 leaves the remainder 1.

Solution : The first odd number greater than 1 is 3 and the first even number is 2. We have $3^2 = 9 = 8 \times 1 + 1$.

Thus, 3^2 when divided by 8 leaves 1 as a remainder.

Now we assume that

$$(2m+1)^2 = 8k + 1 \qquad ....(1)$$

where k is same positive integer. We shall show that $(2m + 3)^2$ when divided by 8 leaves remainder 1.

We have

$$(2m+3)^2 - (2m+1)^2 = (2m+3+2m+1)(2m+3-2m-1)$$
$$= (4m+4)(2) = 8(m+1)$$

or

$$(2m+3)^2 = (2m+1)^2 + 8(m+1)$$

$$= 8k + 1 + 8(m + 1)$$

$$= 8(k + m + 1) + 1 \quad ....(2)$$

This shows that when $(2m + 3)^2$ is divided by 8 the remainder is 1. Hence, by, mathematical induction, it follows that when $(2n+1)^2, \forall n$ is divided by 8, the remainder is 1.

Now we assume that when $(2n + 1)^{2m}$ is divided by 8, the remainder is 1 *i.e.*, we consider

$$(2n + 1)^{2m} = 8k_1 + 1 \quad ....(3)$$

We shall show that when $(2n + 1)^{2m + 2}$, is divided by 8, the remainder is 1.

We have

$$(2n + 1)^{2m + 2} = (2n + 1)^{2m}.(2n + 1)^2$$

$$= (8k_1 + 1)(8k + 1), \quad \text{[using (1) and (2)].}$$

$$= 8[8kk_1 + k + k_1) + 1 \quad ....(4)$$

This shows that when $(2n + 1)^{2m + 2}$ is divided by 8, the remainder is 1.

Hence, by mathematical induction we have that when even power of an odd number greater than 1 is divided by 8, the remainder is 1.

Example 10 : Show that $\frac{(2n)!}{n!(n+1)!}$ is an integer.

Solution : Let $P(n) : \frac{(2n)!}{n!(n+1)!}$ is an integer.

For $n = 1$, we have

$$P(1) : \frac{(2.1)!}{1!(2)!} = 1$$

which is an integer. Therefore, the result is true for $n = 1$.

Now we assume that the result is true for $n = m$, *i.e.*,

$$P(m) : \frac{(2m)!}{m!(m+1)!} = k, \text{ an integer.}$$

We shall prove the result for $n = m + 1$. We have

$$P(m+1) : \frac{[2(m+1)!]}{(m+1)!(m+2)!} = \frac{(2m+2)(2m+1)(2m)!}{(m+1)(m+2)m!(m+1)!}$$

$$= \frac{2(2m+1)}{(m+2)}k$$

It can be seen that k is divisible by $(m + 2)$. Therefore $\frac{2(2m+1)}{m+2}.k$ is an integer.

Hence by mathematical induction $\frac{(2n)!}{n!(n+1)!}$ is an integer.

1.4 Binomial Coefficient

Let n be a positive integer and r another positive integer such that $0 \leqslant r \leqslant n$. Then, binomial coefficient $\binom{n}{r}$ is defined as

$$\binom{n}{r} = \frac{n!}{r!\,(n-r)!} = \frac{n\,(n-1)\,.....\,(n-r+1)\,(n-r)!}{r!\,(n-r)!}$$

$$= \frac{n\,(n-1)\,.....\,(n-r+1)}{r!}$$

Binomial coefficient can also be written as ${}^{n}C_{r}$.

$$\binom{n}{0} = \frac{n!}{0!\,(n-0)!} = \frac{n!}{n!} \qquad [\because 0! = 1]$$

$$= 1$$

$$\binom{n}{n} = \frac{n!}{n!\,(n-n)!} = \frac{n!}{n!\,0!} = \frac{n!}{n!} = 1.$$

Theorem 1 (Pascal's Rule) : Prove that

$$\binom{n}{r} + \binom{n}{r-1} = \binom{n+1}{r}, \ 1 \leqslant r \leqslant n$$

Proof : We have

$$\frac{1}{r} + \frac{1}{n-r+1} = \frac{n-r+1+r}{r\,(n-r+1)} = \frac{n+1}{r\,(n-r+1)}. \qquad ....(1)$$

Multiplying both sides of (1) by $\frac{n!}{(r-1)!\,(n-r)!}$, we get

$$\frac{n!}{r(r-1)!\,(n-r)!} + \frac{n!}{(r-1)!\,(n-r+1)\,(n-r)!}$$

$$= \frac{(n+1)\,n!}{(r-1)!\,r(n-r+1)\,(n-r)!}$$

$$\Rightarrow \quad \frac{n!}{r!\,(n-r)!} + \frac{n!}{(r-1)!\,(n-(r-1))!} = \frac{(n+1)!}{r!\,(n+1-r)!}$$

$$\Rightarrow \quad \binom{n}{r} + \binom{n}{r-1} = \binom{n+1}{r}.$$

Proved.

Theorem 2 : Show that each binomial coefficient $\binom{n}{r}$ $\forall\, n \geqslant 1$, and $\forall\, r$ satisfying $0 \leqslant r \leqslant n$, is an integer.

Proof : We shall prove this result by induction. For $n = 1$, we have $r = 0$ or 1 and

$$\binom{n}{r} = \binom{1}{0} = 1$$

$$\binom{n}{1} = \binom{1}{1} = 1.$$

Both are integers.

Now suppose the result is true for $n-1 \geqslant 1$ and $\forall\, r$ satisfying $0 \leqslant r \leqslant n-1$ *i.e.*, $\binom{n-1}{r}$ is an integer. We shall prove the result for n

Let $r \leqslant n$ be an integer. If $r = n$

Thus, $$\binom{n}{r} = \binom{n}{n} = 1$$

If $r < n$ then $r \leqslant n-1$ and $$\binom{n}{r} = \binom{n-1}{r-1} + \binom{n-1}{r}$$

But according to our assumption $\binom{n-1}{r}$ and $\binom{n-1}{r-1}$ are integer. Therefore, $\binom{n}{r}$ is an integer. Hence, by induction, the binomial coefficients $\binom{n}{r}$ are integers.

Theorem 3 : Show that

$$(a+b)^n = \sum_{r=0}^{n} \binom{n}{r} a^{n-r} b^r$$

Proof : We shall prove this result by induction.

For $n = 1$

$$(a+b)^1 = \sum_{r=0}^{1} \binom{1}{r} a^{1-r} b^r = \binom{1}{0} a^{1-0} b^0 + \binom{1}{1} a^{1-1} b^1 = a + b$$

which is true.

Now suppose the result is true for $n = m$ *i.e.*,

$$(a+b)^m = \sum_{r=0}^{m} \binom{m}{r} a^{m-r} b^r$$

Then $$(a+b)^{m+1} = (a+b)^m (a+b) = \left[\sum_{r=0}^{m} \binom{m}{r} a^{m-r} b^r\right][a+b]$$

$$= a \sum_{r=0}^{m} \binom{m}{r} a^{m-r} b^r + b \sum_{r=0}^{m} \binom{m}{r} a^{m-r} b^r$$

$$= \sum_{r=0}^{m} \binom{m}{r} a^{m+1-r} b^r + \sum_{r=0}^{m} \binom{m}{r} a^{m-r} b^{r+1}$$

$$= a^{m+1} + \sum_{r=1}^{m} \binom{m}{r} a^{m+1-r} b^r + \sum_{r=1}^{m} \binom{m}{r-1} a^{m+1-r} b^r + b^{m+1}$$

$$= a^{m+1} + \sum_{r=1}^{m} \left[\binom{m}{r} + \binom{m}{r-1}\right] a^{m+1-r} b^r + b^{m+1}$$

$$= \sum_{r=0}^{m+1} \binom{m+1}{r} a^{m+1-r} b^r$$

Proved.

This shows that the result is true for $n = m + 1$. Hence, by induction the result will be true for all positive integral values of n.

1.5 Pascal's Triangle

The configuration given below is called Pascal's triangle

				1		1				
			1		2		1			
		1		3		3		1		
	1		4		6		4		1	
1		5		10		10		5		1

In this Pascal's triangle the binomial coefficient $\binom{n}{r}$ is the $(r + 1)$th element in the nth row.

Solved Examples

Example 1 : Show that product of any r consecutive integers is divisible by $r!$.

Solution : Let $P = (n-r)(n-r+1) \ldots\ldots. (n-1)$ be the product of r consecutive integers.

Thus, $$P = \frac{(n-r)(n-r+1)\ldots(n-1)(n-r-1)\ldots 2.1}{(n-r-1)\ldots 2.1}$$

$$= \frac{1.2\ldots(n-r-1)(n-r)\ldots(n-1)}{2.1\ldots(n-1-r)}$$

$$= \frac{(n-1)!}{(n-1-r)!} = \frac{(n-1)!\, r!}{r!\,(n-1-r)!} = \binom{n-1}{r} r!. \qquad \ldots\ldots.(1)$$

Since $\binom{n-1}{r}$ is an integer, it is obvious from (1) that P is divisible by $r!$.

Example 2 : Prove that

$$\sum_{r=0}^{n-1} \left[\binom{n}{r} + \binom{n}{r+1}\right] = 2[2^n - 1]$$

Solution : We have

$$\text{L.H.S.} = \sum_{r=0}^{n-1} \left[\binom{n}{r} + \binom{n}{r+1}\right] = \sum_{r=0}^{n-1} \binom{n+1}{r+1}$$

$$= \binom{n+1}{1} + \binom{n+1}{2} + \ldots \binom{n+1}{n}$$

$$= 1 + \binom{n+1}{1} + \binom{n+1}{2} + \ldots \binom{n+1}{n} + 1 - 2$$

$$= \binom{n+1}{0} + \binom{n+1}{1} + \binom{n+1}{2} + \ldots.. + \binom{n+1}{n+1} - 2$$

$$= 2^{n+1} - 2 = 2[2^n - 1].$$

Proved.

Example 3 : Prove that for $n \geqslant 1$

$$\binom{2n}{n} = \frac{1.3.5 \ldots (2n-1)}{n!} 2^n$$

Solution : We have

$$\binom{2n}{n} = \frac{(2n)!}{n!\,(2n-n)!}$$

$$= \frac{2n\,(2n-1) \ldots (n+1) n\,(n-1) \ldots 2.1}{n!\,n!}$$

$$= \frac{(2n-1) \ldots 3.1.2n\,(2n-2) \ldots 2}{n!}$$

$$= \frac{1.3 \ldots (2n-1) n\,(n-1) \ldots 1}{n!\,n!} \times 2^n$$

$$= \frac{1.3 \ldots (2n-1) n!}{n!\,n!} \times 2^n$$

$$= \frac{1.3 \ldots (2n-1)}{n!} \times 2^n.$$

Proved

Example 4 : If $2 \leqslant r \leqslant n-2$ then show that

$$\binom{n}{r} = \binom{n-2}{r-2} + 2\binom{n-2}{r-1} + \binom{n-2}{r}$$

Solution : We have

$$\text{R.H.S.} = \binom{n-2}{r-2} + 2\binom{n-2}{r-1} + \binom{n-2}{r}$$

$$= \binom{n-2}{r-2} + \binom{n-2}{r-1} + \binom{n-2}{r-1} + \binom{n-2}{r}$$

$$= \binom{n-1}{r-1} + \binom{n-1}{r} \qquad \left[\because \binom{n}{r-1} + \binom{n}{r} = \binom{n+1}{r}\right.$$

$$= \binom{n}{r}$$

$$= \text{L.H.S.}$$

Proved

Example 5 : Show that

$$\binom{n}{0}-\frac{1}{2}\binom{n}{1}+\frac{1}{3}\binom{n}{2}\ldots+\frac{(-1)^n}{n+1}\binom{n}{n}=\frac{1}{n+1}$$

Solution : We have

$$\text{L.H.S.} = \binom{n}{0}-\frac{1}{2}\binom{n}{1}+\frac{1}{3}\binom{n}{2}\ldots+\frac{(-1)^n}{n+1}\binom{n}{n}$$

$$=\frac{1}{n+1}\left[\binom{n+1}{1}-\binom{n+1}{2}+\binom{n+1}{3}\ldots+(-1)^n\binom{n+1}{n+1}\right]$$

$$=\frac{1}{n+1}\left[1-1+\binom{n+1}{1}-\binom{n+1}{2}+\ldots+(-1)^n\binom{n+1}{n+1}\right]$$

$$=\frac{1}{n+1}\left[1-\left\{\binom{n+1}{0}-\binom{n+1}{1}+\binom{n+1}{2}\ldots\ldots+(-1)^n\binom{n+1}{n+1}\right\}\right]$$

$$=\frac{1}{n+1}\left[1-(1-1)^{n+1}\right]$$

$$=\frac{1}{n+1}$$

= R.H.S. **Proved**

1.6 Basis Representation Theorem

For a fixed integer $k>1$ every positive integer n has a unique representation of the form

$$n = a_0k^r + a_1k^{r-1} + \ldots\ldots + a_r,\quad a_0 \neq 0,\quad 0 \leqslant a_i < n,$$
$$i = 0, 1, \ldots\ldots r.$$

Proof : First we shall show the existence of such representation and then the uniqueness of the representation.

Existence :

Case (i) : $n<k$ then n is the unique representation of n.

Case (ii) : $n=k$. Then $n = 1.k + 0$. This is also unique representation.

Case (iii) : $n>k$. Then there exists unique integers q and r such that

$$n = qk + r,\ 0 \leqslant r < k$$

If $q<k$ we take $q = a_0$ and $r = a$. Thus.

$$n = a_0k + a_1$$

This is unique representation of n.

If $q \geqslant k$ then there exists integers q_1 and r_1 such that $q = q_1k + r_1,\ 0 \leqslant r_1 < k$

If $q_1 < k$ then

$$n = (q_1k + r_1)k + r$$
$$= q_1k^2 + r_1k + r.$$

We take $q_1 = a_0$, $r_1 = a_1$ and $r = a_2$. Then

$$n = a_0 k^2 + a_1 k + a_2 \text{ is the required representation.}$$

If $q_1 \geqslant k$. We continue the process. The process terminates after a finite number of steps and we get

$$n = a_0 k^r + a_1 k^{r-1} + \ldots\ldots + a_r$$

Uniqueness : Suppose if possible n has two different representation

$$n = a_0 k^{r_1} + a_1 k^{r_1 - 1} + \ldots\ldots + a_{r_1},\ a_0 \neq 0,\ 0 \leqslant a_i < k \qquad \ldots\ldots(1)$$
$$0 \leqslant i \leqslant r_1 - 1$$

and
$$n = b_0 k^{r_2} + b_1 k^{r_2 - 1} + \ldots\ldots + br_2,\ b_0 \neq 0,\ 0 \leqslant b_i < k \qquad \ldots\ldots(2)$$
$$0 \leqslant i \leqslant r_2 - 1$$

Now r_1 and r_2 are integers we have either

$$r_1 > r_2 \quad \text{or} \quad r_1 = r_2 \quad \text{or} \quad r_1 < r_2.$$

Suppose $r_1 > r_2$. Then

$$k^{r_1} = (k-1) \sum_{i=0}^{r_1 - 1} k^i + 1$$

$$\therefore \quad n = a_0 \left[(k-1) \sum_{i=0}^{r_1 - 1} k^i + 1 \right] + b_0 k^{r_2} + \ldots + b_{r_2}$$

$$= c_0 k^{r_1} + c_1 k^{r_1 - 1} + \ldots\ldots + c_{r_1},\ 0 \leqslant c_i < k,\ c_0 \neq 0$$
$$0 \leqslant i \leqslant r_1 - 1 \qquad \ldots\ldots(3)$$

Thus, we may assume two different representation of n with same number of terms given below :

$$x = a_0 k^{r_1} + a_1 k^{r_1 - 1} + \ldots\ldots + a_{r_1},\ 0 \leqslant a_i \leqslant k,\ a_0 \neq 0 \qquad \ldots\ldots(4)$$
$$0 \leqslant i \leqslant r_1 - 1$$

and
$$x = b_0 k^{r_1} + b_1 k^{r_1 - 1} + \ldots\ldots + b_{r_1},\ 0 \leqslant b_i < k,\ b_0 \neq 0 \qquad \ldots\ldots(5)$$
$$0 \leqslant i \leqslant r_1 - 1$$

Let i be the largest integer such that $a_i \neq b_i$ then

$$a_{i+1} = b_{i+1},\ \ldots\ldots\ a_{r_1} = b_{r_1}$$

Now from (4) and (5), we have

$$(a_0 - b_0) k^{r_1} + (a_1 - b_1) k^{r_1 - 1} + \ldots\ldots\ (a_i - b_i) k^i = 0$$

Since $k > 1$ and $i < r_1$ we have

$$a_i - b_i = -k[(a_0 - b_0) k^{r_1 - i - 1} + \ldots\ldots\ (a_{i-1} - b_{i-1})]$$

This shows that $k \mid (a_i - b_i)$. This is false as a_i, b_i both are less than k. This is contradiction. Hence, representation must be unique.

Example 1 : Write 308 in decimal system.

Solution : We have

$$308 = 30 \times 10 + 8$$
$$30 = 3 \times 10$$
$$\therefore \quad 308 = 3 \times 10 \times 10 + 8$$
$$= 3 \times 10^2 + 0 \times 10 + 8$$

This can be written as $308 = (308)_{10}$.

Example 2 : Write 347 with base 8.

Solution : We have

$$347 = 43 \times 8 + 3$$
$$43 = 5 \times 8 + 3$$
$$\therefore \quad 347 = (5 \times 8 + 3)\, 8 + 3$$
$$= 5 \times 8^2 + 3 \times 8 + 3$$

This can be written as $347 = (533)_8$.

Example 3 : Add $(5624)_7$ and $(4536)_7$ without change of base.

Solution : We add the given numbers with base 7.

Thus, we have

$$\begin{array}{r} 5624 \\ 4536 \\ \hline (13463)_7 \end{array} \qquad [\because\ 4 +_7 6 = 3 \text{ with carry } 1]$$

Example 4 : Write 25 with base 2.

Solution : We have

$$25 = 12 \times 2 + 1$$
$$12 = 6 \times 2 + 0$$
$$6 = 3 \times 2 + 0$$
$$3 = 1 \times 2 + 1$$
$$\therefore \quad 25 = 12 \times 2 + 1$$
$$= (6 \times 2 + 0)2 + 1$$
$$= 6.2^2 + 1$$
$$= (3.2 + 0)\, 2^2 + 1$$
$$= 3.2^3 + 1$$
$$= [\{(1.2 + 1)\, 2^3\} + 1]$$
$$= 1.2^4 + 1.2^3 + 1$$
$$= 1.2^4 + 1.2^3 + 0.2^2 + 0.2 + 1$$

Thus, $\quad 25 = (11001)_2$.

Example 5 : Prove that if

$$a_r k^r + a_{r-1} k^{r-1} + \ldots\ldots + a_0$$

is a representation of *n* to the base k then $0 < n \leqslant k^{r+1} - 1$.

Solution : We have

$$0 < n = a_r k^r + a_{r-1} k^{r-1} + \ldots\ldots + a_0$$

$$\leqslant 1.k^r + 1.k^{r-1} + \ldots\ldots + 1.$$

$$= k^r + k^{r-1} + \ldots\ldots + 1 = \frac{k^{r+1} - 1}{k - 1}$$

$$\leqslant \frac{k^{r+1} - 1}{2 - 1} \qquad [\because k \geqslant 2]$$

$$= k^{r+1} - 1.$$

Proved

Example 6 : We have a set of standard weights of

$$1, 2, 2^2, \ldots\ldots 2^{k-1}.$$

What is the maximum weight which can be weighs with the help of these weights?

Solution : The maximum weight that can be weighed with the help of these weights will be equal to

$$1 + 2 + 2^2 + \ldots\ldots 2^{k-1} = \frac{[2^k - 1]}{[2 - 1]}$$

$$= 2^k - 1.$$

∎

EXERCISE

1. Establish the following by mathematical induction

$$1.2 + 2.3 + 3.4 + \ldots\ldots + n(n+1) = \frac{n(n+1)(n+2)}{3}, n \geq 1$$

2. Establish the following by mathematical induction.

$$1^2 + 3^2 + 5^2 + \ldots\ldots + (2n-1)^2 = \frac{n(4n^2-1)}{3}, n \geq 1$$

3. Prove by mathematical induction

$$\frac{1}{1^2} + \frac{1}{2^2} + \frac{1}{3^2} + \ldots \frac{1}{n^2} < 2 - \frac{1}{n}$$

4. Show that

$$\binom{n}{0} + \binom{n}{1} + \binom{n}{2} + \ldots \binom{n}{n} = 2^n$$

5. Show that

$$\binom{n}{0} + 2\binom{n}{1} + 2^2\binom{n}{2} + \ldots 2^n\binom{n}{n} = 3^n$$

6. Show that

$$\binom{n}{0} + \binom{n}{2} + \binom{n}{4} + \ldots = \binom{n}{1} + \binom{n}{3} + \binom{n}{5} + \ldots = 2^{n-1}$$

7. Show that

$$\binom{2}{2} + \binom{3}{2} + \binom{4}{2} + \ldots \binom{n}{2} = \binom{n+1}{3}, n \geq 2.$$

8. Show that $\frac{(2n)!}{n!\,(n+1)!}$ is an integer.

9. Prove that

$$\frac{1}{1.2} + \frac{1}{2.3} + \frac{1}{3.4} + \ldots + \frac{1}{n(n+1)} = \frac{n}{n+1}$$

10. Prove that

$$1 + 3 + 5 + \ldots\ldots (2n-1) = n^2.$$

11. If $F_1 = 1, F_2 = 1, F_n = F_{n-1} + F_{n-2}$. For $n \geq 3$. (F_n is called Fibonacci number), then show that

$$F_1 + F_2 + \ldots\ldots + F_n = F_{n+2} - 1.$$

12. If $L_1 = 1$ and $L_n = F_{n+1} + F_{n-1}$ for $n \geq 2$. (L_n is the Lucas numbers). Then show that

$$L_n = L_{n-1} + L_{n-2}.\ (n \geq 3).$$

13. Convert 4385 to the base 9. **[Ans. $(6012)_9$]**

14. We have a set of standard weights of 1, 3, 3^2, ... 3^{k-1}.
What is the maximum weight that can be weight with the help of these weights ?

[Ans. $(\frac{1}{2})3^k - 1)$].

❑

CHAPTER 2

DIVISIBILITY THEORY

2.1 Introduction

Divisibility property in the set of integers is an important property in number theory. When we divide an integer by another integer the result is not always an integer. It seems like an obstacle. But it is not so. The existence of number theory depends on this very fact. If the division of one integer by another integer always produced an integer then it is not an exaggeration to say that there would be no existence of number theory. Consequently then mathematicians would have been deprived of this fascinating branch of Mathematics. In this chapter we shall discuss divisibility theory of integers.

2.2 Divisibility

An integer a is said to be divisible by an integer b ($\neq 0$) if there exists an integer q such that $a = bq$. It is denoted as $b|a$.

In other words we can say that a is a multiple of b.

For example 39 is divisible by 13 as $39 = 13 \times 3$. Thus, $13|39$.

If b divides a then $-b$ also divides a because $a = bq \Rightarrow a = (-b)\cdot(-q)$. Therefore, **we will discuss the divisibility by positive integers unless stated otherwise.**

Some Important Results

For integers a, b, c and d, we have

(*i*) $a|0$, $1|a$ and $a|a$

(*ii*) $a|b$ and $c|d \Rightarrow ac|bd$

(*iii*) $a|b$ and $b|c \Rightarrow a|c$ (Transitivity)

(*iv*) $a|b$ and $b|a \Rightarrow a = \pm b$.

(*v*) $a|b$ and $a|c \Rightarrow a|bx + cy$, for all integers x, y.

Some Theorems

Theorem 1 : If $c = ax + by$ and $d|a$ but $d \nmid c$ then $d \nmid b$.

Proof : We have

$d|a \Rightarrow \exists$ an integer q_1 such that

$$a = dq_1$$

Therefore, $$c = ax + by = dq_1x + by$$

Suppose $d|b \Rightarrow \exists$ an integer q_2 such that $b = dq_2$.

Therefore, $c = dq_1x + dq_2y = d(q_1x + q_2y)$

$$\Rightarrow d \mid c$$

Contrapositively

$$d \nmid c \Rightarrow d \nmid b$$

Theorem 2 : If integer *b* divides a positive integer *a* then *b* is not numerically greater than *a*.

Proof : We have

$b \mid a \Rightarrow \exists$ an integer q (with $|q| \geqslant 1$)

such that $a = bq$

Hence, $a = |a| = |bq|$

$$= |b||q|$$

$$\geqslant |b|$$

2.3 Division Algorithm

Theorem 1 : For given integers *a* and *b* > 0 there exist unique integers *q* and *r* such that

$$a = bq + r,\ 0 \leqslant r < b$$

The integers *q* and *r* are called the quotient and the remainder respectively.

(C.C.S.U. 2004)

Proof : We consider the infinite sequence of multiples of b given below :

$$\ldots\ldots\ldots, -b, 0, b, \ldots\ldots\ bq \ldots\ldots$$

Then obviously either a must be equal to one of the multiples of b say bq in this sequence or it must lie between two consecutive multiples say bq and $b(q + 1)$. Thus, we have

$$bq \leqslant a < b(q+1) \text{ for some } q$$

$$\Rightarrow \quad 0 \leqslant a - bq < b$$

Let $a - bq = r$. Then we have

$$a = bq + (a - bq)$$

$$= bq + r,\ 0 \leqslant r < b$$

This completes the existence part of the theorem. For uniqueness we assume the possibility of two different representations of a as given below :

$$a = bq + r,\quad 0 \leqslant r < b$$

and $a = bq_1 + r_1,\ 0 \leqslant r_1 < b$

for some integers q, q_1, r and r_1.

These two equations imply that

$$bq + r = bq_1 + r_1$$

or $bq - bq_1 = r_1 - r$

or $b(q - q_1) = r_1 - r$

or $r_1 - r = b(q - q_1)$

This shows that b divides $r_1 - r$. But this is not possible because both r and r_1 are positive integers less than b. Hence, q and r must be unique.

This theorem is known as Division Algorithm **Proved.**

Theorem 2 : For any two integers a and $b > 0$ there exists integers q_1 and r_1 such that

$$a = bq_1 + er_1,\ 0 \leqslant r_1 < b/2,\ e = +1 \text{ or } -1.$$

Proof : By division algorithm, we have

$$a = bq + r,\ 0 \leqslant r < b. \qquad \text{.......(1)}$$

Now we consider the following cases :

Case I : $r < b/2$. If we take $q_1 = q$, $r_1 = r$ and $e = 1$ then from (1), we have

$$a = bq_1 + er_1,\ 0 \leqslant r_1 < b/2$$

Case II : $r > b/2$. Then $0 < b - r < b/2$. If we take $q_1 = q + 1$, $r_1 = b - r$ and $e = -1$ then from (1), we have

$$a = b(q + 1) - (b - r)$$
$$= bq_1 + er_1,\ 0 \leqslant r_1 < b/2$$

Case III : $r = b/2$: If we take

$$q_1 = q,\ r_1 = r$$

and $e = 1$ in (1) we have

$$a = bq_1 + er_1,\ r_1 = b/2$$

Also if we put $q_1 = q + 1$, $r_1 = b - r$ and $e = -1$, we have

$$a = b(q + 1) - (b - r)$$
$$= bq_1 + er_1,\ r_1 = b/2.$$

Proved

Theorem 3 : Every integer is of the form

(i) **$3q$ or $(3q \pm 1)$**

(ii) **$4q$, $(4q \pm 1)$ or $(4q \pm 2)$**

(iii) **$5q$, $(5q \pm 1)$ or $(5q \pm 2)$**

Proof : Let a be an integer.

(i) Taking $b = 3$ in theorem (2) we have

$$a = 3q_1 + er_1,\ 0 \leqslant r_1 \leqslant 3/2,\ e = \pm 1.$$

Therefore, $r_1 = 0$ or 1. Hence,

$$a = 3q \quad \text{or} \quad 3q \pm 1.$$

(ii) Taking $b = 4$ in theorem (2) we have

$$a = 4q_1 + er_1,\ 0 \leqslant r_1 \leqslant 4/2,\ e = \pm 1.$$

Therefore, $r_1 = 0, 1, 2$. Hence,

$$a = 4q,\ (4q \pm 1) \text{ or } (4q \pm 2).$$

(iii) Taking $b = 5$ in theorem (2) we have

$$a = 5q_1 + er_1,\ 0 \leqslant r_1 \leqslant 5/2,\ e = \pm 1.$$

Therefore, $r_1 = 0, 1, 2$. Hence,

$$a = 5q,\ (5q \pm 1) \text{ or } (5q \pm 2).$$

Proved.

Theorem 4 : Every odd integer is of the form

(*i*) $2q + 1$
(*ii*) $2q - 1$
(*iii*) $4q \pm 1$
(*iv*) $\pm (4q + 1)$

Proof : Since $2q$ is an even integer, we have $2q + 1$ and $2q - 1$ are odd integers. Also we know that every integer has one of the form $4q$, $(4q \pm 1)$, $(4q \pm 2)$ in which $4q$ and $4q \pm 2$ are even integers. Therefore, $(4q \pm 1)$ are odd integers. Now $4q - 1 = -(-4q + 1) = -(4(-q) + 1)$. So $\pm (4q + 1)$ is an odd integer. Thus, every odd integer is of the form (*i*) $2q + 1$, (*ii*) $2q - 1$, (*iii*) $4q \pm 1$, (*iv*) $\pm (4q + 1)$.

Theorem 5 : The square of an odd integer is of the form $8q + 1$.

Proof : Let n be an odd integer. Then we have $a = (4q_1 + 1)$ or $a = -(4q_1 + 1)$ for same integer q_1.

Now

$$\begin{aligned} a^2 &= [\pm (4q_1 + 1)]^2 \\ &= 16q_1^2 + 8q_1 + 1 \\ &= 8(2q_1^2 + q_1) + 1 \\ &= 8q + 1, \qquad \text{where } q = 2q_1^2 + q_1 \text{ is an integer.} \end{aligned}$$

This shows that square of an odd integer is of the form $8q + 1$.

Theorem 6 : One of every three consecutive integers is divisible by 3.

(C.C.S.U. 2005, B.P. 2006)

Proof : Let a, $(a + 1)$, $(a + 2)$ be any three consecutive integers. Then a is of the form $3q$, $(3q + 1)$ or $(3q - 1)$. If $a = 3q$ then it is divisible by 3. If $a = 3q + 1$ then $a + 2 = 3q + 1 + 2 = 3q + 3 = 3(q + 1)$ is divisible by 3. If $a = 3q - 1$ then $a + 1 = 3q - 1 + 1 = 3q$ is divisible by 3. Thus, one of every three consecutive integers is divisible by 3.

Theorem 7 : The product of any three consecutive integers is divisible by 3 !

(C.C.S.U. 2004)

Proof : Let a, $(a + 1)$ and $(a + 2)$ be any three consecutive integers. Then we have to show that $a(a + 1)(a + 2)$ is divisible by 3 ! we shall prove this result by mathematical induction.

For $a = 1$ we have

$$a(a + 1)(a + 2) = 1.2.3$$

which is obviously divisible by 3 ! Thus, result is true for $a = 1$.

Let the result be true for $a = k$ *i.e.*, $k(k + 1)(k + 2)$ is divisible by 3!. Then for $a = k + 1$ we have

$$\begin{aligned} a(a + 1)(a + 2) &= (k + 1)(k + 2)(k + 3) \\ &= k(k + 1)(k + 2) + 3(k + 1)(k + 2) \qquad \text{.......(1)} \end{aligned}$$

The first form on the R.H.S. of (1) is divisible by 3! by our assumption. The second term on the R.H.S. of (1) is also divisible by 3! because $(k + 1)(k + 2)$ is divisible by $2! = 2$

Thus, $a(a + 1)(a + 2)$ is divisible by 3! for $a = k + 1$ *i.e.*, the result is true for $a = k + 1$.

Hence, by mathematical induction the product of any three consecutive integers is divisible by 3!

Example 1 : Find the minimal remainder of 217 with respect to 39.

Solution : We have

$$217 = 39 \times 5 + 22.$$

Here the remainder $22 > \frac{39}{2}$. Therefore, the minimal remainder

$$= -(39 - 22) = -17$$

This is verified as follows :

$$217 = 39 \times 6 - 1\ (17)$$

where $$0 < 17 < (39/2).$$

Example 2 : If a and b are any two odd integers. Then one of the two numbers $\frac{a+b}{2}$ and $\frac{a-b}{2}$ is odd and the other is even.

Solution : Let $a = 2n_1 + 1$ and $b = 2n_2 + 1$ where n_1 and n_2 are any two integers. Then we have,

$$\frac{a+b}{2} = \frac{2n_1 + 1 + 2n_2 + 1}{2} = (n_1 + n_2) + 1 \quad ....(1)$$

and $$\frac{a-b}{2} = \frac{(2n_1 + 1) - (2n_2 + 1)}{2} = (n_1 + n_2). \quad ....(2)$$

From (1) and (2) we see that if n_1 and n_2 are both even (or both odd) then $\frac{(a+b)}{2}$ is an odd integer and $\frac{(a-b)}{2}$ is an even integer.

If one of n_1 and n_2 is even and the other is odd then from (1) and (2) we see that $\frac{(a+b)}{2}$ is an even integer and $\frac{(a-b)}{2}$ is an odd integer.

Thus, if a and b are any two integers then one of the two numbers $\frac{(a+b)}{2}$ and $\frac{(a-b)}{2}$ is odd and the other is even.

Example 3 : Show that the number of the form $\frac{a(a^2+2)}{3}$ is an integer where a is an integer $\geqslant 1$.

Solution : We know that every integer a is of the form $3q$, $3q + 1$ or $3q + 2$.

Now if $a = 3q$ then

$$\frac{a[a^2+2]}{3} = \frac{3q[(3q)^2+2]}{3} = q[9q^2+1]$$

which is an integer.

If $a = 3q + 1$ then

$$\frac{a[a^2+2]}{3} = \frac{(3q+1)[(3q+1)^2+2]}{3}$$

$$= \frac{(3q+1)[9q^2+6q+1+2]}{3}$$

$$= \frac{(3q+1)[9q^2+6q+3]}{3}$$

$$= (3q+1)[3q^2+2q+1]$$

which is an integer.

If $a = 3q + 2$ then

$$\frac{a[a^2+2]}{3} = \frac{(3q+2)[(3q+2)^2+2]}{3}$$

$$= \frac{(3q+2)[(9q^2+12q+4+2]}{3}$$

$$= (3q+2)[3q^2+4q+2]$$

which is an integer.

Thus, a number of the form $\frac{a[a^2+2]}{3}$ is an integer where a is an integer $\geqslant 1$.

Example 4 : If a is an odd integer then show that $\frac{a^4+4a^2+11}{16}$ is an integer.

Solution : Let $a = 2k + 1$ then

$$= \frac{a^4+4a^2+11}{16} = \frac{(2k+1)^4+4[2k+1]^2+11}{16}$$

$$= \frac{16k^4+4.(2k)^3+6(2k)^2+4(2k)+1+4(4k^2+4k+1)+11}{16}$$

$$= \frac{16k^4+32k^3+24k^2+8k+1+16k^2+16k+4+11}{16}$$

$$= \frac{16k^4+32k^3+40k^2+24k+16}{16}$$

$$= k^4+2k^3+1+\frac{k[5k+3]}{2}$$

Now obviously $\frac{k[5k+3]}{2}$ an integer if k is even integer. If k is an odd then $5k+3$ is an even integer. Therefore, $\frac{k[5k+3]}{2}$ is an even integer. Hence, the given quantity $\frac{a^4+4a^2+11}{16}$ is an integer.

Example 5 : If *a* is odd integer then show that $\frac{a^4+(a+2)^3+(a+4)^2+1}{12}$ is an integer.

Solution : Let $a = 2k+1$ then

$$= \frac{a^4+(a+2)^2+(a+4)^2+1}{12}$$

$$= \frac{(2k+1)^4+(2k+1+2)^2+(2k+1+4)^2+1}{12}$$

$$= \frac{4k^2+4k+1+4k^2+12k+9+4k^2+20k+25+1}{12}$$

$$= \frac{12k^2+26k+36}{12} = k^2+3k+3$$

which is an integer. Therefore, $\frac{a^2+(a+2)^2+(a+4)^2+1}{12}$ is an integer when a is an odd integer.

Example 6 : If $(a-s) \mid (ab+st)$ then $(a-s) \mid (at+bs)$.

Solution : We have

$$(ab+st)-(at+bs) = (a-s)(b-t) \qquad ....(1)$$

We are given that $(a-s) \mid (ab+st)$. then (1) implies that $at+bs$ is also a multiple of $(a-s)$ consequently $(a-s) \mid (at+bs)$.

Example 7 : Show that if one of the two integers $2a+3b$ or $9a+5b$ is divisible by 17 then so can the other.

Solution : Let $2a+3b$ be divisible by 17. Then

$$2a+3b = 17k$$

$\Rightarrow$ $9[2a+3b] = 9 \times 17k$

$\Rightarrow$ $2[9a+5b]+17b = 17.9k$

$\Rightarrow$ $2[9a+5b] = 17[9k-1]$

$\Rightarrow$ $(9a+5b)$ is divisible by 17 [$\because$ 2 is not divisible by (7)]

Conversely let $9a+5b$ is divisible by 17. Then

$$9a+5b = 17k_1$$

$\Rightarrow$ $2[9a+5b] = 2.17k_1$

$\Rightarrow$ $9[2a+3b]-17b = 17.2k_1$

$\Rightarrow$ $9[2a+3b] = 17[2k_1+b]$

$\Rightarrow$ $(2a + 3b)$ is divisible by 17 [$\because$ 9 and 17 are relatively prime].

Example 8 : Show that if k is any positive integer then $k^2 + k + 1$ is not a square.

Solution : We have

$$k^2 < k^2 + k + 1 < k^2 + 2k + 1 = (k + 1)^2$$

Since there is no integer whose square lies between k^2 and $(k + 1)^2$, $k^2 + k + 1$ is not the square of a positive integer.

Example 9 : Show that the number of 300 digits of each digit 1 is divisible by 3 and 11.

Solution : Since the sum of digits of the given number is 300 is divisible by 3 the given number is divisible by 3. Also the given number has 150 pairs of 11 as digits. So it is divisible by 11. Thus, the given number is divisible by 3 and 11.

Example 10 : Show that $5^{10} - 3^{10}$ is divisible by 11.

Solution : We have

$$\begin{aligned} 5^{10} - 3^{10} &= (5^5)^2 - (3^5)^2 \\ &= (5^5 - 3^5).(5^5 + 3^5) \\ &= (3125 - 243).(3125 + 243) \\ &= 2882 \times 3368 \end{aligned}$$

Now 2882 is divisible by 11. Therefore $5^{10} - 3^{10}$ is divisible by 11.

Example 11 : Show that every square number is of the form $9k$ or $3k + 1$, k is an integer.

Solution : We know that any integer a is of the form $3q$ or $3q \pm 1$. Therefore,

$$\begin{aligned} (3q)^2 : 9q^2 = 9k \text{ where } k = q^2 \text{ is an integer and } (3q \pm 1)^2 &= 9q^2 \pm 6q + 1 \\ &= 3[3q^2 \pm 2q] + 1 \\ &= 3k + 1, \text{ where } k = 3q^2 \pm 2q \text{ is an integer.} \end{aligned}$$

Thus, square of any integer is expressible in the form $9k$ or $3k + 1$.

Example 12 : If n is a positive odd integer expressible as product of two integers a and b then it can be expressed as difference of two squares.

Solution : Let $n = ab$ such that n, a and b are positive odd integers. Then

$$n = ab = \left(\frac{a+b}{2}\right)^2 - \left(\frac{a-b}{2}\right)^2$$

Since a and b are odd integers $\left(\frac{a+b}{2}\right)$ and $\left(\frac{a-b}{2}\right)$ will be integers. Thus, n is expressible as difference of two square.

Example 13 : Show that $3^n + 1$ is divisible by 2 if n is even and is divisible by 2^2 if n is odd. It is not divisible by $2r$ for $k \geqslant 3$.

Solution : Since square of an odd number minus 1 is divisible by 8 for $n = 2m$, we have

$$3^n = 3^{2m} = (3^m)^2 = 8k + 1$$

This gives

$$3^n + 1 = 8k + 2$$
$$= 2[4k + 1]. \quad ....(1)$$

Thus, $3^n + 1$ is divisible by 2 when n is even. For $n = 2m + 1$, we have

$$3^n + 1 = 3^{2m+1} + 1 = 3.(3^m)^2 + 1$$
$$= 3(8k + 1) + 1$$
$$= 4(6k + 1). \quad ....(2)$$

Thus, $3^n + 1$ is divisible by 2^2 when n is odd.

Also $(4k + 1)$ and $(6k + 1)$ both are odd. Therefore, for any n, $3^n + 1$ is not divisible by 2^r for $r \geqslant 3$.

Example 14 : Show that $a^{n+1} - (a - 1)n - a$ can be divided by $(a - 1)^2$.

Solution : We have

$$a^{n+1} - (a - 1)n - a = a[a^n - 1] - (a - 1)n$$
$$= a(a - 1)(a^{n-1} + a^{n-2} + ... + 1) - (a - 1)n$$
$$= (a - 1)[(a^n + a^{n-1} + ... a) - n]$$
$$= (a - 1)(a^n - 1) + (a^{n-1} - 1) + ... (a - 1)]$$
$$= (a - 1)^2[(a^{n-1} + a^{n-2} + ... 1)$$
$$+ (a^{n-2} + a^{n-3} + ... 1) + ... + 1]$$

This shows that the given expression is divisible by $(a - 1)^2$.

2.4 Greatest Common Division

Let a and b be any two given integers in which at least one is non-zero. Then the greatest common divisor of a and b denoted by $gcd\,(a, b)$ [or (a, b)] is the positive integer d such that

(*i*) $d|a$ and $d|b$

(*ii*) If $c|a$ and $c|b$ then $c \leqslant d$

For example $gcd.\ (10, 15) = 5$ and $gcd\,(a, b) = a$ if $a|b$.

2.5 Euclid's Algorithm

The *gcd* of two integers a and b can be determined by a process known as Euclid's algorithm which is as follows :

Let a and b both are positive and $a > b$. Then there exist integers q_1 and r_1 such that

$$a = bq_1 + r_1,\ 0 \leqslant r_1 < b \quad ....(1)$$

(By division algorithm)

Again there exist integers q_2 and r_2 such that

$$b = r_1q_2 + r_2,\ 0 \leqslant r_2 < r_1 \quad ....(2)$$

Continuing this process, we get

$$r_1 = r_2 q_3 + r_3, \; 0 \leqslant r_3 < r_2 \qquad ....(3)$$
$$\vdots$$
$$r_{n-2} = r_{n-1} q_n + r_n, \; r_n = 0 \qquad ....(4)$$

where $\qquad q_n \geqslant 2$

Here we have

$$a > b > r_1 > r_2 ....$$

Thus, these numbers form a decreasing sequence of non-negative integers. It follows that $r_n = 0$ for some integer n. The process ends at this stage. The set of equations (1) to (4) is called Euclids algorithm for *gcd* (a, b). The *gcd* of a and b will be r_{n-1}.

This is proved in theorem 1 given below :

Theorem 1 : Let a and b be positive integers such that $a > b$ and let $r_n = 0$ in Euclid's algorithm. Then r_{n-1} is the *gcd* of a and b.

Proof : From equation (4) of Euclid's algorithm we have

$$r_{n-2} = r_{n-1} q_n + 0$$

$$\Rightarrow \quad r_{n-1} / r_{n-2} \qquad ....(1)$$

Again we have

$$r_{n-3} = r_{n-2}\, q_{n-1} + r_{n-1}$$
$$= r_{n-1}\, q_n q_{n-1} + r_{n-1} \qquad \text{[Using (1)]}$$
$$= r_{n-1}[q_n q_{n-1} + 1]$$

$$\Rightarrow \quad r_{n-1} / r_{n-3} \qquad ....(2)$$

Continuing in this way we finally reach at the result that

$$r_{n-1}/a \quad \text{and} \quad r_{n-1}/b$$

Thus, r_{n-1} satisfies condition (1) of *gcd.*

Further let c divides a and b. Since $a = bq_1 + r_1$ it follows that c divides b and r_1. Also $b = r_1 q_2 + r_2$ it follows c divides r_1 and r_2. Continuing this process we finally have that c divides r_{n-1}. This shows that r_{n-1} satisfies condition (2) of *gcd.*

Hence, *gcd* $(a, b) = r_{n-1}$. **Proved**

Minimal Algorithm (Absolutely Least Remainder Algorithm)

Let a and b both are positive and $a > b$. Then there exist integers Q_1 and R_1 such that

$$a = bQ_1 + e_1 R_1, \; 0 < R_1 \leqslant \frac{b}{2} \qquad ....(1)$$

Again there exist integers Q_2 and R_2 such that

$$b = R_1 Q_2 + e_2 R_2, \; 0 < R_2 \leqslant \frac{R_1}{2} \qquad ....(2)$$

Continuing this process, we get

$$R_1 = R_2Q_3 + e_3R_3, 0 < R_3 \leqslant \frac{R_2}{2} \quad ....(3)$$

$$\vdots$$

$$R_{n-3} = R_{n-2}\, Q_{n-1} + e_{n-1}\, R_{n-1}, 0 < R_{n-1} \leqslant \frac{R_{n-2}}{2} \quad -(n-1)$$

$$R_{n-2} = R_{n-1}\, Q_n + e_n\, R_n, R_n = 0 \quad ....(4)$$

where $e_1, e_2 .... e_n$ all are + 1 or – 1.

Since $a > b > R_1 > R_2 ...... > R_n$ form a decreasing sequence of non-negative integers. If follows that $R_n = 0$, for some integer n. The process ends at this stage. The *gcd* of a and b will be R_{n-1} as in Euclid's algorithm.

Theorem 2 : If a and b are any two integers not both zero then *gcd* (a, b) exists and is unique. **(R.U. 2005)**

Proof : Existence. Obviously the *gcd* (a, b) is not affected by the signs of a and b. Therefore, we assume that both a and b are positive and $a \geqslant b$. By division algorithm

$$a = bq_1 + r_1, 0 \leqslant r_1 < b \quad ....(1)$$

If $r_1 = 0$ then $b|a$ and *gcd* $(a, b) = b$. Thus, *gcd* (a, b) exists.

If $r_1 \neq 0$ then by division algorithm, we have

$$b = r_1q_2 + r_2, \quad 0 \leqslant r_2 < r_1 \quad ....(2)$$

If $r_2 = 0$ then $r_1|b$ and therefore from (1)

$$a = (r_1q_2)\, q_1 + r_1$$
$$= r_1[q_2q_1 + 1]$$

$$\Rightarrow r_1|a$$

Let $s|a, s|b \Rightarrow s|a - bq_1$

$\Rightarrow s/r_1$ [By (1)]

Therefore, $gcd(a, b) = r_1$. Thus, *gcd* (a, b) exists. If $r_2 \neq 0$ we repeat the process. This process terminates in finite steps n. In this way we will arrive at zero remainder after nth step. Thus, we have a sequence of integers r_i such that

$$0 \leqslant r_n < r_{n-1} ...... < r_2 < r_1 < b, r_{n-2} = r_{n-1}q_n + r_n, n \geqslant 3.$$

and $\quad r_{n-1} = q_{n+1}r_n.$

Thus, $r_n|r_{n-1}, r_n|r_{n-2}, ... r_n|b$ and $r_n|a$.

Now if s is *a* common divisor of a and b then $s|a$ and $s|b \Rightarrow s|a - bq$ [By (1)]

$$\Rightarrow s|r_1$$
$$\Rightarrow s|r_2$$
$$\vdots$$
$$= s|r_n$$

Therefore, *gcd* $(a, b) = r_n$. Thus, *gcd* (a, b) exists.

Uniqueness : If d_1 and d_2 are two *gcds* of a and b then by definition of *gcd* we have

$$d_1 \geqslant d_2 \quad \text{and} \quad d_2 \geqslant d_1 \Rightarrow d_1 = d_2$$

This shows that *gcd* (a, b) is unique. **Proved**

Theorem 3 : If a and b are any two integers not both zero then there exists integers x and y such that $gcd\ (a, b) = ax + by$.

Proof : Let $gcd(a, b)$ be d and let

$$S = \{ax_1 + by_1 : ax_1 + by_1 > 0, x_1, y_1 \text{ are integers}\}.$$

Since at least one of a or b is non-zero either $|a|$ or $|b| \in S$. Thus, S is non-empty. By well-ordering principle S has a least element $d = ax_0 + by_0$. By definition

$$d \leqslant |a|, |b|$$

Now by division algorithm we have

$$|a| = dq + r, 0 \leqslant r < d$$

$$\Rightarrow \quad r = |a| - dq$$

$$= \pm a - q(ax_0 + by_0)$$

$$= a(\pm 1 - x_0 q) + b(-y_0 q)$$

This is of the form $ax + by$.

If $r > 0$ then this representation implies that r is a member of S which contradicts the fact that d is the least integer in S. Therefore, $r = 0$ consequently

$$|a| = dq.$$

$$\Rightarrow \quad d \mid |a|$$

$$\Rightarrow \quad d \mid a$$

In a similar manner we can show that d/b. Thus, d is a common divisor of a and b.

Now if c is an arbitrary positive common divisor of a and b *i.e.*,

$$c \mid a \quad \text{and } c \mid b \quad \text{then}$$

$$c \mid ax + by = c \mid d.$$

Thus, d is the greatest common divisor of a and b *i.e.*,

$$d = gcd\ (a, b) = ax + by.$$ **Proved**

Corollary : If a, b are any two given integers, not both zero, then the set

$$S_1 = \{ax + by : x, y \text{ are integers}\}$$

consists of multiple of $d = gcd\ (a, b)$.

Proof : Since $d \mid a$ and $d \mid b$ we have

$$d \mid (ax + by)$$

for all integers x, y. Thus, every member of S_1 is *a* multiple of d.

Let $\quad d = ax_0 + by_0$

where x_0, y_0 are suitable integers.

Now $$nd = n(ax_0 + by_0)$$
$$= a(nx_0) + b(ny_0)$$
$$\in S_1 .$$ [∵ nd is a linear combination of a and b].

Proved.

Theorem 4 : If a, b are any two integers, not both zero and k is any integer then $(ka, kb) = |k| (a, b)$.

Proof : Let $d = (a, b)$ and $d_1 = (ka, kb)$, k is positive.

Since $d = (a, b)$ there exists integers x and y such that
$$d = ax + by.$$

Therefore, $dk = x(ka) + y(kb)$.
$$= d_1 r.$$ [By the corollary].

This shows that $$d_1 | dk \quad \text{.......(1)}$$

Also $d|a$, $d|b \Rightarrow dk|ka$ and $dk|kb$

This shows that dk is a common multiple of ka and kb

$$\therefore \quad dk | d_1 \quad \text{.......(2)}$$

From (1) and (2) we have
$$d_1 = dk$$
or $$(ka, kb) = k(a, b).$$ **Proved.**

Corollary : If $d = (a, b)$ then $\left(\frac{a}{d}, \frac{b}{d}\right) = 1$.

Proof : Since $d = gcd(a, b)$ we have d/a and d/b. Therefore a/d and b/d both are integers.

Also, $$d = (a, b)$$
$$= \left(d\frac{a}{d}, d\frac{b}{d}\right) = d\left(\frac{a}{d}, \frac{b}{d}\right)$$

This gives $$\left(\frac{a}{d}, \frac{b}{d}\right) = 1.$$ **Proved.**

Prime Number : A positive integer p other than 1 is said to be prime number if its only positive divisors are 1 and p.

For example, 2, 3, 5, 7, 11, 13, ... are prime numbers.

Relatively Prime : Two integers, not both zero, are said to be relatively prime (coprime) if $(a, b) = 1$.

For example 7 and 9 are relatively prime.

Theorem 1 : Two integers a and b, not both zero, are relatively prime iff there exist integers x and y such $ax + by = 1$

Proof : Let a and b be two relatively prime so that $gcd(a, b) = 1$. Therefore, there exist integers x and y such that $gcd(a, b) = ax + by = 1$.

Conversely suppose $ax + by = 1$ for some integers x and y and $d = gcd(a, b)$. Now $d|a$ and $d|b$ implies $d|ax + by$ or $d|1$. Since d is a positive integer and $d|1$ we have $d = 1$.

Corollary 1 : If $gcd(a, b) = d$ then $gcd\left(\frac{a}{d}, \frac{b}{d}\right) = 1$

Proof : Since $gcd(a, b) = d$ we have integers x and y such that $d = ax + by$

$$\Rightarrow \quad 1 = \frac{a}{d}x + \frac{b}{d}y \qquad ....(1)$$

Now $d|a$ and $d|b$. Therefore, a/d and b/d are integers. Hence, by (1) we have a/d and b/d are relatively prime.

Corollary 2 : If $a|c$ and $b|c$ with $gcd(a, b) = 1$, then ab/c.

Proof : Since $a|c$ and $b|c$ there exists integers q_1 and q_2 such that $c = aq_1$ and $c = bq_2$. Now $gcd(a, b) = 1 \Rightarrow$ there exist integers x and y such that

$$ax + by = 1 \Rightarrow c(ax + by) = c\,|.$$

$$\Rightarrow \quad c = a(bq_2)x + b(aq_1)y$$

$$= ab[q_2x + q_1y]$$

$$\Rightarrow ab/c.$$

Proved.

Theorem 2 : (Euclid's Lemma)

If a/bc and $(a, b) = 1$ then a/c.

Proof : We have

$$(a, b) = 1 \Rightarrow \text{there exists integers } x \text{ and } y \text{ such that } 1 = ax + by$$

$$\Rightarrow c.1 = c[ax + by]$$

$$\Rightarrow \quad c = cax + cby$$

Now $\qquad a|ac \quad \text{and} \quad a|bc$

$$\Rightarrow [acx + bcy]$$

$$\Rightarrow a|c$$

If a and b are not relatively prime then the conclusion of Euclid's Lemma fails. For example,

$6|4.9$ but $6 \nmid 4$ and $6 \nmid 9$

Corollary 1 : If a and b are integers, p is a prime such that $p|ab$ and $p \nmid a$ then $p|b$.

Proof : If $p \nmid a$ then $gcd(a, p) = 1$. Hence, by Euclid Lemma we have $p|b$.

Corollary 2 : If $p|a_1a_2, ... a_n$ then these exists some i such that $p|a_i$.

Proof : We shall prove this result by mathematical induction. For $n = 1$.

The result is obviously true. For $n = 2$ the result is true by corollary 1. Now suppose the result is true for n less than or equal to k. Then for $n = k + 1$ we take

$$p|(a_1a_2 \ldots a_k)a_{k+1}$$

By corollary 1 either $p|a_{k+1}$ ($\therefore\ i = k + 1$) or $p|a_1a_2 \ldots a_k$ for some $i(1 \leqslant i \leqslant k)$. Thus, the result is true for $n = k + 1$. Hence, by mathematical induction the result is true.

Theorem 3 : If a and b are any two integers, not both zero. Then a positive integer $d = gcd\ (a, b)$ iff

(i) $d|a$ and $d|b$

(ii) Whenever, $c|a$ and $c|b$ then $c|d$.

Proof : Let $d = gcd\ (a, b)$. Then obviously $d|a$ and $d|b$. Thus, condition (i) is satisfied. Since $d = gcd\ (a, b)$ there exist integers x and y such that $d = ax + by$. Now $c|a$ and $c|b$ implies $c|ax + by$ implies $c|d$. Thus, (ii) condition holds.

Conversely let d be any positive integer satisfying conditions (i) and (ii). Then we have to show that $d = gcd\ (a, b)$. According to the condition (ii) if c is a common divisor of a and b then $c|d$. This shows that $d \geqslant c$ and consequently d is greatest common divisor of a, b i.e.,

$$d = gcd(a, b).$$

Proved.

2.6 Least Common Multiple

If a and b are two non-zero integers then a positive integer m is called their least common multiple if

(i) $a|m$ and $b|m$ and

(ii) there exists a positive integer n such that if a/n and b/n then $m \leqslant n$ equivalently m/n.

It is denoted as $[a, b]$

Theorem 1 : The least common multiple is unique.

Proof : Let a and b be two non-zero integers. We have to show that least common multiple of a and b is unique. Suppose if possible there are two least common multiples m and m' of a and b. Then a and b divides m as well as m'. By (ii) condition of definition we have

$$m \text{ divides } m' \quad \ldots\ldots(1)$$

and $$m' \text{ divides } m \quad \ldots\ldots(2)$$

From (1) and (2) we have

$$m = m'$$

Thus, least common multiple is unique.

Theorem 2 : If a and b are two positive integers then

$$(a, b).[a, b] = ab$$

Proof : Let a and b be two positive integers. Let $d = (a, b)$ and $m = [a, b]$. We have to show that $dm = ab$

Now $d = (a, b) \Rightarrow$ there exist integers x and y such that

$a = dx$, $b = dy$ and $(x, y) = 1$

and $d = ax + by$

Also $m = [a, b] \Rightarrow$ there exists integers q_1 and q_2 such that

$$m = aq_1 \quad \text{and} \quad m = bq_2 \qquad \text{.......(2)}$$

Now $d = ax + by$

$$\Rightarrow \quad md = m(ax + by)$$
$$= max + mby$$
$$= bq_2ax + aq_1by \qquad \text{[By (2)]}$$
$$= ab[q_2x + q_1y]$$
$$\Rightarrow \quad ab|md \qquad \text{.......(3)}$$

Further $\dfrac{ab}{d} = \dfrac{dx\,b}{d} = x\,b$ [By (1)]

and $\dfrac{ab}{d} = \dfrac{ady}{d} = ay$ [By (1)]

Thus, $a \left| \dfrac{ab}{d} \right.$, $b \left| \dfrac{ab}{d} \right.$ i.e. $\dfrac{ab}{d}$ is a common multiple of a and b.

Therefore $m \left| \dfrac{ab}{d} \right.$ ....(4)

or $md = ab$. [By (3) and (4)]. **Proved.**

Corollary 1 : If a, b are positive integers then $[a, b] = ab$ if $(a, b) = 1$

Proof : From theorem 2 we have

$$[a, b]\,(a, b) = ab \qquad \text{.......(1)}$$

Putting $(a, b) = 1$ in (1) we get

$$[a, b].1 = ab \quad \text{or} \quad [a, b] = ab. \qquad \textbf{Proved.}$$

Theorem 3 : If $[a_1, a_2] = m_2$, $[m_2, a_3] = m_3$, ... $[m_{n-1}, a_n] = m_n$ then $[a_1, ... a_n] = m_n$.

Proof : We have

$[m_{n-1}, a_n] = m_n \Rightarrow m_{n-1} \mid m_n$ and $a_n \mid m_n$. ....(1)

Again $[m_{n-2}, a_{n-1}] = m_{n-1} \Rightarrow m_{n-2} \mid m_{n-1}$ and $a_{n-1} \mid m_{n-1}$

Therefore, from (1) we see that $m_{n-2} \mid m_n$ and $a_{n-1} \mid m_n$

Continuing this process we can show that

$a_n, a_{n-1}, ... a_1$ all divide m_n. Thus, condition (*i*) of definition of l c.m. is satisfied for n numbers.

Further let $a_1, a_2, ... a_n$ all divide and integer c then $[a_1, a_2] = m_2$ and a_1 and a_2 divide c. Therefore, m_2 also divides c. Again $[m_2, a_3] = m_3$ and m_2 and a_3 divide c. Therefore, m_3 also divides c. Continuing in this way we can show that m_n divides c. Thus, m_n satisfies (*ii*) condition of the definition of l.c.m. Hence, $[a_1, a_2, ... a_n] = m_n$

Corollary 1 : If $a_1, a_2 \ldots. a_n$ are all pairwise prime integers then

$$[a_1, a_2, \ldots. a_n] = a_1.a_2. \ldots. a_n.$$

Example 1 : Find the gcd of 117 and 45.

Solution : We have

$$117 = 45.2 + 27$$
$$45 = 27.1 + 18$$
$$27 = 18.1 + 9$$
$$18 = 9.2 + 0.$$

Here $r_4 = 0$. Therefore, $r_3 = 9$ is the required *gcd.*

Example 2 : Find the gcd of 108 and 243.

Solution : We have

$$243 = 108.2 + 27$$
$$108 = 27.4 + 0.$$

Here $r_2 = 0$. Therefore, $r_1 = 27$ is the required *gcd* of 243 and 108.

Example 3 : Find gcd of 272 and 1479.

Solution : We have

$$1479 = 272.5 + 119$$
$$272 = 119.2 + 34$$
$$119 = 34.3 + 17$$
$$34 = 17.2 + 0.$$

Here $r_4 = 0$. Therefore $r_3 = 17$ is the required *gcd* of 272 and 1479.

Example 4 : Find gcd of 396 and 671 by minimal algorithm.

Solution : We have

$$671 = 396.2 - 121$$
$$396 = 121.3 + 33$$
$$121 = 33.4 - 11$$
$$33 = 11.3 + 0.$$

Here $r_4 = 0$. Therefore, $r_3 = 11$ is the required *gcd* of given numbers 396 and 671.

Example 5 : Find *gcd* of 256 and 1166 and express *gcd* as linear combination of 256 and 1166.

Solution : We have

$$1166 = 256.4 + 142$$
$$256 = 142.1 + 114$$
$$142 = 114.1 + 28$$
$$114 = 28.4 + 2$$
$$28 = 2.14 + 0.$$

Here $r_5 = 0$. Therefore, $r_4 = 2$ is the required *gcd* of the given numbers.

Further *gcd* of 256 and 1166.

$$
\begin{aligned}
2 &= 114 - 28.4 \\
&= 114 - 4[142 - 114.1] \\
&= 114 - 4.142 + 4.114 \\
&= 5.114 - 4.142 \\
&= 5.(256 - 142.1) - 4.142 \\
&= 5.256 - 5.142 - 4.142 \\
&= 5.256 - 9.142 \\
&= 5.256 - 9.[1166 - 256.4]. \\
&= 5.256 - 9.1166 + 36.256 \\
&= 41.256 - 9.1166 \\
&= 256x + 1166y
\end{aligned}
$$

where $x = 41$ and $y = -9$. Thus, *gcd* 2 has been expressed as linear combination of 256 and 1166.

Example 6 : Find the *gcd* and *lcm* of 119 and 272. Also express the *gcd* as a linear combination of 119 and 272.

Solution : We have

$$
\begin{aligned}
272 &= 119.2 + 34 \\
119 &= 34.3 + 17 \\
34 &= 17.2 + 0.
\end{aligned}
$$

Here $r_3 = 0$. Therefore $r_2 = 17$ is the *gcd* of 119 and 272.

Further *gcd* of 119 and 272.

$$
\begin{aligned}
17 &= 119 - 34.3 \\
&= 119 - 3(272 - 119.2) \\
&= 119 - 3.272 + 6.119 \\
&= 7.119 - 3.272 \\
&= 119x + 272y
\end{aligned}
$$

where $x = 7$ and $y = -3$. Thus, *gcd* 17 has been expressed as linear combination of 119 and 272.

Further, we have

$$[119, 272]\ (119, 272) = 119 \times 272$$

$$\therefore \qquad [119, 272] = \frac{119 \times 272}{(199, 272)} = \frac{119 \times 272}{17} = 7 \times 272$$

$$= 1904.$$

Therefore, l.c.m. of 119 and 272 = 1904.

Example 7 : Find the l.c.m. of 8, 12, 15, 20 and 25.

Solution : We know that

$$[a, b] = \frac{a \times b}{(a, b)}$$

$$\therefore \quad [8, 12] = \frac{8 \times 12}{(8, 12)} = \frac{8 \times 12}{4} = 24$$

$$[24, 15] = \frac{24 \times 15}{(24, 15)} = \frac{24 \times 15}{3} = 120$$

$$[120, 20] = \frac{120 \times 20}{(120, 20)} = \frac{120 \times 20}{20} = 120$$

$$[120, 25] = \frac{120 \times 25}{(120, 25)} = \frac{120 \times 25}{5} = 600.$$

Therefore, l.c.m. of 8, 12, 15, 20 and 25 is given by [8, 12, 15, 25] = 600.

Example 8 : Find *gcd* of 28 and 49. Express it as linear combination of 28 and 49. **[C.C.S. (B.P.) 2006]**

Solution : We have

$$49 = 28.1 + 21$$
$$28 = 21.1 + 7$$
$$21 = 7.3 + 0$$

Here, $r_3 = 0$ therefore

$r_2 = 7$ is the required *gcd*

Further
$$\begin{aligned} 7 &= 28 - 21.1 \\ &= 28 - (49 - 28.111) \\ &= 28.2 - 49.1 \\ &= 28x + 49y \end{aligned}$$

When $x = 2, y = -1$.

Example 9 : If $a > 1$ and m, n are positive integers then $(a^m - 1, a^n - 1) = a^{(m, n)} - 1$.

Solution : For $m = n$ the result is obvious. If $m \neq n$ suppose $m > n$. So it can be written as $m = nq + r$. Therefore,

$$\begin{aligned} a^m - 1 &= (a^n - 1)a^{m-n} + a^{m-n} - 1 \\ &= (a^n - 1)\, a^{m-n} + (a^n - 1)\, a^{m-2n} + a^{m-2n} - 1 \\ &= (a^n - 1)[a^{m-1} + \ldots .\ a^{m-qn}] + a^{m-qn} - 1 \\ &= (a^n - 1)(a^{m-1} + \ldots .\ a^r) + a^r - 1 \end{aligned}$$

Hence,

$$\begin{aligned} (a^m - 1, a^n - 1) &= (a^n - 1, a^r - 1) \\ &= (a^r - 1, a^{r_1} - 1), \text{ where } r_1 < r \\ &= (a^d - 1, a^0 - 1) \\ &= a^d - 1 \text{ where } d = (m, n) \\ &= a^{(m, n)} - 1. \end{aligned}$$

Example 10 : If a, b are two positive integers then

$(a + b)\,[a, b] = b[a, a + b]$.

Solution : We have R.H.S. $= b[a, a + b]$

$$= \frac{ba\,(a+b)}{(a,\, a+b)}$$

$$= \frac{(a+b)\,ab}{(a,b)}$$

$$= (a+b)[a,\, b]$$

$$= \text{L.H.S.}$$

2.7 Fibonacci Sequence

The sequence $a_1, a_2, a_3, \ldots$, in which $a_1 = 1$, $a_2 = 2$ and $a_n = a_{n-1} + a_{n-2}$ for every $n > 2$ is called a Fibonacci Sequence.

The first few terms of this sequence are 1, 2, 3, 5, 8 13, 21, ...

(C.C.S.U. 2001, 2005, BP 2006)

Theorem 1 : If a_n is the nth term of the Fibonacci sequence and $\alpha = \frac{1+\sqrt{5}}{2}$ then $a_n > \alpha^{n-1}$ for all $n > 1$ (C.C.S.U. 2001, 2004, 2005, BP 2006)

Proof : We have

$$\alpha^2 = \left(\frac{1+\sqrt{5}}{2}\right)^2$$

$$= \frac{1+5+2\sqrt{5}}{4}$$

$$= \frac{6+2\sqrt{5}}{4}$$

$$= \frac{3+\sqrt{5}}{2}$$

$$= \frac{1+\sqrt{5}}{2} + 1 = \alpha + 1. \quad \text{.......(1)}$$

Therefore, for any $k > 1$ we have

$$\alpha^k = \alpha^{k-2}.\alpha^2 = \alpha^{k-2}\,[\alpha + 1] \quad \text{[using (1)]}$$

$$= \alpha^{k-1} + \alpha^{k-2} \quad \text{.......(2)}$$

Now $a_2 = 2$ and $\alpha = \frac{1+\sqrt{5}}{2}$

$$\therefore \quad a_2 > \alpha = \alpha^{2-1}. \quad \text{.......(3)}$$

This shows that the result is true for $n = 2$.

From definition of Fibonacci sequence we have

$$a_3 = a_2 + a_1$$

$$> \alpha + 1 \quad \text{[Using (1) and (3)]}$$

$$= \alpha^2 = \alpha^{3-1}$$

This shows that the result is true for $n = 3$.

Now suppose the result is true for

$n = 2, 3, \ldots.\, k$ then

$$a_k > \alpha^{k-1} \quad \text{and} \quad a_{k-1} > \alpha^{k-2}.$$

Therefore,
$$\begin{aligned} a_{k+1} &= a_k + a_{k-1} \\ &> \alpha^{k-1} + \alpha^{k-2} \\ &= \alpha^{k-2}[\alpha + 1] \\ &= \alpha^{k-2}.\alpha^2 = \alpha^k \\ &= \alpha^{k+1} - 1 \end{aligned}$$

This shows that the result is true for $n = k + 1$. Hence, by mathematical induction the result is true for all values of $n > 1$.

2.8 Lame's Theorem

If a and b are any two positive integers with $a > b$ and n is the number of divisions in Euclid's algorithm then $n \leqslant 5t$ where t is the number of digits in b.

Proof : Let a and b be two positive integers and let n be the number of divisions in Euclid's algorithm. Then we have the following sequence of positive numbers : $r_{n-1}, r_{n-2}, \ldots\ldots, r_2, r_1, b, a$ in non-decreasing form. Comparing this sequence with Fibonacci sequence we have

$$r_{n-1} \geqslant 1 = a_1. \quad \ldots\ldots(1)$$

Also
$$r_{n-2} = r_{n-1}\, q_1 \quad \text{and} \quad q_1 \geqslant 2.$$

$\therefore$
$$r_{n-2} \geqslant a_2 \quad \ldots\ldots(2)$$

Further for any $k > 2$ we have

$$\begin{aligned} r_{n-k} &= r_{n-(k-1)} q_{n-(k-2)} + r_{n-(k-2)} \\ &\geqslant r_{n-(k-1)} + r_{n-(k-2)} \quad \ldots\ldots(3) \end{aligned}$$

Putting $k = 3, 4, \ldots\ldots, n - 1$ in (3) we have

$$\begin{aligned} r_{n-3} &\geqslant r_{n-2} + r_{n-1} \geqslant a_2 + a_1 = a_3 \\ r_{n-4} &\geqslant r_{n-3} + r_{n-2} \geqslant a_3 + a_2 = a_4 \\ &\vdots \\ r_2 &\geqslant r_3 + r_4 \geqslant a_{n-2} \\ r_1 &\geqslant r_2 + r_3 \geqslant a_{n-1} \end{aligned}$$

Also we have

$$\begin{aligned} b &= r_1 q_2 + r_2 \\ &\geqslant r_1 + r_2 \\ &\geqslant a_{n-1} + a_{n-2} \\ &= a_n \\ &> \alpha^{n-1}, \text{ where } \alpha = \frac{1+\sqrt{5}}{2} \end{aligned}$$

$\therefore$
$$\log_{10} b > (n-1)\log_{10} \alpha$$

$$= (n-1)\log_{10}\left(\frac{1+\sqrt{5}}{2}\right)$$

$$> 1/5 \qquad \text{.......(4)}$$

Also t = number of digits in b

$$> \log_{10} b \qquad \text{.......(5)}$$

From (4) and (5) we have

$$t > (n-1)\,1/5$$

$$\Rightarrow \quad n < 5t + 1$$

$$\Rightarrow \quad n \leqslant 5t.$$

Proved

Corollery : Show that $n \leqslant \dfrac{1}{\log_{10}\alpha}, \alpha = \dfrac{1+\sqrt{5}}{2}$

Proof : We have

$$t > \log_{10} b > (n-1)\log_{10}\alpha$$

$$\Rightarrow \quad t \geqslant n \log_{10}\alpha$$

$$\Rightarrow \quad n \leqslant \frac{1}{\log_{10}\alpha}$$

Theorem 2 : If a and b are any two positive integers with $a > b$ and n is the number of divisions in minimal algorithm for a and b. Then $(n-1) < \dfrac{10}{3}$ t where t is the number of digits in b.

Proof : Let a and b be two positive integers such that $a > b$. Then in the minimal algorithm we have

$$R_1 \leqslant \frac{b}{2}$$

$$R_2 \leqslant \frac{R_1}{2} \leqslant \frac{b}{2^2}$$

$$R_3 \leqslant \frac{R_2}{2} \leqslant \frac{b}{2^3}$$

$$\vdots$$

$$R_{n-1} \leqslant \frac{R_{n-2}}{2} \leqslant \frac{b}{2^{n-1}}$$

and $\quad R_{n-1} \geqslant 1.$

Therefore,

$$b \geqslant 2^{n-1} R_{n-1}$$

$$\geqslant 2^{n-1}$$

or

$$\log_{10} b \geqslant (n-1)\log_{10}{}^2$$

$$\geqslant (n-1)\frac{3}{10} \qquad \left[\because \log_{10}^2 > \frac{3}{10}\right] \qquad \text{.......(1)}$$

Also

$$t > \log_{10} b \qquad \text{.......(2)}$$

From (1) and (2) we have

$$t > (n-1)(3/10)$$

or

$$(n-1) < (10/3t).$$

2.9 Kroneeker's Theorem

The number of divisions in the minimal algorithm for two positive integers a and b is not greater then number of divisions in Euclid's algorithm for the same integers *i.e.*, $M(a, b) \leqslant E(a, b)$ where $M(a, b)$ is the number of division in minimal algorithm and $E(a, b)$ is the number of divisions in the Euclid's algorithm. **(C.C.S.U. 2001)**

Proof : We shall prove this theorem by mathematical induction method.

For $a = 2$ and $b = 1$ we have

$$2 = 2.1 + 0$$

Therefore, $E(a, b) = 1$ and $M(a, b) = 1$

Thus, $M(a, b) \leqslant E(a, b)$.

Hence, result holds for $a = 2$

For $a = 3, b = 1$ we have

$$3 = 3.1 + 0$$

Therefore, $E(a, b) = 1, M(a, b) = 1$

Thus, $M(a, b) \leqslant E(a, b)$

For $a = 3, b = 2$ we have

$$3 = 2.1 + 1$$

$$2 = 1.2 + 0$$

Therefore, $E(a, b) = 2, M(a, b) = 1$

Thus, $M(a, b) \leqslant (a, b)$

Hence the result holds for $a = 3$

Now let the theorem holds for $a = 2, 3, \ldots. k - 1$. We shall show that the result holds for $a = k$. Let b be a positive integer less than k. Then we have

$$k = bQ + eR. \quad \text{where } e = \pm 1 \text{ and } 0 \leqslant R \leqslant b/2$$

Hence, $M(k, b) = 1 + M(b, R)$ ....(1)

Also $k = bq + r, 0 \leqslant r < b$

Hence, $E(k, b) = 1 + E(b, r)$ ....(2)

Now there may be three possibilities

(*i*) $0 = R = r$

(*ii*) $0 < R = r$

(*iii*) $0 < R < r$

In case (*i*) we have

$$M(k, b) = 1 \quad \text{and} \quad E(k, b) = 1$$

Therefore, the theorem holds for $a = k$ in this case.

In case (*ii*)

$$E(k, b) = 1 + E(b, R).$$

But $b < k$ and $R < b$. Therefore, by assumption

$$E(b, R) \geqslant M(b, R) \qquad ....(3)$$

Hence, by (2), (3) and (1) we have

$$E(k, b) = 1 + E(b, R)$$
$$\geqslant 1 + M(b, R) = M(k, B).$$

Therefore, the theorem holds for $a = k$ in this case.

In the third case we have $r = b - R$.

Substituting the value of r in (2) we get

$$E(k, b) = 1 + E(b, b - R) \quad \text{.......(4)}$$

Now, $b < k$ and $b - R < b$, therefore by induction

$$E(b, b - k) \geqslant M(b, b - k) \quad \text{.......(5)}$$
$$E(k, b) = 1 + E(b, b - R)$$

By (4) and (5) we have

$$E(k, b) = 1 + E(b, b - R)$$
$$\geqslant 1 + M(b, b - R)$$
$$\geqslant 1 + M(b, R) = M(k, b).$$

Therefore, the theorem holds for $a = k$, in this case also. Hence by mathematical induction the result is true for $a > 1$.

Example 1 : Verify Lame's theorem for a = 249 and b = 113.

Solution : We have

$$249 = 113.2 + 23$$
$$113 = 23.4 + 21$$
$$23 = 21.1 + 2$$
$$21 = 2.10 + 1$$
$$2 = 1.2 + 0.$$

Thus, here number of division $n = 5$. The number of digits of $b = 113$, $t = 3$.

$$\therefore \quad 5t = 5.3 = 15$$

Thus, $5 < 15$ *i.e.*,

$$n < 5t.$$

Example 2 : If 0 < b ⩽ a/3 then show that M(a, b) < M(a, a – b).

Solution : From the given condition $0 < b \leqslant a/3$ we have

$$0 < b \leqslant \frac{a - (a/3)}{2} \leqslant \frac{a - b}{2} \quad \text{.......(1)}$$

Now there will be two cases :

(*i*) b divides a

In this case the first in the minimal algorithm (M.A.) for a and b we have

$$a = bQ_1 + 0 \quad \text{.......(2)}$$

for some integer Q_1. Therefore, $M(a, b) = 1$.

Also the first step in the *MA* for a and $(a - b)$ is

$$a = (a - b).1 + b \qquad \left[\because \quad 0 < b < \frac{a-b}{2}\right]$$

In the second step the dividend is $(a - b)$ and divisor is b. In this step we have

$$a - b = bQ_1 - b \qquad \text{[From (2)]}$$
$$= b[Q_1 - 1] + 0$$

Thus, $M(a, a - b) = 2$. Therefore, in this case

$$M(a, b) < M(a, a - b).$$

(*ii*) a is not divisible by b. In this case the given condition implies that

$$0 < b < \frac{b - a/3}{2} < \frac{a-b}{2} \qquad \text{.......(3)}$$

Now the first step in the *MA* for a and b is

$$a = bQ_1 + e_1R_1 \qquad \text{.......(4)}$$

for some integer Q_1, $e_1 = \pm 1$ and $0 < R_1 < b/2$

Therefore,

$$M(a, b) = 1 + M(b, R_1). \qquad \text{.......(5)}$$

The first step in the M, A for a and $a - b$ is

$$a = (a - b).1 + b \qquad \left[\because \quad 0 < b < \frac{a-b}{2}\right]$$

For the second step the dividend is $a - b$ and the divisor is b. In this step we have

$$a - b = bQ_1 + e_1R_1 - b \qquad \text{[From (4)]}$$
$$= b(Q_1 - 1) + e_1R_1,\ 0 < R_1 \leqslant b/2.$$

Therefore,

$$M(a, b - b) = 2 + M(b, R_1) \qquad \text{.......(6)}$$

From (5) and (6) we have

$$M(a, b) - 1 = M(a, a - b) - 2$$

or
$$M(a, b) = M(a, a - b) - 1$$
$$< M(a, a - b).$$

Proved.

Example 3 : Show that M(a, b) = M(a ± b, b).

Solution : The first step in the *MA* for a and b is

$$a = bQ_1 + e_1R_1 \qquad \text{.......(1)}$$

for some integer Q_1, $e_1 = \pm 1$ and $0 < R_1 < b/2$

Therefore,

$$M(a, b) = 1 + M(a, R_1) \qquad \text{.......(2)}$$

Now adding $\pm b$ to both sides of (1) we get

$$a \pm b = bQ_n + e_1R_1 \pm b$$
$$= b[Q_n \pm 1] + e_1R_1$$

This is first step in the *MA* for $a \pm b$ and b.

Therefore,

$$M(a \pm b, b) = 1 + M(b, R_1) \qquad ....(3)$$

From (2) and (3) we have

$$M(a, b) = M(a \pm b, b).$$ **Proved.**

Example 4 : If a/3 < b < 2/5a then show that M(a, a – b) = 1 + M[b, b – (3b – a)].

Solution : From the given inequality we have

$$a < 3b \quad \text{and} \quad a - 2b > a - (5/2)b > 0.$$

Also we have

$$a - 2b = \frac{2a - 4b}{2}$$

$$= \frac{a + a - 4b}{2}$$

$$< \frac{a + 3b - 4b}{2} \qquad [\because a < 3b]$$

$$= \frac{a - b}{2}$$

Now the first step in the *MA* for a and $(a - b)$ is given by

$$a = (a - b)2 + e_1(a - 2b).$$

where $e_1 = \pm 1$.

Therefore,

$$M(a, a - b) = 1 + M(a - b, a - 2b) \qquad ....(1)$$

Also
$$a - b = -(-a) + 2b - 3b$$
$$= b + b - (-a + 3b)$$
$$= b + (b - (3b - a))$$

and
$$a - 2b = b - (3b - a).$$

Therefore, $M(a - b, a - 2b) = M[b + (b - (3b - a)), b - (3b - a)]$

$$= M[b, b - (3b - a)]$$

[Using the result of example 3]. **Proved.**

2.10 The Linear Diophantine Equation

An equation of the form

$$ax + by + c = 0 \qquad ....(1)$$

with $a \neq 0$, $b \neq 0$ and c integer, is called a linear diophantine equation in two unknowns x and y. A pair x_0, y_0 of integers is called a solution of (1) if

$$ax_0 + by_0 + c = 0.$$

For example

$$2x + 3y = 12$$

is a linear Diophantine equation $x = 3$ and $y = 2$ is the solution of this equation. We may write this solution as (3, 2).

But $8x + 17y = 7$ has no solution.

Theorem 1 : **If $(a, b) = d$ then the equation $ax + by = c$ has a solution (integral solution) iff $d | c$.**

Proof : Suppose $d | c$. Then $c = rd$, r is an integer.

Since $(a, b) = d$ there exists integers x_1 and y_1 such that

$$ax_1 + by_1 = d \quad \text{.......(1)}$$

Multiplying both sides of (1) by $\frac{c}{d}$ we have

$$\frac{c}{d}\, ax_1 + \frac{c}{d}\, by_1 = d.\frac{c}{d} = c$$

or
$$c = a\left(\frac{c}{d}\, x_1\right) + b\left(\frac{c}{d}\, y_1\right) = ax + by.$$

This shows that $\left(\frac{c}{d}\, x_1\right)$ and $\left(\frac{c}{d}\, y_1\right)$ satisfy the equation

$$ax + by = c$$

Thus, the linear Diophantine equation has a solution.

Conversely, suppose the equation

$$ax + by = c$$

has a solution say (x_0, y_0)

Then

$$ax_0 + by_0 = c$$

But $ax_0 + by_0$ must be a multiple of d.

i.e., $ax_0 + by_0 = rd$, r is an integer

$\therefore$ $c = rd$

$\Rightarrow$ $d | c$. **Proved.**

Theorem 2 : If (x_0, y_0) is one solution of

$$ax + by = c, (a, b) = d \quad \text{.......(1)}$$

then $x_1 = x_0 - \frac{b}{d}\, t,\ y_1 = y_0 + \frac{a}{d}\, t$ is the general solution of (1).

Proof : Since (x_0, y_0) is a solution of (1), we have

$$ax_0 + by_0 = c \quad \text{.......(2)}$$

Now let (x_1, y_1) be a general solution of (1). Then we have

$$ax_1 + by_1 = c \quad \text{.......(3)}$$

Subtracting (2) from (3) we get

$$a[x_1 - x_0] + b[y_1 - y_0] = 0$$

or
$$a[x_1 - x_0] = -\, b[y_1 - y_0] \quad \text{.......(4)}$$

Since $(a, b) = d$ there exist, integers r_1 and r_2 such that $a = r_1 d$, $b = r_2 d$. Putting these values in (4) we get

$$r_1 d[x_1 - x_0] = - r_2 d(y_1 - y_0]$$

or $$r_1[x_1 - x_0] = - r_2[y_1 - y_0] \qquad ....(5)$$

$$\Rightarrow \quad r_1 \mid - r_2(y_1 - y_0)$$

$$\Rightarrow \quad r_1 \mid (y_1 - y_0).$$

Therefore, $y_1 = y_0 + tr_1$ for some integer t.

or $$y_1 = y_0 + \frac{a}{d} t.$$

From (5) we have

$$r_1(x_1 - x_0) = - r_2 r_1 t.$$

or $$x_1 - x_0 = - r_2 t$$

or $$x_1 = x_0 - r_2 t$$

$$= x_0 - \frac{b}{d} t.$$

Thus, $x_1 = x_0 - \frac{b}{d} t$ and $y_1 = y_0 + \frac{a}{d} t$ is the general solution of (1).

Corollary 1 : If (x_0, y_0) is one solution of

$$ax + by = c, \ (a, b) = d \text{ then}$$

$$\boldsymbol{x_1 = x_0 + b/dt, \ y_1 = y_0 - a/dt}$$

is the general solution of (1).

Proof : Replacing t by $-t$ in the result of the above theorem we get the required result.

Corollary 2 : If (x_0, y_0) is one solution of

$$ax + by = c, \ (a, b) = 1$$

then $x_1 = x_0 + bt$, $y_1 = y_0 - at$ is the general solution of the equation $ax + by = c$.

Proof : Putting $d = 1$ in the result of the above theorem we get the required result.

Corollary 3 : If (x_0, y_0) is one solution of

$$ax + by = c, \ (a, b) = 1$$

them $x_1 = x_0 + bt$, $y_1 = y_0 - at$ is the general solution of the equation $ax + by = 1$.

Proof : Replacing t by $-t$ in the result of corollary (2) we get the required result.

Theorem 3 : If

$$\boldsymbol{ax + by = c, \ (a, b) = 1} \qquad ....(1)$$

b is numerically smaller of the two coefficients a and b and a_1 and c_1 are the minimal remainders of a and c respectively with respect to $|b|$. Then (1) can be written in the form

$$\boldsymbol{a_1 x + |b| x_1 = c_1} \qquad ....(2)$$

in which $|a_1| \leqslant \frac{|b|}{2}$ **and** $|c_1| \leqslant \frac{|b|}{2}$

Proof : Since a_1 and c_1 are minimal remainders of a and c with respect to $|b|$ we have

$$a = |b|Q_1 + a_1,\ 0 < |a_1| \leqslant \frac{|b|}{2}$$

$$c = |b|Q_2 + c_1,\ 0 < |c_1| \leqslant \frac{|b|}{2}$$

Therefore, (1) can be written as

$$(|b|Q_1 + a_1)x + by = |b|Q_2 + c_1$$

or $$a_1x + |b|\left(Q_1x + \frac{b}{|b|}y - Q_2\right) = c_1$$

Putting $x_1 = Q_1x + \frac{b}{|b|}y - Q_2$ the above equation reduces to

$$a_1x + |b|x_1 = c_1.$$

Proved.

Example 1 : Find the general solution of 170x – 455y = 625.

Solution : First we find *gcd* of 170 and 455, we have

$$455 = 170.2 + 115$$
$$170 = 115.1 + 55$$
$$115 = 55.2 + 5$$
$$55 = 5.11 + 0$$

This, gives (170, 455) = 5

Now 5/625. Therefore, $170x - 455y = 625$ has a solution.

We see that $x = 1$ and $y = -1$ is a particular solution of the given equation. Therefore, its general solution is given by

$$x_1 = 1 - \left(-\frac{455}{5}\right)t \qquad\qquad x = x_0 - \frac{b}{d}t$$

$$= 1 + 91t,\ t \text{ is an integer} \qquad\qquad y = y_0 + \frac{a}{d}t$$

and $$y_1 = 1 + \frac{170}{5}t$$

$$= -1 + 34t,\ t \text{ is an integer.}$$

Example 2 : Find the general solution of

$$\mathbf{70x + 112y = 168.} \qquad \text{.......(1)}$$

Solution : First we find the *gcd* of 70 and 112. We have

$$112 = 70.1 + 42$$
$$70 = 42.1 + 28$$
$$42 = 28.1 + 14$$
$$28 = 14.2 + 0$$

$\therefore$ $gcd\,(70, 112) = 14.$

Now 14/168. Therefore, equation (1) has a solution.

Dividing (1) by 14 we get

$$5x + 8y = 12$$

We see that $x = -4$, $y = 4$ satisfy the above equation. Its general solution is given by

$$x_1 = x_0 - \frac{112}{14}t = -4 - 8t$$

$$y_1 = y_0 - \frac{70}{14}t = 4 + 5t.$$

Example 3 : Find the general solution of

$$\mathbf{21x + 13y = 1791.}$$

Solution : We have

$$21x + 13y = 1791 \qquad \text{.......(1)}$$

$$\therefore \qquad y = \frac{1791 - 21x}{13}$$

[∵ Coefficient 13 is smaller numerically]

$$= \frac{138 \times 13 - 3 - 26x + 5x}{13}$$

$$= 138 - 2x + \frac{5x - 3}{13} \qquad \text{.......(2)}$$

Now putting $y_1 = \dfrac{5x - 3}{13}$ we get

$$13y_1 - 5x = -3$$

This, gives

$$x = \frac{3 + 13y_1}{5} \qquad \text{.......(3)}$$

$$= \frac{5 - 2 + 15y_1 - 2y_1}{5}$$

$$= 1 + 3y_1 - \frac{2 + 2y_1}{5}.$$

Again putting $x_1 = \dfrac{2 + 2y_1}{5}$

This gives

$$5x_1 = 2 + 2y_1$$

or

$$5x_1 - 2y_1 = 2$$

or

$$y_1 = \frac{5x_1 - 2}{2}. \qquad \text{.......(4)}$$

If we put $x_1 = 0$ in (4) we get $y_1 = -1$. Then from (3) we get

$$x = \frac{3 + 13(-1)}{5}$$

$$= \frac{3 - 13}{5} = -\frac{10}{5}$$

$$= -2$$

Further from (2) we get

$$y = \frac{1791 - 21(-2)}{13}$$
$$= \frac{1791 + 42}{13}$$
$$= \frac{1833}{13} = 141.$$

Therefore, the general solution of the equation (1) is given by

$$x = -2t,\ y = 141 + 13t.$$

Example 4 : Find the general solution of

$$\mathbf{311x - 112y = 73.}$$

Solution : We have

$$311x - 112y = 73. \qquad \text{......(1)}$$

Here (112, 311) = 1.

Therefore, equation (1) is solvable.

Here, 112 is numerically smaller.

We consider 311 and 73.

$$311 = 112.3 - 25$$
$$73 = 112.1 - 39.$$

Therefore, (1) can be written as

$$(112.3 - 25)x - 112y = 112.1 - 39$$

or $$-25x + 112\,[3x - y - 1] = -39$$

or $$-25x + 112u = -39 \qquad \text{......(2)}$$

where $$u = 3x - y - 1.$$

Now (2) is satisfied by $u = 3, x = 15$.

Thus, we have

$$-25x + 112u = -39,\ u = 3,\ x = 15. \qquad \text{......(3)}$$

In this equation neither of the two coefficients is unity. Therefore equation (2) can be treated in the same way as (1).

We consider 112 and 39.

$$112 = 25.4 + 12$$
$$39 = 25.1 + 14.$$

Therefore, (2) can be written as

$$-25x + (25.4 + 12)u = -(25.2 - 11)$$

or $$25[-x + 4u + 2] + 12u = 11$$

or $$25v + 12u = 11 \qquad \text{......(4)}$$

where $v = -x + 4u + 2$

Now (4) is satisfied by $v = -1$, $u = 3$.

Thus, we have

$$25v + 12u = 11$$
$$v = -1$$
$$u = 3. \quad ....(5)$$

In this equation neither of the two coefficients is unity. Therefore, we again treat equation (4) in the same manner as 1.

We consider 25 and 11.

$$25 = 12.2 + 1.$$
$$11 = 12.1 - 1.$$

Therefore, (4) can be written as

$$(12.2 + 1)v + 12u = 12.1 - 1$$

or $$12[2v + u - 1] + v = -1$$

or $$12w + v = -1 \quad ....(6)$$

where $$w = 2v + u - 1.$$

In this one coefficient is unity. Now putting $w = 0$ we get $v = -1$, from (6)

$u = 3$, from (5)

$x = 15$, from (2)

$y = 41$, from (1)

Thus, $x = 15$, $y = 41$ is one solution.

The general solution is given by

$$x = 15 + 112t$$
$$y = 41 + 311t, \ t \text{ is only integer.}$$

Example 5 : Find the positive solution of the equation

$$\mathbf{11x + 5y = 79.} \quad ....(1)$$

Solution : Here we have (11, 5) = 1. Therefore, the given equation is solvable.

Now considering 11 and 79 we have

$$11 = 5.2 + 1$$
$$79 = 5.16 - 1.$$

Therefore, (1) can be written as

$$(5.2 + 1)x + 5y = 5.16 - 1$$

or $$5[2x + y - 16] + x = -1$$

or $$5u + x = -1. \quad ....(2)$$

Here one coefficient is unity.

Putting $u = 0$ we get $x = -1$ from (1) $y = 18$.

Thus, $x = -1, y = 18$ is one solution.

Therefore, the general solution is given by

$$x = -1 + 5t, y\ 18 - 11t.$$

Now the required solutions are to be positive.

Therefore, we have to find the value of t for which x and y are positive.

Putting $t = 1$ we get

$$x = -1 + 5.1 = 4,$$
$$y = 18 - 11.1 = 7.$$

For $t = 2$ and $> 2y$ will be negative.

Therefore, the only positive solution is $x = 4$ and $y = 7$.

Example 6 : Find a positive integer n such that $n!$ is a perfect square.

Solution : For $n = 1$ we have

$$1! = 1$$

Also $1^2 = 1$

Thus $1! = 1^2$.

Hence $n = 1$ is the required number.

Further for $n = 1$ we have

$$n! + (n+1)! + (n+2)! = 1! + 2! + 3!$$
$$= 1 + 2 + 6$$
$$= 9$$
$$= 3^2.$$

Thus, for $n = 1$, $n! + (n+1)! + (n+2)!$ is also a perfect square.

Example 7 : Prove that if $5 \nmid (n-1)$, $5 \nmid n$ and $5 \nmid (n+1)$ then $5 \nmid n^2 + 1$.

(C.C.S. Univ. 1998, 2000, 2003)

Solution : We know that a positive integer is divisible by 5 if the digit of unit place of the given number is either 0 or 5. Therefore, the digit of unit place of a number not divisible by 5 must be 1, 2, 3, 4, 6, 7, 8 or 9. We are given that $5 \nmid (n-1)$, $5 \nmid n$ and $5 \nmid (n+1)$. Now unit digit of n cannot be 1 or 6 otherwise $n - 1$ will be divisible by 5. Similarly the unit digit of n cannot be 4 or 9 otherwise $(n + 1)$ will be divisible by 5. If the unit digit of n is 2 or 8 then the unit digit of $n^2 + 1$ will $4 + 1 = 5$. This shows that $5 \mid (n^2 + 1)$.

If the unit digit of n is 3 or 7 then unit digit of $n^2 + 1$ will be $9 + 1 = 0$. This shows that $5 \mid n^2 + 1$.

Thus, if $5 \nmid (n-1)$, $5 \nmid n$ and $5 \nmid (n+1)$ then $5 \mid (n^2 + 1)$. **Proved.**

Example 8 : Solve the equation $50x + 45y + 36z = 10$.

Solution : The given equation can be written as

$$50x + 45y = 5u,\ 5u + 36 = 10$$

Thus, the given linear Diophantine equation in three unknowns has been broken into two linear equations.

Now $u = -70$, $z = 36$ is the solution of second equations. Therefore, general solution of the above two equation is given by

$$u = -70 + 36k_1$$
$$z = 10 - 5k_1$$
$$x = u + 9k_2$$
$$y = -u - 10k_2$$

Eliminating t from the above equations, we get

$$x = -70 + 9k_2 + 36k_1$$
$$y = 70 - 90k_2 - 36k_1$$
$$z = 10 - 5k_1$$

or

$$x = 2 + 9k_2{}^* + 36k_1$$
$$u = -2 - 10k_2 - 36k_1$$
$$z = -5k_1{}^*$$

2nd method : The given equation can be written as

$$36[x + y + z] + 14x + 9y = 10$$

or $36k_1 + 14x + 9y = 10$, where $x + y + z = k_1$ ....(1)

or $9(x + y + 4k_1) + 5x = 10$

or $45k_2 + 5x = 10$, where $x + y + 4k_1 = 5k_2$ ....(2)

or $x + 9k_2 = 2$

This gives $x = 2 - 9k_2$

Putting this value of x in (2), we get

$$y = -2 + 14k_2 - 4k_1$$

Finally putting the values of x and y in (1), we get

$$z = 5k_1 + 5k_2$$

Here k_1 and k_2 are integers

Thus, we have

$$x = 2 - 9k_1$$
$$y = -2 - 4k_1 + 14k_2$$
$$z = 5k_1 - 5k_2.$$

∎

EXERCISE

1. Find *gcd* of 527, 765. **(Ans. 17)**
2. Find *gcd* of 12321, 8658. **(Ans. 333)**
3. Compute l.c.m of 27, 81. **(Ans. 81)**
4. Compute l.c.m. of 25, 30. **(Ans. 150)**
5. If a, b and c are integers such that $(a, b, c) = 1$. Find $(a + b, b + c, c)$. **(Ans. 1)**
6. Prove that $(n - 1)^2 \mid n^k - 1$ iff $(n - 1) \mid k$
7. Find *gcd* of 27, 30, 48 and 72. **(Ans. 3)**
8. Find the general solution of $39x - 56y = 11$.
   (Ans. $x_1 = 29 + 56t$, $y_1 = 20 + 34t$, t is an integer).
9. Write 100 as the sum of numbers are of which is divisible by 7 and the other by 11.
   (Ans. 56, 44)
10. Find all positive solution of $5x + 14y = 620$.
    (Ans. $x_1 = 110 - 14t$, $y_1 = 5 + 5t$, $t = 1, 2, 3, 4, 5, 6, 7$)
11. Show that $(2^m - 1, 2^n - 1) = 2^d - 1$ where $d = (m, n)$.

❑

CHAPTER 3

PRIMES AND THEIR DISTRIBUTIONS

3.1 Introduction

Prime numbers play an important role in number theory. The idea of prime numbers is quite simple. But some problems related with them are extremely difficult. It is well known fact that every integer is divisible by 1 and itself. There are so many integers like 6, 9, 18 etc., which have a number of divisors while the others like 7, 13, 17 etc., have no other divisors except 1 and itself. The formers are called composite numbers and the laters are called prime number. In this chapter, we will discuss the prime numbers and there distributions.

3.2 Prime Number

An integer $p > 1$ which has no divisor except 1 and the number itself is called a prime number. **(C.C.S.U. 2004, BP 2006)**

For example 2, 3, 5, 7, 11, 13, 17, 19, 23, 29 and 31 are first few prime numbers. A prime number is denoted by p. The nth prime is denoted by p_n.

An integer > 1 is called a composite number if it is not a prime number.

Twin Primes : Two successive odd integers p and $p + 2$ which are prime are called twin primes.

For example 3, 5; 5, 7; 11, 13 etc.

Theorem 1 : The smallest divisor (other than 1) of a composite number is a prime.

Proof : Let a be any given composite number. Then a has atleast one divisor other than 1 and a. This implies that a has a smallest divisor d which is less than a. If d is a composite number then it has atleast one divisor d_1 other than 1 and d. Thus, d_1 is less than d and divides a. This contradicts our assumption that d is the smallest divisor of a. Therefore d cannot be a composite number. Hence, d is a prime. **Proved.**

Theorem 2 : If p is a prime and a is any integer. Then either $(a, p) = 1$ or a is a multiple of p.

Proof : Since p is a prime, it has two divisors 1 and p. Therefore,

$$(a, p) = 1 \text{ or } (a, p) = p$$

If $(a, p) = 1$ then theorem is proved. If $(a, p) = p$ then obviously a is a multiple of p. **Proved.**

Theorem 3 : If p is a prime and $p|ab$ then either $p|a$ or $p|b$.

Proof : If $p|a$ then theorem is proved.

Suppose $p \nmid a$. Now the only divisors of p are 1 and p therefore $gcd\ (p, a) = p$ or $gcd(p, a) = 1$. Accordingly $p|a$, $p \nmid a$. Therefore, by Euclid's lemma we have $p|b$.

Proved

Theorem 4 : If p is a prime and $p|a_1a_2 \ldots\ldots a_n$ then $p|a_k$, where $1 \leqslant k \leqslant n$.

Proof : Suppose if possible p does not divide any of the numbers $a_1, a_2, \ldots\ldots a_n$. Then p is relatively prime to each of these numbers. Therefore, $(p, a_1, a_2, \ldots\ldots a_n) = 1$. Hence, $a_1a_2 \ldots\ldots a_n$ is not a multiple of p. But this is contradiction. Hence p divides atleast one of the numbers $a_1, a_2, \ldots\ldots a_n$ *i.e.* p/a_k, $1 \leqslant k \leqslant n$.

Corollary 1 : If $p, q_1, q_2, \ldots\ldots a_n$ are all primes and $p|q_1q_2 \ldots\ldots q_n$ then $p = q_k$ where $1 \leqslant k \leqslant n$.

Proof : By the above theorem $p|q_k$ for same k with $1 \leqslant k \leqslant n$. But q_k is divisible by 1 or q_k as q_k is a prime. Since $p > 1$ we have $p = q_k$.

3.3 Fundamental Theorem of Arithmetic

Every positive integer $n > 1$ can be expressed as the product of prime factors uniquely. **(C.C.S.U. 2001, 2004, BP 2006)**

Proof : Let $n > 1$ be an integer. If n is a prime we have nothing to do. If n is a composite number then there exists a prime p_1 such that $n = p_1n_1$ for same integer n_1. If n_1 is a prime then n is expressed as the product of prime factors.

If n_1 is a composite number then there exists a prime p_2 such that

$$n = p_1n_1 = p_1p_2n_2$$

for some integer n_2

If n_2 is a prime then n is expressed as the product of prime factors. If n_2 is a composite number then we continue the process.

Since $$n > n_1 > n_2 \ldots\ldots$$

the process cannot continue infinitely. Therefore, after finite number of steps we get

$$n = p_1p_2 \ldots\ldots p_k$$

where all p_i's are primes.

Uniqueness : Suppose if possible n can be represented as a product of primes in two ways as given below

$$n = p_1p_2 \ldots\ldots p_r = q_iq_i \ldots\ldots q_s,\ r < s \qquad \ldots\ldots(1)$$

where p_i and q_i are primes in the increasing order *i.e.*,

$$p_1 \leqslant p_2 \leqslant p_3 \ldots\ldots \leqslant p_r$$

and $$q_1 \leqslant q_2 \leqslant q_3 \ldots\ldots \leqslant q_s$$

Since $p_1|q_1q_2 \ldots\ldots q_s$ there exists some q_k such that $p_1|q_k$. But p_1 and q_k are both primes. Therefore, $p_1 = q_k$. We rearrange q_i's such that $p_1 = q_1$

Now cancelling p_1 and q_1 in (1) we get

$$p_2.p_3 \text{ ...... } p_r = q_2q_3 \text{ ...... } q_n.$$

We continue the process till all p_i's are exhausted. Also $r < s$ we left with

$$1 = q_{r+1}.q_{r+2} \text{ ...... } q_s$$

But it is not possible as q_i's are primes. Therefore r cannot be less than s. Similarly, we can show that s cannot be less than r. Hence, $r = s$ and

$$p_i = q_i \; \forall_i.$$

Thus, the representation is unique.

Corollary 1 : Any positive integer $n > 1$ can be written uniquely in a canonical form

$$n = p_1^{a_1}.p_2^{a_2} \text{ ...... } p_r^{a_r}$$

where a_i is a positive integer, $i = 1, 2, \text{......} r$ and each p_i is a prime such that $p_1 < p_2 < \text{......} p_r$.

Proof : By fundamental theorem of arithmetic we have

$$n = p_1.p_2.p_3 \text{ ...... } p_s. \quad \text{.......(1)}$$

In this decomposition primes $p_1, p_2 \text{ ...... } p_s$ may be repeated. Combining the repeated factors (1) can be written as

$$n = p_1^{a_1}.p_2^{a_2} \text{ ...... } p_r^{a_r}$$

where $p_1 < p_2 < \text{......} p_r$ and $a_i \geqslant 1$.

Uniqueness can be proved as in the proof of fundamental theorem of arithmetic.

Note : Suppose 1 is allowed to be a prime then for any n we have

$$n = p_1^{a_1}.p_2^{a_2} \text{ ...... } p_r^{a_r}$$
$$= 1^s.p_1^{a_1}.p_2^{a_2} \text{ ...... } p_r^{a_r}$$
$$= 1^t.p_1^{a_1}.p_2^{a_2} \text{ ...... } p_r^{a_r}$$

where $s \neq t$. Thus n has several representation. This violates the uniqueness condition.

Theorem 2 : If n is not divisible by any prime $\leqslant \sqrt{n}$ then n is a prime.

Proof : Suppose if possible n is not a prime. Then it is composite number. So it can be written as

$$n = p_1^{a_1}.p_2^{a_2} \text{ ...... } p_r^{a_r}$$
$$\geqslant p_1.p_2$$

But $p_1, p_2 > \sqrt{n}$. ($\because$ n is not divisible by any prime $\leqslant \sqrt{n}$).

Therefore, $n > \sqrt{n}\sqrt{n}$.

which is impossible. Hence, n is a prime.

Corollary : If n is a composite number then the smallest prime divisor of n is $\leqslant \sqrt{n}$.

Example 1 : Represent 144 as the product of prime factors.

Solution : We have

$$144 = 2 \times 72$$
$$= 2 \times 2 \times 36$$
$$= 2 \times 2 \times 2 \times 18$$
$$= 2 \times 2 \times 2 \times 2 \times 9$$
$$= 2 \times 2 \times 2 \times 2 \times 3 \times 3$$
$$= 2^4 \times 3^2.$$

Example 2 : Express 560 as the product of prime factors.

Solution : Use have

$$560 = 2 \times 280$$
$$= 2 \times 2 \times 140$$
$$= 2 \times 2 \times 2 \times 70$$
$$= 2 \times 2 \times 2 \times 2 \times 35$$
$$= 2 \times 2 \times 2 \times 2 \times 5 \times 7$$
$$= 2^4 \times 5 \times 7.$$

Example 3 : Show that $\sqrt{2}$ is not a rational number.

Solution : Suppose if possible $\sqrt{2}$ is a rational number then $\sqrt{2} = \frac{p}{q}$ where p, q are positive integers and $(p, q) = 1$

Now $\sqrt{2} = \frac{p}{q}$

$$\Rightarrow \quad 2 = \frac{p^2}{q^2}$$

$$\Rightarrow p^2 = 2q.q$$

$$\Rightarrow q | p^2$$

If $q > 1$ then by fundamental at theorem of arithmetic there exists atleast one prime p_1 such that $p_1 | q \Rightarrow p_1 | p^2$ $[\because q | p^2]$.

$$\Rightarrow p_1 | p$$

Therefore, $(p, q) = p_1$

But $(p, q) = 1$. Therefore, $p_1 = 1 \Rightarrow q = 1$

Now $q = 1 \Rightarrow p = \sqrt{2}$

which is not possible because p is a positive integer. Hence, $\sqrt{2}$ is not a rational number.

Example 4 : Show that 503 is a prime.

Solution : We have that 2, 3, 5, 7, 11, 13, 17 and 19 are the only primes $\leqslant \sqrt{(503)}$. Also none of these primes divides 503. Therefore, 503 is a prime.

Example 5 : Show that every prime of the form 3m + 1 is necessarily of the form 6k + 1.

Solution : Let $n = 3m + 1$ be a prime where m is a positive integer. Now m may be even or odd *i.e.*, $m = 2k$ or $m = 2k + 1$

If $m = 2k$ then

$$n = 3m + 1 = 3 \times 2k + 1 = 6k + 1$$

If $m = 2k + 1$ then

$$\begin{aligned} n &= 3(2k + 1) + 1 = 6k + 3 + 1 \\ &= 6k + 4 = 2[3k + 1] \end{aligned}$$

which is not possible as $2(3k + 1)$ is not a prime. Therefore, prime n of the form $3m + 1$ will also be of the form $6k + 1$. **Proved**

Example 6 : If a and b are two odd integers then show that $a^2 + b^2$ cannot be a perfect square.

Solution : Let $a = 2k_1 + 1$ and $b = 2k_2 + 1$ be two odd integers. Then

$$\begin{aligned} a^2 + b^2 &= (2k_1 + 1)^2 + (2k_2 + 1)^2 \\ &= 4k_1^2 + 4k_1 + 1 + 4k_2^2 + 4k_2 + 1 \\ &= 4k_1^2 + 4k_1 + 4k_2^2 + 4k_2 + 2 \\ &= 2[2k_1^2 + 2k_2^2 + 2k_1 + 2k_2 + 1]. \end{aligned}$$

This is obviously not a perfect square. **Proved.**

3.4 Sieve of Eratosthenes **(C.C.S.U. 2004)**

Let n be a given integer. Then we can construct a table of primes not exceeding n by a method which is known as the Sieve of Eratosthenes. We explain this method by taking $n = 100$ as follows :

First we write down all integers from 1 to 100 in their natural order as

	2	3	4	5	~~6~~	7	~~8~~	~~9~~	~~10~~
11	~~12~~	13	~~14~~	~~15~~	~~16~~	17	~~18~~	19	~~20~~
~~21~~	~~22~~	23	~~24~~	~~25~~	~~26~~	~~27~~	~~28~~	29	~~30~~
31	~~32~~	~~33~~	~~34~~	~~35~~	~~36~~	37	~~38~~	~~39~~	~~40~~
41	~~42~~	43	~~44~~	~~45~~	~~46~~	47	~~48~~	~~49~~	~~50~~
~~51~~	~~52~~	53	~~54~~	~~55~~	~~56~~	~~57~~	~~58~~	59	~~60~~
61	~~62~~	~~63~~	~~64~~	~~65~~	~~66~~	67	~~68~~	~~69~~	~~70~~
71	~~72~~	73	~~74~~	~~75~~	~~76~~	~~77~~	~~78~~	79	~~80~~
~~81~~	~~82~~	83	~~84~~	~~85~~	~~86~~	~~87~~	~~88~~	89	~~90~~
~~91~~	~~92~~	~~93~~	~~94~~	~~95~~	~~96~~	97	~~98~~	~~99~~	~~100~~

Now 2 is the first integer in the table which is a prime. We retain 2 and strike all integers multiple of 2.

After 2 number 3 is the next smallest integer which is prime. We retain 3 and strike out the multiple of 3.

After 3 number 5 is the next smallest integer which is a prime. We retain 5 and strike out the multiple of 5.

After 5 number 7 is the next smallest integer which is prime we retain 7 and strike out the multiple of 7.

After 7 number 11 is the next prime which is $> \sqrt{(100)}$. Hence, unstriked number in the table are not divisible by any prime $< \sqrt{(100)}$. Therefore, the unstriked numbers will be primes.

Theorem 1 : If the smallest prime factor of n is $> n^{1/3}$ then n has only two factors which are prime.

Proof : Suppose $n = p_1^{a_1}.p_2^{a_2} \ldots\ldots p_r^{a_r}$. Suppose if possible p_1, p_2, p_3 are prime $> n^{1/3}$ and $n \geqslant p_1 p_2 p_3$. Therefore,

$$n > n^{1/3} n^{1/3} n^{1/3} = n$$

which is not possible. Hence, $n = p_1.p_2$. **Proved**

Theorem 2 : If

$$m = p_1^{a_1}.p_2^{a_2} \ldots\ldots p_r^{a_r} = \pi p^a$$

$$n = p_1^{b_1}.p_2^{b_2} \ldots\ldots p_r^{b_r} = \pi p^b$$

Then

$$(m, n) = \pi\, p^{\min(a,\, b)}$$

Proof : Let $d = \pi p^{\min(a,\, b)}$. We have to show that d is the *gcd* of m and n.

Since $\min(a, b) \leqslant a$ we have $\pi p^{\min(a,\, b)} | \pi p^a$

$$\Rightarrow d | m$$

Similarly, $\min(a, b) \leqslant b$ we have

$$\pi^{p\min(a,\, b)} | \pi p^b$$

$$\Rightarrow d | n$$

Thus, d divides both m and n.

Let an integer c divides both m and n.

Then c is the product of primes from among $p_1, p_2, \ldots\ldots p_r$. Let $c = p_1^{c_1}.p_2^{c_2} \ldots\ldots p_r^{c_r} = \pi p^c$

Therefore, $\pi p^c | \pi p^a$ and $\pi p^c | \pi p^b$. This implies $c \leqslant a$ and $c \leqslant b$. This implies $c \leqslant \min(a, b)$.

Hence, πp^c divides $\pi p^{\min(a,\, b)}$, Thus, $c | d$.

This shows that d is *gcd* of m and n.

Theorem 3 : If $m = \pi p^a$ and $n = \pi p^b$ then

$$[m, n] = \pi p^{\max(a,\, b)}$$

Proof : Let $\pi p^{\max(m,\, n)} = m$. Then we have to show that $M = [m, n]$

We have

$$a \leqslant \max(a, b) \text{ and } b \leqslant \max(a, b)$$

$\Rightarrow \pi p^a | M$ and $\pi p^b | M$

Further let πp^a and πp^b both divide an integer c. Then $e = e_1\, \pi p^{\max(a,\, b)}$ for some integer $e_1 \geqslant 1$. Therefore. $c = c_1 M$. This imples M divides c. Hence, M is the lcm of m and n. **Proved**

Theorem 4 : (Euclid's Theorem)

There are infinite number of primes.

Proof : Suppose there are only finite number of primes $p_1.p_2 ......p_r$ in ascending order.

Let $p = p_1.p_2 ...... p_r + 1$. Then obviously $p > p_r$. If p is a prime then it shows that there exists a prime greater than p_r. If p is a composite number then it is not divisible by any primes $p_1, p_2, ... p_r$ as such a division leaves 1 as the remainder. This shows that if p is composite it must be divisible by a prime greater than p_r. Thus, in either case there exists a prime greater than p_r. But this contradicts our assumption that there are only a finite number of primes. Hence, there are infinitely many primes.

Theorem 5 : If p_r is the rth prime number then $p_r \leqslant 2^{2^r-1}$

Proof : We shall prove this result by mathematical induction. For $r = 1$ we have L.H.S. $= p_1 = 2$ and R.H.S. $= 2^{2^1-1} = 2^1 = 2$

Thus, $p_1 \leqslant 2$

This shows that the result is true for $r = 1$.

New let the result be true for $r = m$ *i.e.*, $p_m \leqslant 2^{2^m-1}$

We have to prove the result for $r = m + 1$ *i.e.*, we have to show that

$$p_{m+1} \leqslant 2^{2^{m+1-1}}$$

We have

$$p_{m+1} \leqslant p_1.p_2 ...... p_r + 1$$
$$\leqslant 2.2^2 ...... 2^{2^{m-1}} + 1$$
$$= 2^{1+2+2^2+ - 2m-1} + 1$$
$$= 2^{2^m-1} + 1$$

But $$1 \leqslant 2^{2^m-1} \quad \forall m$$

$\therefore$ $$p_{m+1} \leqslant 2^{2^m-1} + 2^{2^m-1}$$
$$= 2.2^{2^m-1}$$
$$= 2^{2^m}$$

This shows that the result is true for $r = m + 1$. Hence, by mathematical induction the result will be true for all value of r.

Corollary 1 : For $n > 1$ there are atleast $(n + 1)$ primes less than 2^{2^n}.

Proof : From theorem 5 we have that there are primes $p_1, p_2, ... p_{n+1}$ which are less than 2^{2^n}. So there are atleast $(n + 1)$ prime less than 2^{2^n}.

Theorem 6 : There are infinitely many primes of the form $4q + 3$

Proof : Suppose there are only n primes of the form $4q + 3$. Let these primes be $p_1, p_2, ... p_n$ in ascending order. Then the remaining primes if any are of the form $4q + 1$. Let

$$n = 4p_1p_2 ...... p_n - 1$$
$$= 4(p_1p_2 ...... p_n - 1) + 3 \quad ....(1)$$

This is of the form $4q + 3$. Now if n is a prime then it is a prime greater then p_n. If n is a composite number then it cannot be in product of the primes of the form $4q + 1$ because the product of $(4q_1 + 1)$ and $(4q_2 + 1)$ is given by

$$(4q_1 + 1)(4q_2 + 1) = 4[4q_1q_2 + q_1 + q_2] + 1$$

which is of the form $4q + 1$. Therefore, n must have atleast one prime factor of the form $(4q + 3)$. But this prime factor cannot be any one of $p_1, p_2 \ldots\ldots p_n$ due to (1). Therefore, this prime must be greater than p_n. Thus, there exists a prime which is of the form $4q + 3$ and which is greater than p_n. This is contradiction. Hence, there are infinitly many primes of the form $4q + 3$.

Theorem 7 : There are infinitely many primes of the form $6k + 5$.

Proof : We observe that

(*i*) Every prime > 3 is of the form $6q + 1$ or $6q + 5$ because the other possible form $6q$, $6q + 2$, $6q + 3$, $6q + 4$ are not primes.

(*ii*) The product of two factors of the form $6q + 1$ is of the same form as shown below :

$$(6q_1 + 1)(6q_2 + 1) = 6(6q_1q_2 + q_1 + q_2) + 1 \qquad \ldots\ldots.(1)$$

This shows that a number of the form $6k + 1$ need not be a prime. Therefore, primes will be of the form $6k + 5$. We have to show that there are infinitely many primes of the form $6q + 5$.

Suppose there are on n such primes $p_1, p_2, \ldots\ldots. p_n$ is ascending order. We consider a number

$$n = 6p_1p_2 \ldots\ldots. p_n - 1$$
$$= 6(p_1p_2 \ldots\ldots p_n - 1) + 5 \qquad \ldots\ldots.(2)$$

This is of the form $6q + 5$. Now if n is a prime then it is a prime greater than p_n. If n is a composite number then it cannot be the product of the primes of the form $6q + 1$ only as shown in (1). Therefore, n must be divisible by atleast one prime of the form $6q + 5$. But this prime factor cannot be anyone of $p_1, p_2, \ldots\ldots p_n$ due to (2). Therefore, this prime must be greater than p_n. Hence, there are infinitely many primes of the form $6q + 5$.

Theorem 8 : (Dirichlet's theorem) : If $(a, b) = 1$ then there are infinitely many primes of the form $aq + b$.

Theorem 9 : If $n > 2$ terms of an A.P.

$$p, p + d, p + 2d, \ldots\ldots p + (n - 1)d$$

are all prime numbers then the common difference d is divisible by every prime $q < n$.

Proof : We consider a prime $q < n$ and suppose if possible $q \mid d$. We take first q terms of the progression $p, p + d, p + 2d, \ldots\ldots p + (q - 1)d$.

If we divide these terms by q then we will get non-zero divisors. Suppose there are two integers i and j with $0 \leqslant i < j < q$ such that the numbers $p + id$ and $p + jd$ give the same remainder on division by q. Then obviously q divides their difference $(j - i)d$. But $gcd(q, d) = 1$ implies $q|j - i$ which is absurd as $j - i < q$. Therefore, all the remainder will be different. Thus, q remainder will be from 0, 1, 2, ... $q - 1$. Therefore, one remainder must be zero. This gives that $q/p + kd$ for some k satisfying $0 \leqslant k < q$. Now

$$q < n \leqslant p \leqslant p + kd$$

We conclude that $p + kd$ is composite. This is contradiction. Hence $q|d$.

Theorem 10 : For each positive integer n there exist n consecutive numbers each one of which is composite.

Proof : We consider the sequence

$$(n + 1)! + 2, (n + 1)! + 3 + \ldots\ldots (n + 1)! + (n + 1) \text{ of } n \text{ integers.}$$

Then general term of this sequence

$$(n + 1)! + k = (n + 1)n(n - 1) \ldots\ldots (k.k - 1) \ldots\ldots 2.1 + k$$
$$= k[(n + 1)n \ldots\ldots (k + 1).(k - 1) \ldots\ldots 2.1 + 1]$$

This is a composite number. Thus, for each positive integer n there exist n consecutive numbers each one of which is composite.

Theorem 11 : If $n > 3$ then $p_n > n + 2$.

Proof : We have

$$p_4 = 7 > 4 + 2$$

This shows that the given result is true for $n = 4$

Let the given result holds for $n = m$ then

$$p_m > m + 2$$

Now $p_{m+1} \geqslant p_{m+2}$ [$\because$ The difference between two consecutive primes is atleast 2]

$$> m + 2 + 2$$
$$> (m + 1) + 2$$

This shows that the given result holds for $n = m + 1$. Hence, by mathematical induction the given result is true for all integral values of $n > 3$.

Theorem 12 : If $m = [n/2]$ then

(i) $n \geqslant 2m \ \forall \ n \in N$.

(ii) $n - (m - 1) < p_m$ for $n \geqslant 8$

Proof : (*i*) We have

$$m = \left[\frac{n}{2}\right]$$

$$\Rightarrow \quad m = \frac{n}{2} \quad \text{or} \quad m = \frac{n-1}{2}$$

$$\Rightarrow \quad n = 2m \quad \text{or} \quad n = 2m + 1$$

$$\Rightarrow \quad n \geqslant 2m.$$

(*ii*) Let $n > 8$. Then $m = \left[\frac{n}{2}\right] = 4 > 3$

Now if $n = 2m + 1$ then by previous theorem we have

$$n - (m - 1) = 2m + 1 - (m - 1)$$
$$= m + 2 < p_m.$$

Proved

Theorem 13 : (Bonse's inequality)

If $n > 3$ then $p^2_{n+1} < p_1.p_2 \text{......} p_n$

Proof : We have

For $n = 4$, $11^2 < 2.3.5.7$

For $n = 5$, $13^2 < 2.3.5.7.11$

For $n = 6$, $17^2 < 2.3.5.7.11.13$

For $n = 7$, $19^2 < 2.3.5.7.11.13.17$

Thus, the given result is true for $n = 4, 5, 6, 7$.

For $n = 8$. We have $m = \left[\frac{n}{2}\right] = \left[\frac{8}{2}\right] = 4 > 3$

Therefore, by theorem 12 we have

$$p_m > n - (m - 1) \quad \text{.......(1)}$$

and $$n \geqslant 2m \quad \text{.......(2)}$$

Let $$t = p_1p_2 \text{......} p_{m-1} \text{ and let}$$

$$S = \{t - 1, 2t - 1, \text{......} p_m t - 1\}$$

Suppose $r_1t - 1$ and $r_2t - 1$ of S are divisible by a prime p_{m+i} where $i = 0, 1, \text{......} n - m$.

Then

$$p_{m+1} \mid [(r_1t - 1) - (r_2t - 1)] \Rightarrow p_{m+1} \mid t(r_1 - r_2) \text{ because } (p_{m+i}, t) = 1$$

and $$(r_1 - r_2) < p_{m+i}.$$

This shows that none of the primes

$$p_m, p_{m+1}, \text{......} p_n \quad \text{.......(3)}$$

divides more then one element of S.

Since $p_m > n - (m - 1)$, there are more integers in S then the number of primes given by (3). This shows that there are one or more elements of S which are not divisible by any of the primes given by 3. Also no element of S is divisible by the primes $p_1, p_2, \text{......} p_m$. Thus, we conclude that there exist atleast one integer in S which is not divisible by any of the primes $p_1, p_2, \text{......} p_n$. Suppose this integer is $rt - 1$. For some r such that $1 \leqslant r \leqslant p_m$. This implies that $rt - 1$ is a prime $> p_n$. Therefore,

$$p_{n+1} \leqslant r_{n-1} \leqslant p_m 4 - 1$$

$$\Rightarrow \quad p_{n+1} < p_1p_2 \text{......} p_m$$

$$\Rightarrow \quad p^2_{n+1} < (p_1.p_2 \text{......} p_m)(p_1p_2 \text{......} p_m)$$

$$< (p_1.p_2 \text{......} p_m)(p_{m+1}p_{m+2} - p_{2m})$$

$$\leqslant p_1p_2 \text{......} p_n. \quad [\because n \geqslant 2m].$$

Proved

3.5 The Goldbach Conjecture **(C.C.S.U. 2004)**

It is a famous unsolved problem concerning primes given by C. Goldbach. The Goldbach conjecture is that every even integer can be written as sum of two numbers that are either primes or 1.

For example

$$2 = 1 + 1 \qquad 8 = 7 + 1 = 3 + 5$$
$$3 = 2 + 1 \qquad 10 = 5 + 5 = 3 + 7$$
$$4 = 3 + 1 = 2 + 2 \qquad 12 = 11 + 1 = 7 + 5$$
$$6 = 3 + 3 = 5 + 1$$

Property P : If an integer n possess the property that numbers less than n and relatively prime to n are only unity and the primes less than n then it is said that n possess the property P.

No integer greater than 30 possess property P.

Example 1 : If $n \geqslant 9$ then $p_n > 2n + 3$

Solution : We will prove this result by mathematical induction.

For $n = 9$ we have

$$p_9 = 23 > 2 \times 9 + 3$$

This show that the result holds good for $n = 9$

Let the result holds for $n = m$ *i.e.*,

$$p_m > 2m + 3$$

Now $\quad p_{m+1} \geqslant p_m + 2$
$$> 2m + 3 + 2$$
$$= 2[m + 1] + 3$$

This show that the result is true for $n = m + 1$. Hence, by mathematical induction the result is true for all values of $n \geqslant 9$.

Example 2 : Prove that $n^4 + 4^n$ is composite for all integers $n > 1$.

Solution : We will prove this result by mathematical induction.

For $n = 2$ we have

$$2^4 + 4^2 = 16 + 16$$
$$= 32$$

This is a composite number. Therefore, the result is true for $n = 2$.

Let the result be true for $n = m$ *i.e.*, $m^4 + 4^m$ is a composite number. We have to show that $(m + 1)^4 + 4^{m+1}$ is also a composite number.

Now $(m + 1)^4 + 4^{m+1} = m^4 + 4m^3 + 6m^2 + 4m + 1 + 4.4^m$.

$$= (m^4 + 4^m) + 2m[2m^2 + 3m + 1] + (2m + 1) + 3.4^m$$

$$= (m^4 + 4^m) + (2m + 1)[2m(m + 1) + 1] + 3.4^m$$

Every term of this expression is a composite number. Therefore, their sum is also a composite number. Hence, by mathematical induction the given result is true for all integer $n > 1$.

Example 3 : Prove that for each prime $p \geqslant 5$, $p^2 + 2$ is a composite number.

Solution : Since p is a prime it must be of the form $(3k + 1)$ or $(3k + 2)$ for some integer. Also $p \geqslant 5$.

Case I : If $p = 3k + 1$ then

$$p^2 + 2 = (3k + 1)^2 + 2$$
$$= 9k^2 + 6k + 1 + 2$$
$$= 9k^2 + 6k + 3$$
$$= 3[3k^2 + 2k + 1].$$

This is a composite number. Thus $p^2 + 2$ is a composite number if $p = 3k + 1$.

Case II : If $p = 3k + 2$ then

$$p^2 + 2 = (3k + 2)^2 + 2$$
$$= 9k^2 + 10k + 4 + 2$$
$$= 9k^2 + 12k + 6$$
$$= 3[3k^2 + 4k + 2].$$

This is a composite number. Thus, $p^2 + 2$ is a composite number if $p = 3k + 2$.

Hence, $p^2 + 2$ is a composite number for all primes $p \geqslant 5$.

Note : For $p = 3$ we have

$$3^2 + 2 = 9 + 2 = 11$$

This is a prime number.

Example 4 : If p and q are twin primes then show that (pq + 1) is a perfect square.

Solution : Let p and q are twin primes such that $q = p + 2$. Then

$$pq + 1 = p[p + 2] + 1$$
$$= p^2 + 2p + 1$$
$$= (p + 1)^2.$$

Thus, $pq + 1$ is a perfect square.

Example 5 : If p and q are twin primes then show that 12| (p + q) whenever p > 3

Solution : Let p and q are twin primes such that $q = p + 2$. Then

$$p + q = p + p + 2$$
$$= 2p + 2$$
$$= 2(p + 1)$$
$$= 2[3k + 2 + 1] \quad \text{[Taking } p = 3k + 2\text{]}$$
$$= 2[3k + 3]$$
$$= 6[k + 1]$$
$$= 6.2\,m \quad [\because k \text{ cannot be even}]$$
$$= 12\,m.$$

This gives that $12/(p + q)$.

Example 6 : Show that 1949 and 1951 are twin primes.

Solution : We have

$$1949 = 3 \times 649 + 2$$

and

$$1951 = 3 \times 650 + 1$$

Thus 1949 and 1951 are of the form $3k + 2$ and $3k + 1$. Therefore, these number are primes. Also 1951-1949 = 2. Hence, they are twin primes.

Example 7 : Determine whether the integer 701 is a prime by testing all primes $p \leqslant \sqrt{(701)}$ as possible divisors.

Solution : We have

$$26 < \sqrt{(701)} < 27$$

The primes less than 26 are 2, 3, 5, 7, 11, 13, 17, 19, 21, 23. We can show that none of these primes divides 701. Therefore, 701 must be a prime.

Example 8 : Determine whether the integer 1009 is a prime.

Solution : We have

$$31 < \sqrt{(1009)} < 32 \text{ or equal to}$$

The primes less than 31 are 2, 3, 5, 7, 11, 13, 17, 19, 23, 29, 31. We can show that none of these primes divides 1009. Therefore, 1009 must be a prime.

Example 9 : Prove that every odd number $\geqslant 9$ is the sum of three odd primes.

(C.C.S. 2001, 2003, 2004)

Solution : We see that the smallest number which is the sum of three odd prime is $3 + 3 + 3 = 9$. Let n be any given odd integer greater than or equal to 9 *i.e.*, $n \geqslant 9$. Let p_1 be an odd prime such that $p_1 < n - 4$. Then $n - p_1$ is even and greater than 4. Therefore, by Goldbach's conjecture it can be expressed as the sum of two odd primes p_2 and p_3 *i.e.*, $n - p_1 = p_2 + p_3$. This gives $n = p_1 + p_2 + p_3$.

Thus, the given odd integer n is expressible as the sum of three odd primes.

Example 10 : Find a prime which can be expressed as $x^7 - 1$ where x is an integer.

Solution : Putting $x = 2$ in $x^7 - 1$ we have

$$2^7 - 1 = 128 - 1$$
$$= 127$$

This is a prime number. Thus, 127 is the required prime number.

Example 11 : If a prime number is greater than 3, then show that $2p + 1$ and $4p + 1$ are not prime numbers simultaneously.

Solution : Since p is a prime number, it is of the form $3k + 1$ or $3k - 1$.

If $p = 3k + 1$ then

$$2p + 1 = 2(3k + 1) + 1 = 3(2k + 1).$$

This shows that $2p + 1$ is a composite number.

If $p = 3k - 1$ then

$$4p + 1 = 4(3k - 1) + 1 = 3(4k - 1)$$

This shows that $4p + 1$ is a composite number.

Hence, $2p + 1$ and $4p + 1$ can not be prime simultaneously.

EXERCISE

1. Show that for every odd integer a, $a^2 + (a + 2)^2(a + 4)^2 + 1$ is divisible by 12.
2. Show that 2093 is not a prime.
3. Show that there exists a prime p such that $n < p < 2n$ where $n > 2$.
4. If a and b are any two odd integers then show that $a^2 + b^2$ is not a perfect square.
5. For what positive integer values of n, $2^n + 1$ is divisible by 3.

   (Ans. All odd integers)

6. If $n > 1$, show that $n!$ is never a perfect square.
7. Find the values of $n \geqslant 1$ for which $n! + (n + 1)! + (n + 2)!$ is a perfect square.
8. If $\frac{1}{a} + \frac{1}{b} = \frac{1}{c}$ where a, b and c are positive integers with no common factor, then prove that $a + b$ is a square.

❑

CHAPTER 4

THEORY OF CONGRUENCE

4.1 Introduction

The concept of congruence was first introduced by the great German Mathematician Karl Friedrich Gauss. Gauss (1777-1855) worked in all known branches of mathematics in his time such as geometry, analysis, algebra, mechanics, astronomy, complex numbers, electricity and magnetism and above all the theory of numbers. He always held number theory in high esteem. His interest in number theory was so great that he called it the 'Queen of Mathematics.'

A congruence is a refined statement of divisibility. Congruences provide us with an algebraic machinary for the study of divisibility property of integers. In this chapter we shall discuss the theory of congruences.

4.2 Congruence

Let m be a fixed integer. Then an integer a is said to be congruent to another integer b modulo m if $m \mid (a - b)$. This is symbolically written as

$$a \equiv b \pmod{m}. \qquad \text{.......(1)}$$

Expression (1) is called the congruence, m is called the modulo of the congruence and b is called a residue of a (mod m).

For example

$$67 \equiv 2 \pmod{13}$$

because $13 \mid (67 - 2)$.

4.3 Basic Properties of Congruence

Theorem 1 : If $m > 0$ is fixed and a, b, c and d are integers then the following properties hold :

(i) $a \equiv a \pmod{m}$

(ii) If $a \equiv b \pmod{m}$ then $b \equiv a \pmod{m}$

(iii) If $a \equiv b \pmod{m}$, $b \equiv c \pmod{m}$ then $a \equiv c \pmod{m}$.

(iv) If $a \equiv b \pmod{m}$ and $c \equiv d \pmod{m}$ then

$(a + c) \equiv (b + d) \pmod{m}$ and $ac \equiv bd \pmod{m}$

(v) If $a \equiv b \pmod{m}$ then $(a + c) \equiv (b + c) \pmod{m}$

(vi) If $a \equiv b \pmod{m}$ then $a^k \equiv b^k \pmod{m}$ for all $k \geqslant 1$

But if $a^k \equiv b^k \pmod{m}$ for $k > 2$ then $a = b \pmod{m}$ may not be true.

Proof

(*i*) We have

$$a - a = 0 = 0.m$$
$$\Rightarrow m \mid (a - a)$$
$$\Rightarrow a \equiv a \pmod{m}.$$

(*ii*) $a \equiv b \pmod{m} \Rightarrow m \mid (a - b)$
$$\Rightarrow m \mid (b - a)$$
$$\Rightarrow b \equiv a \bmod m.$$

(*iii*) $a \equiv b \pmod{m}$, $b \equiv c \pmod{m}$
$$\Rightarrow m \mid (a - b),\ m \mid (b - c)$$
$$\Rightarrow m \mid (a - b) + (b - c)$$
$$\Rightarrow m \mid (a - c)$$
$$\Rightarrow a \equiv c \pmod{m}.$$

(*iv*) $a \equiv b \pmod{m}$, $c \equiv d \pmod{m}$
$$\Rightarrow m \mid (a - b),\ m \mid c - d$$
$$\Rightarrow m \mid (a - b) + (c - d)$$
$$\Rightarrow m \mid (a + c) - (b + d)$$
$$\Rightarrow (a + c) \equiv (b + d) \pmod{m}.$$

Also $a \equiv b \pmod{m}$, $c \equiv d \pmod{m}$
$$\Rightarrow\ a = b + k_1 m,\ c = d + k_2 m$$
$$\Rightarrow ac = (b + k_1 m)(d + k_2 m)$$
$$= bd + k_1 dm + k_2 bm + k_1 k_2 m^2$$
$$= bd + m(k_1 d + k_2 b + k_1 k_2 m)$$
$$\Rightarrow m \mid (ac - bd)$$
$$\Rightarrow ac \equiv bd \pmod{m}.$$

(*v*) $a \equiv b \pmod{m} \Rightarrow m \mid (a - b)$
$$\Rightarrow m \mid [(a + c) - (b + c)]$$
$$\Rightarrow (a + c) \equiv (b + c) \pmod{m}.$$

(*vi*) $a \equiv b \pmod{m}$
$$\Rightarrow m \mid (a - b)$$
$$\Rightarrow\ m \mid (a^k - b^k) \qquad [\because a^k - b^k = (a - b)(a^{k-1} + a^{k-2} b + ... + b^{k-1})$$
$$\Rightarrow a^k \equiv b^k \pmod{m}.$$

If we take $a = 8$, $b = 4$, $m = 3$ then

$$\begin{aligned} a^2 - b^2 &= 8^2 - 4^2 \\ &= 64 - 16 \\ &= 48 \\ &= 3.16 \end{aligned}$$

$$\Rightarrow 3 \mid (a^2 - b^2)$$

$$\Rightarrow a^2 \equiv b^2 (\text{mod } 3).$$

But $3 \nmid (8 - 4)$

$\therefore \quad 8 \not\equiv 4 \ (\text{mod } 3).$

Theorem 2 : (Cancellation law) : If a, b and c are integers such that $ac \equiv bc$ (mod m), $m > 0$ is a fixed integer and $d = (c, m)$ then

$$a \equiv b \left(\text{mod } \frac{m}{d}\right).$$

Proof : Since $d = (c, m)$ there exist integers q_1, q_2 such that $c = q_1 d$ and $m = q_2 d$ and $(q_1, q_2) = 1$

Now we have

$$ac = bc \ (\text{mod } m)$$

$$\Rightarrow m \mid (ac - bc)$$

$$\Rightarrow m \mid (a - b)q_1 d$$

$$\Rightarrow \frac{m}{d} \mid (a - b)q_1$$

$$\Rightarrow q_2 \mid (a - b)q_1$$

$$\Rightarrow q_2 \mid (a - b) \qquad [\because \ (q_2, q_1) = 1]$$

$$\Rightarrow a \equiv b \ (\text{mod } q_2)$$

$$\Rightarrow a \equiv b \left(\text{mod } \frac{m}{d}\right).$$

Proved.

Corollary 1 : If a, b and c are integers such that $ac \equiv bc$ (mod m) and $(c, m) = 1$ then

$$a \equiv b \ (\text{mod } m).$$

Proof : Putting $d = 1$ in the proof of the above theorem we get the proof of this corollary.

Corollary 2 : If $ac \equiv bc$ (mod p) and $p \nmid c$ where p is a prime number then

$$a \equiv b \ (\text{mod } p).$$

Proof : Here $p \nmid c$ and p is a prime. Therefore, $(c, p) = 1$.

Hence, $a \equiv b$ (mod p).

Theorem 3 : Prove that $a \equiv b$ (mod m) iff a and b have the same remainders with respect to m.

Proof : Let $a \equiv b$ (mod m). Let r_1 and r_2 be the remainders of a and b respectively with respect to m *i.e.*,

$$\left.\begin{aligned} a &= mq_1 + r_1, \quad 0 \leqslant r_1 < m \\ \text{and} \quad b &= mq_2 + r_2, \quad 0 \leqslant r_2 < m \end{aligned}\right\} \quad \text{.......(1)}$$

We have to show that $r_1 = r_2$.

Since $a \equiv b \pmod m$ we have

$$(mq_1 + r_1) \equiv (mq_2 + r_2) \pmod m$$
$$\Rightarrow m \mid (mq_1 + r_1) - (mq_2 + r_2)$$
$$\Rightarrow m \mid m(q_1 - q_2) + (r_1 - r_2)$$
$$\Rightarrow m \mid (r_1 - r_2)$$
$$\Rightarrow r_1 - r_2 = 0. \qquad [\because r_1, r_2 \text{ are positive integers less than } m]$$

This gives $r_1 = r_2$

Conversely, let $r_1 = r_2$. Then from (1) we have

$$a - b = m(q_1 - q_2)$$
$$\Rightarrow a \equiv b \pmod m.$$

Proved

Least Residue : If $a \equiv b \pmod m$, $0 \leqslant b < m$ then b is called the least residue of $a \pmod m$.

Minimal Residue : If $a \equiv b \pmod m$ and $0 \leqslant |b| \leqslant (m/2)$ then b is called the minimal residue of $a \pmod m$.

It is also called the absolutely least residue of $a \pmod m$.

Example 1 : Show that 41 divides $2^{20} - 1$. **[C.C.S. (B.P.) 2006]**

Solution : We have

$$\begin{aligned} 2^{20} &= (2^5)^4 \\ &= (32)^4 \\ &= [-9 \pmod{41}]^4 \\ &= [(-9)^4 \pmod{41}] \\ &= 81 \times 81 \pmod{41} \\ &= 1 \pmod{41} \qquad [\because 81 = -1 \pmod{41}) \end{aligned}$$

$$\therefore \quad 2^{20} - 1 = 0 \pmod{41}.$$

This gives $41 \mid (2^{20} - 1)$. Thus 41 divides $2^{20} - 1$.

Example 2 : Find the remainder when 5^{48} is divided by 24.

Solution : We have

$$\begin{aligned} 5^{48} &= (5^2)^{24} \\ &= (25)^{24} \\ &= (1)^{24} \pmod{24} \\ &= 1 \pmod{24} \end{aligned}$$

Thus, when 5^{48} is divided by 24 the remainder is **1**.

Example 3 : Find the remainder when the sum

$S = 1! + 2! + 3! + ... + 1000!$ is divisible by 8.

Solution : Since k ! is divisible by 8 for all $k \geqslant 4$ we have

$$S = 1! + 2! + 3! + ... + 1000!$$
$$= 1! + 2! + 3! \pmod 8$$
$$= 1 + 2 + 6$$
$$= 9$$
$$= 1 \pmod 8.$$

This shows that the remainder is 1 when S is divided by 8.

Example 4 : Find the remainder when 2^{24} is divided by 17.

Solution : We have

$$2^{24} = (2^4)^6$$
$$= (16)^6$$
$$= [-1 \pmod{17}]^6$$
$$= (-1)^6 \pmod{17}$$
$$= 1 \pmod{17}.$$

This shows that the remainder is 1 when 2^{24} is divided by 17.

Example 5 : Find the remainder when 2^{340} is divided by 341. [C.C.S. (B.P.) 2006]

Solution : We have

$$341 = 11 \times 31$$

and $$340 = 68 \times 5.$$

Now $$2^5 = 32$$
$$= -1 \pmod{11}.$$

Therefore,

$$(2)^{340} = (2^5)^{68} = 32^{68}$$
$$= [(-1 \pmod{11})]^{68}$$
$$= (-1)^{68} \pmod{11}$$
$$= 1 \pmod{11}.$$

Similarly, $$2^5 = 1 \pmod{31}.$$

Therefore, $$(2^5)^{68} = 1 \pmod{31}.$$

This gives $$2^{340} = [(\text{mod } (11.\ 31)]$$
$$= 1 \pmod{341}.$$

Example 6 : Find the remainder when 3^{287} is divided by 23. [C.C.S. (B.P.) 2006]

Solution : We have

$$3^2 \equiv 9 \pmod{23}$$
$$3^4 \equiv 81 \equiv -11 \pmod{23}$$
$$3^8 \equiv 121 \equiv 6 \pmod{23}$$
$$3^{16} \equiv 36 \equiv -10 \pmod{23}$$

$$3^{32} \equiv 100 \equiv 8 \pmod{23}$$
$$3^{64} \equiv 64 \equiv -5 \pmod{23}$$
$$3^{128} \equiv 25 \equiv 2 \pmod{23}$$
$$3^{256} \equiv 4 \equiv \pmod{23}.$$

Therefore,

$$3^{287} = 3^{256} \times 3^{16} \times 3^{8} \times 3^{4} \times 3^{2} \times 3$$
$$\equiv 4 \times (-10) \times 6 \times (-11) \times 9 \times 3 \pmod{23}$$
$$\equiv (-40) \times (-66) \times 27 \pmod{23}$$
$$\equiv 6 \times 3 \times 4 \pmod{23}$$
$$\equiv 24 \times 3 \pmod{23}$$
$$\equiv 1 \times 3 \pmod{23}$$
$$\equiv 3 \pmod{23}.$$

This shows that the required remainder is 3.

Example 7 : What is remainder when 11^{35} is divided by 13.

Solution : We have

$$11^{2} \equiv 121 = 4 \pmod{13}$$
$$11^{4} \equiv 16 \equiv 3 \pmod{13}$$
$$11^{8} \equiv 9 \equiv -4 \pmod{13}$$
$$11^{16} \equiv 16 \equiv 3 \pmod{13}$$
$$11^{32} = 9 \equiv -4 \pmod{13}.$$

Therefore,

$$11^{35} = 11^{32} \times 11^{2} \times 11$$
$$\equiv (-4) \times 4 \times (-2) \pmod{13}$$
$$\equiv (-16)(-2) \pmod{13}$$
$$\equiv (-3)(-2) \pmod{13}$$
$$= 6 \pmod{13}.$$

Thus, the required remainder is 6.

Example 8 : What is the remainder when the sum
$1^5 + 2^5 + 3^5 + ... + 100^5$
is divided by 4 ?

Solution : We have

$$1^{5} \equiv 1 \pmod{4}$$
$$2^{5} = 32 \equiv 0 \pmod{4}$$
$$3^{5} = 243 \equiv 3 \pmod{4}$$
$$4^{5} \equiv 0 \pmod{4}$$

$$5^5 = 15625 \equiv 1 \pmod 4$$
$$6^5 = 2^5.3^5 \equiv 0 \pmod 4$$
$$7^5 = 7^2.7^2.7 \equiv 1.1.3 \pmod 4 \equiv 3 \pmod 4$$
$$8^5 = (2^5)^3 \equiv 0 \pmod 4$$
$$9^5 = (3^5)^2 \equiv 3^2 \pmod 4 \equiv 1 \pmod 4$$
$$10^5 = 2^5.5^5 \equiv 0 \pmod 4.$$

Thus, $1^5 + 2^5 + 3^5 + ... + 100^5$

$$\equiv 1 \pmod 4 + 0 \pmod 4 + 3 \pmod 4 + ... 0 \pmod 4$$
$$\equiv 9 \times 10 \pmod 4 \equiv (0 + 25 + 3 \times 25) \pmod 4$$
$$\equiv 100 \pmod 4$$
$$\equiv 0 \pmod 4.$$

Therefore 0 is the required remainder.

Example 9 : What is the remainder when $3^{12} + 5^{12}$ is divided by 13 ?

Solution : We have

$$3^2 \equiv 9 \pmod{13}$$
$$3^4 \equiv 9^2 \pmod{13}$$
$$\equiv 3 \pmod{13}$$
$$3^{12} \equiv 3^3 \pmod{13}$$
$$\equiv 27 \pmod{13}$$
$$\equiv 1 \pmod{13} \quad ....(1)$$

and
$$5^2 \equiv -1 \pmod{13}$$
$$5^{12} \equiv (-1)^6 \pmod{13}$$
$$\equiv 1 \pmod{13} \quad ....(2)$$

Adding (1) and (2) we have

$$3^{12} + 5^{12} \equiv 1 \pmod{13} + 1 \pmod{13}$$
$$= 2 \pmod{13}$$

Therefore the required remainder is 2.

4.4 Residue System

Let m be a fixed positive integer. A set $a_1, a_2, ... a_k$ of integers is called a Complete Residue System modulo m written as CRS (mod m) if

(i) $a_i \not\equiv a_j \pmod m$ for each $i \neq j$

(ii) For each integer n there exist a unique $a_i : n \equiv a_i \pmod m$.

In this way 0, 1, 2, ..., $m - 1$ is a CRS (mod m).

Theorem 1 : If $a_1, a_2, ..., a_k$ form a CRS (mod m) then $m = k$.

Proof : Since 0, 1, 2, ... $m - 1$ form a CRS (mod m) for each j, $1 \leqslant j \leqslant k$ these exists a unique integer i such that $0 \leqslant i \leqslant m - 1$ and $a_i \equiv i \pmod{m}$.

This gives $k \leqslant m$. ....(1)

But then $(a_1, a_2, ... a_k)$ is also a CRS (mod m). Therefore, for all i, $0 \leqslant i \leqslant m - 1$ there exists a unique, $1 \leqslant j \leqslant k$ such that $i \equiv a_j \pmod{m}$

This gives $m \leqslant k$. ....(2)

From (1) and (2) we get $m = k$

Example 1 : Show that the set {5, 12, – 3, – 4, 7, 22} (mod 6) is a complete system of residue.

Solution : The given set is a complete system of residue because the set consists of 6 integers whose least residue (mod 6) are 5, 0, 3, 2, 1, 4 which is a permutation of the number 0, 1, 2, 3, 4, 5.

Example 2 : Show that the set

{49, 20, 10, 17, – 18, – 27} (mod 6)

is a complete system of residue.

Solution : The given set is a complete system of residue because the set consists of 6 integers whose least residue (mod 6) are 1, 2, 4, 5, 0, 3 which is a permutation of the numbers 0, 1, 2, 3, 4, 5.

Example 3 : Show that the set {–3, 14, 3, 12, 37, 57, – 1} (mod 7) is a complete system of residue.

Solution : The given set as a complete system of residue because the set consists of seven integers whose least residue (mod 7) are 4, 0, 3, 5, 2, 1, 6 which is permutation of the numbers 0, 1, 2, 3, 4, 5, 6.

Reduced Residue System

The set of integers $a_1, a_2, ... a_k$ is called a reduced residue system modulo m written as RRS (mod m) if

(*i*) $(a_i, m) = 1 \ \forall \ i = 1, 2, ... k$

(*ii*) $a_i \equiv a_j \pmod{m} \ \forall \ i \neq j$ and

(*iii*) If n is an integer relatively prime to m then $n \equiv a_i \pmod{m}$ for a unique i, $1 \leqslant i \leqslant k$

Example 1 : Show that the set of integers {1, 5, 7, 11} is a RRS (mod 12).

Solution : We have

$$(1, 12) = 1, (5, 12) = 1, (7, 12) = 1 \text{ and } (11, 12) = 1.$$

Thus, condition (*i*) of definition of RRS is satisfied. (ii) condition is also obviously true.

Let m be any integer such that

$$(m, 12) = 1.$$

By division algorithm

$$m \equiv r \pmod{12},\ 0 \leqslant r < 12.$$

Now if $(r, 12) = 1$ then r will be 1 or 5 or 7 or 11.

Therefore, $m \equiv r \pmod{12}$.

Example 2 : Show that the set of integers

$\{-19, -1, 22, 43, 46, 79, 113, 452\}$ is a RRS (mod 15).

Solution : We see that the least residues (mod 15) of the integers of the given set are

$$11, 14, 7, 13, 1, 4, 8, 2. \quad \text{.......(1)}$$

Also the integers less than 15 and prime to 15 are

$$1, 2, 4, 7, 8, 11, 13, 14. \quad \text{.......(2)}$$

It is obvious that (1) is a permutation of (2). Therefore, the given set of integers is RRS (mod 15).

4.5 Tests of Divisibility

Congruences can be used to test whether a given integer is divisible by another given integer. These tests may be based on decimal notational system or binary notational system.

Theorem 1 : Let N be a positive integer such that

$$N = a_m 10^m + a_{m-1} 10^{m-1} + ... + a_1.10 + a_0$$

where $a_m \neq 0,\ 0 \leqslant a_i < 10,\ 0 \leqslant i \leqslant m-1$

then

(*i*) $2 | N \Leftrightarrow 2 | a_0$

(*ii*) $3 | N \Leftrightarrow 3 \left| \sum_{i=1}^{m} a_i \right.$

(*iii*) $4 | N \Leftrightarrow 4 | a_0 + 2a_1$

(*iv*) $5 | N \Leftrightarrow 5 | a_0$

(*v*) $9 | N \Leftrightarrow 9 \left| \sum_{i=1}^{m} a_i \right.$

and (*vi*) $11 | N \Leftrightarrow 11 \left| \sum_{i=0}^{m} (-1)^i a_i \right.$

Proof : We have

$$10 = \begin{cases} 0 \pmod 2 \text{ and } \pmod 5 \\ 1 \pmod 3 \text{ and } \pmod 9 \\ 2 \pmod 4 \\ -1 \pmod{11} \end{cases}$$

Therefore,

$$N = \begin{cases} a_0 \pmod 2 \text{ and } \pmod 5 \\ \Sigma\, a_i \pmod 3 \text{ and } \pmod 9 \\ 2a_1 + a_0 \pmod 4 \\ \Sigma(-1)^i\, a_i \pmod{11} \end{cases}$$

This gives that

(*i*) $2 | N \Leftrightarrow 2 | a_0$

(*ii*) $3 | N \Leftrightarrow 3 \left| \sum_{i=1}^{m} a_i \right.$

(*iii*) $4 | N \Leftrightarrow 4 | a_0 + 2a_1$

(*iv*) $5 | N \Leftrightarrow 5 | a_0$

(*v*) $9 | N \Leftrightarrow 9 \left| \sum_{i=1}^{m} a_i \right.$

(*vi*) $11 | N \Leftrightarrow 11 \left| \sum_{i=0}^{m} (-1)^i a_i \right.$.

Theorem 2 : (Dividisbility by 7 or 13)

A number $N = (a_{k-1}\, a_{k-2} \ldots\, a_1 a_0)$ is divisible by 7 or 13 iff

$(a_2\, a_1\, a_0) - (a_5\, a_4\, a_3) + (a_8\, a_7\, a_6)$ .... is divisible by 7 or 13.

Proof : Let $N = (a_{k-1}\, a_{k-2} \ldots\, a_1 a_0)$. Then it can be written as

$$N = (a_2\, a_1\, a_0) + (a_5\, a_4\, a_3) \times 1000 + (a_8\, a_7\, a_6) \times 1000^2 + \ldots$$

But $\quad 1000 \equiv -1 \pmod{7 \text{ or } 13}$

Therefore,

$$N \equiv (a_2\, a_1\, a_0) + (a_5\, a_4\, a_3) \times (-1) + (a_8\, a_7\, a_6) \times (-1)^2 + \ldots \pmod{7 \text{ or } 13}$$

Hence, N is divisible by 7 or 3 iff the right hand side of the above congruence is divisible by 7 or 13.

Theorem 3 : (Divisibility by 37)

A number $N = (a_{k-1}\, a_{k-2}, \ldots\, a_1 a_0)$ is divisible by 37 if

$(a_2\, a_1\, a_0) + (a_5\, a_4\, a_3) + \ldots$ is divisible by 37.

Proof : Here

$$N = (a_{k-1}\, a_{k-2} \,....\, a_1 a_0)$$

which can be written as

$$N = (a_2\, a_1\, a_0) + (a_5\, a_4\, a_3) \times 1000 + (a_8\, a_7\, a_6) \times 1000^2 + ...$$

But $1000 \equiv 1 \pmod{37}$

Therefore, $N = (a_2\, a_1\, a_0) + (a_5\, a_4\, a_3) + ... \pmod{37}$

Hence, N is divisible by 37 if $(a_2\, a_1\, a_0) + (a_5\, a_4\, a_3) + ...$ is divisible by 37.

Theorem 4 : (Divisibility by 101) : A number $N = (a_{k-1}\, a_{k-2} \,....\, a_1 a_0)$ divisible by 101.

Proof : N can be written as

$$N = (a_1\, a_0) + (a_3\, a_2) \times 100 + (a_5\, a_4) \times 100^2 + ...$$

But $100 \equiv -1 \pmod{101}$

Therefore, $N = (a_1\, a_0) - (a_3\, a_2) + (a_5\, a_4) .... \pmod{101}$

Theorem 5 : (Divisibility by 2^h) : A number $N = (a_{k-1}\, a_{k-2} .... a_1 a_0)$ is divisible by 2^h iff the number represented by the last h digits is divisible by 2^h.

Proof : Here

$$N = a_{k-1} \times 10^{k-1} + a_{k-2} \times 10^{k-2} + ... + a_h \times 10^h + a_{h-1} \times 10^{h-1} + ... a_0$$

Now 2^h divides 10^h and higher powers of 10. It follows that 2^h divides N iff 2^h divides $a_{h-1}\, 10^{h-1} + ... a_0$.

Example 1 : Show that 125671221 is divisible by 9.

Solution : The given number can be written as

$$125671221 = 1.10^8 + 2.10^7 + 5.10^6 + 6.10^5 + 7.10^4 + 1.10^3 + 2.10^2 + 2.10 + 1$$

The sum of coefficients

$$= 1 + 2 + 5 + 6 + 7 + 1 + 2 + 2 + 1$$

$$= 27$$

Obviously $9|27$. Therefore, $9|125671221$.

Example 2 : Show that the number 5117247 is divisible by 9.

Solution : The given number can be written as

$$5117247 = 5.10^6 + 1.10^5 + 1.10^4 + 7.10^3 + 2.10^2 + 4.10 + 7$$

The sum of coefficients

$$= 5 + 1 + 1 + 7 + 2 + 4 + 7$$

$$= 27$$

Since $9\,|\,27$, we have $9\,|\,5117247$.

Example 3 : Show that the number 1571427 is divisible by 11.

Solution : Here the alternating sum

$$= 1 - 5 + 7 - 1 + 4 - 2 + 7$$
$$= 11$$

which is divisible by 11. Therefore, the given number is divisible by 11.

Example 4. Test the number 67058902 for divisibility by 7.

Solution : To test the divisibility of 67058902 by 7 we first ignore the unit digit 2 to get the numbers 6705890. Subtracting twice the unit digit of this new number we get the same number. We again ignore the unit digit to get 670589. Subtraction twice the unit place digit number we get 67071. Again ignoring the unit place digit 1 we get 6707. Subtracting twice the unit place digit 7 we get 6693. Ignoring unit place digit 3 we get 669. Subtracting twice the unit digit place we get 651. Ignoring 1 we get 65. Such 65 is not divisible by 7, the given number is not divisible by 7.

Alternate method : Here. $N = 67058902$.

Now, $902 - 058 + 67 = 921$ is not divisible by 7. Therefore, the given number is not divisible by 7.

Example 5 : Show that the number 5233779 is divisible by 9.

Solution : Here, the sum of the digits

$$5 + 2 + 3 + 3 + 7 + 7 + 9 = 36$$

is divisible by 9. Therefore, the given number is divisible by 9.

Example 6 : Show that the number 2587322568103 is divisible by 7 and 13.

Solution : Here we have

$$103 - 568 + 322 - 587 + 2 = -728$$

which is divisible by 7 and 13. Therefore, the given number is divisible by 7 and 13.

Example 7 : Show that the number 22125744515 is divisible by 37.

Solution : Here we have

$$515 + 744 + 125 + 22 = 1406$$

which is divisible by 37. Therefore, the given number is divisible by 37.

Example 8 : Show that the number 58533742 is divisible by 101.

Solution : We have

$$42 - 37 + 53 - 58 = 0$$

which is divisible by 101. Therefore, the given number is divisible by 101.

4.6 Linear Congruence

(C.C.S.U. 2004

An expression of the form

$$ax \equiv b \pmod{m},\ a \not\equiv 0 \pmod{m} \qquad \text{.......(1}$$

is called a linear congruence mod m.

An integer x_0 for which $ax_0 \equiv b \pmod{m}$ is called a solution of linear congruence $ax \equiv b \pmod{m}$.

Now, $\quad ax_0 \equiv b \pmod{m} \Rightarrow m \mid (ax_0 - b)$

$\Rightarrow \exists$ an integer y_0 such that $ax_0 - b = my_0$

$\Rightarrow ax_0 - my_0 = b.$

This shows that (x_0, y_0) is a solution of the linear Diophantine equation

$$ax - my = b. \qquad ....(2)$$

Linear Diophantine equation (2) has a solution if $d = (a, m)$ divides b. If (x_0, y_0) is a particular solution of (2) then general solution is given by $x = x_0 + \frac{m}{d}t, y = y_0 + \frac{a}{d}t$ where t is an integer.

Theorem 1 : The linear congruence $ax \equiv b \pmod{m}$ has a solution iff $d|b$ where $d = (a, m)$.

Proof : We have observed that the linear congruence $ax \equiv b \pmod{m}$ is equivalent to the linear Diophantine equation $ax - my = b$ which is soluble iff $d \mid b$. If (x_0, y_0) is its solution then

$$x = x_0 + \frac{m}{d}t, \quad y = y_0 + \frac{a}{d}t$$

are the other solution.

We consider the solution

$$x_0, \; x_0 + \frac{m}{d}, \; x_0 + \frac{2m}{d}, \ldots \; x_0 + \frac{(d-1)m}{d}.$$

Now we shall show that these solutions are mutually in congruent solution of the linear congruent

$$ax \equiv b \pmod{m}.$$

If $x_0 + \frac{m}{d}t_1 = x_0 + \frac{m}{d}t_2 \pmod{m}, \quad 0 \leqslant t_1 < t_2 \leqslant d - 1$

then we have

$$\frac{m}{d}t_1 = \frac{m}{d}t_2 \pmod{m}. \qquad ....(1)$$

Now $gcd\left(\frac{m}{d}, m\right) = \frac{m}{d}$ therefore (1) implies

$$t_1 \equiv t_2 \pmod{m}$$

$$\Rightarrow \quad d \mid (t_2 - t_1)$$

But this is impossible as $0 < t_2 - t_1 < d$

Theorem 2 : Let $ax \equiv b \pmod{m}$, $(a, m) = d$ and $d \mid b$. Then the given linear congruence has exactly d incongruent solutions (mod m). **(C.C.S. 2005)**

Proof : We have already shown that $x_0 + \frac{m}{d}t$ is the solution of the given linear congruence. We have to show that they are exactly d incongruent solutions (mod m).

By division algorithm we can write

$$t = qd + r, \text{ where } 0 \leqslant r \leqslant d - 1.$$

Therefore,

$$x_0 + \frac{m}{d}t = x_0 + \frac{m}{d}(qd + r)$$

$$= x_0 + mq + \frac{m}{d}r$$

$$\equiv x_0 + \frac{m}{d}r \pmod{m},$$

These solutions are d in number. Thus, the given linear congruence has exactly d incongruent solution (mod m).

Corollary 1 : The linear congruence $ax \equiv b \pmod{m}$ has a unique solution iff $(a, m) = 1$.

Theorem 3 : (Chinese Remainder Theorem)

Let $m_1, m_2, \ldots, m_r$ be pairwise relatively prime numbers such that gcd $(m_i, m_j) = 1$ for $i \neq j$. Then, the system of linear congruences

$$x \equiv a_1 \pmod{m_1}$$
$$x \equiv a_2 \pmod{m_2}$$
$$\vdots$$
$$x \equiv a_r \pmod{m_r}$$

has a simultaneous solution which is unique modulo $m_1, m_2, \ldots, m_r$. (R.U. 2005)

Proof : Let $m = m_1 m_2 \ldots, m_r$ and let for each $k = 1, 2, \ldots, r$

$$M_k = = \frac{m}{m_k} = m_1 m_2 \ldots m_{k-1} m_{k+1} \ldots m_r.$$

Since m_i are relatively prime in pairs, we have

$$\gcd(M_k, m_k) = 1.$$

Therefore, it is possible to solve the linear congruence $M_k x \equiv 1 \pmod{m_k}$. It will have a unique solution x_k (say).

Now we shall show that

$$\bar{x} = a_1 M_1 x_1 + a_2 M_2 x_2 + \ldots a_r M_r x_r$$

is a simultaneous solution of the given system.

We have $M_i \equiv 0 \pmod{m_k}$ for $i \neq k$ as m_k / m_i.

Therefore $\bar{x} = a_1 M_1 x_1 + \ldots a_r M_r x_r \equiv a_k M_k x_k \pmod{m_k}$.

But x_k satisfies the congruence $M_k x \equiv 1 \pmod{m_k}$.

$\therefore \quad \bar{x} \equiv a_k.1 \equiv a_k \pmod{m_k}$

This shows that a solution to the given system of congruence exists.

Uniqueness : Suppose $\bar{x}_1$ and $\bar{x}_2$ are two solutions of the given system.. Then

$$\bar{x}_1 \equiv a_k \equiv \bar{x}_2 \pmod{m_k},\ k = 1, 2, ..., r.$$

$$\Rightarrow m_k | \bar{x}_1 - \bar{x}_2) \text{ for each } k.$$

Since gcd $(m_i, m_j) = 1$ for $i \neq j$ we have $m_1 m_2 - m_r | (\bar{x}_1 - \bar{x}_2)$.

Therefore $\bar{x}_1 = \bar{x}_2 \pmod{m}$. This proves uniqueness.

Example 1 : Solve the following linear congruence

$$9x \equiv 12 \pmod{15}$$

Solution : Here we have

$$(9, 15) = 3 \text{ and } 3 | 12.$$

Therefore the given linear congruence has a solution. It will have 3 incongruent solutions. $x_0 = 3$ is a solution of the linear congruence

$$9x \equiv 12 \pmod{15}.$$

Hence, $3, 3 + \frac{15}{3}, 3 + 2.\frac{15}{3}$, *i.e.*, 3, 8, 13 are 3 incongruent solutions (mod 15).

Example 2 : Solve the linear congruence.

$$6x \equiv 15 \pmod{21}$$

Solution : Here we have

$$(6, 21) = 3 \text{ and } 3 | 15.$$

Therefore, the given linear congruence has a solution. It will have 3 incongruent solution

$x_0 = 6$ is a solution of the linear congruence

$6x \equiv 15 \pmod{21}$.

Hence $6, 6 + \frac{21}{3}, 6 + 2.\frac{21}{3}$, *i.e.*, 6. 13. 20 are 3 incongruent solution (mod 21).

Example 3 : (Method of Diophantine equation)

Solve $9x \equiv 21 \pmod{30}$. **(C.C.S.U. 2004)**

Solution : Here $(9, 30) = 3$. Therefore, there are 3 solutions. To solve the given linear congruence. We solve the Diophantine equation

$$9x + 30y = 21 \quad ....(1)$$

$$\Rightarrow 9x + (9 \times 3 + 3)y = 9 \times 2 + 3$$

$$\Rightarrow 9(x + 3y - 2) + 3y = 3$$

$$\Rightarrow 9u + 3y = 3, \quad \text{where } u = x + 3y - 2$$

$$\Rightarrow 3u + y = 1. \quad ....(2)$$

Putting $u = 0$ in (2) we get

$$y = 1.$$

Putting $y = 1$ in (1) we get

$$9x + 30\,(1) = 21$$

or $$9x = 21 - 30 = -9$$

or $$x = -1.$$

The least residue $-1 \pmod{30}$ is 29.

The other two solution will be $29 - \frac{30}{3}$ and $-1 - 2.\frac{30}{3}$ *i.e.*, 19 and 9.

Example 4 : Solve $49x \equiv 47 \pmod{81}$.

Solution : Here $(49, 81) = 1$. Therefore, there is only one solution. To find this solution we solve the Diophantine equation.

$$49x + 81y = 47. \qquad \text{........(1)}$$

Now equation (1) can be written as

$$49x + (49 \times 2 - 17)y = 49 \times 1 - 2$$

or $$49[x + 2y - 1] - 17y = -2$$

or $$49u - 17y = -2, \quad \text{where } u = x + 2y - 1 \qquad \text{.......(2)}$$

or $$(17 \times 3 - 2)u - 17y = -2$$

or $$17[3u - y] - 2u = -2$$

or $$17v - 2u = -2, \quad \text{where } v = 3u - y \qquad \text{.......(3)}$$

This gives $v = 0$, $u = 1$.

Putting $u = 1$ in (2), we get. $y = 3$

Putting $y = 3$ in (1), we get

$$49x + 81 \times 3 = 47$$

or $$49x = 47 - 243$$

$$= -196$$

or $$x = -4.$$

The least residue of $-4 \pmod{81}$ is 77.

Hence, the solution of the given congruence is $77 \pmod{81}$.

Example 5 : Solve the linear congruence

$$12x \equiv 44 \pmod{59}$$

Solution : The given linear congruence

$$ax \equiv b \pmod{m},\ (a, m) = 1$$

can be written as

$$x \equiv \frac{b}{a} \pmod{m}$$

$$\equiv \frac{b + mh}{a} \pmod{m}$$

Here, $a = 12$, $b = 44$ and $m = 59$

Also $(12, 59) = 1$. Therefore,

$$12x \equiv 44 \pmod{59}$$

$$\Rightarrow \quad x \equiv \frac{44}{12} \pmod{59}$$

$$\equiv 3 + \frac{2}{3} \pmod{59}$$

$$\equiv 3 + \frac{2 + 2 \times 59}{3} \pmod{59}$$

$$\equiv 43 \pmod{59}.$$

Example 6 : Find the solution of

$47x \equiv 11 \pmod{249}$. **(C.C.S. U. 2004)**

Solution : Here, $(47, 249) = 1$. Therefore, the given congruence can be written as

$$x \equiv \frac{11}{47} \pmod{249}$$

$$\equiv \frac{11 + 16 \times 249}{47} \pmod{249}$$

$$\equiv 85 \pmod{249}.$$

Example 7 : Find the last two digits of the number 9^{9^9}.

Solution : We have

$$9^2 \equiv 1 \pmod{10}$$

$$\Rightarrow (9^2)^4 \equiv 1 \pmod{10}$$

$$\Rightarrow \quad 9^8 \equiv 1 \pmod{10}$$

$$\Rightarrow \quad 9^9 \equiv 9 \pmod{10}$$

$$\therefore \quad 9^9 = 10k + 9. \quad \text{.......(1)}$$

Now $$9^{9^9} = 9^{9 + 10k}$$

$$= 9^9 \times 9^{10k} \quad \text{.......(2)}$$

But $$9^{10} \equiv 1 \pmod{100}.$$

$$\therefore \quad 9^{10k} \equiv 1 \pmod{100}. \quad \text{.......(3)}$$

Using (3) in (2) we have

$$9^{9^9} \equiv 9^9 \times 1 \pmod{100}$$

$$\equiv 9 \times 9^8 \pmod{100}$$

$\equiv 9 \times 21 \pmod{100}$

$\equiv 89 \pmod{100}$.

Example 8 : Solve the system of linear congruence

$$x \equiv 2 \pmod 3$$
$$x \equiv 3 \pmod 5$$
$$x \equiv 2 \pmod 7$$

Solution : Here $m = 3.5.7 = 105$, $a_1 = 2$, $a_2 = 3$, $a_3 = 2$, $m_1 = 3$, $m_2 = 5$ and $m_3 = 7$

$$M_1 = \frac{m}{m_1} = \frac{105}{3} = 35$$

$$M_2 = \frac{m}{m_2} = \frac{105}{5} = 21$$

$$M_3 = \frac{m}{m_3} = \frac{105}{7} = 15.$$

Now the linear congruences

$$35x \equiv 1 \pmod 3$$
$$21x \equiv 1 \pmod 5$$
$$15x \equiv 1 \pmod 7$$

are satisfied by $x_1 = 2$, $x_2 = 1$, $x_3 = 1$ respectively A solution of the system is given by

$$\bar{x} = a_1M_1x_1 + a_2M_2x_2 + a_3M_3x_3$$
$$= 2.35.2 + 3.21.1 + 2.15.1$$
$$= 233. \text{ Modulo } (105).$$

Thus, we have the unique solution

$$\bar{x} = 233 \equiv 23 \pmod{105}.$$

Example 9 : Solve the system of linear congruence

$$x \equiv 3 \pmod{11}$$
$$x \equiv 5 \pmod{19}$$
$$x \equiv 10 \pmod{29}$$

Solution : Here $m = 11.19.29 = 6061$, $a_1 = 3$, $a_2 = 5$, $a_3 = 10$, $m_1 = 11$, $m_2 = 19$, $m_3 = 29$

$$M_1 = \frac{m}{m_1} = \frac{6061}{11} = 551$$

$$M_2 = \frac{m}{m_2} = \frac{6061}{19} = 319$$

$$M_3 = \frac{m}{m_3} = \frac{6061}{29} = 209.$$

Now the linear congruences.

$$551x \equiv 1 \pmod{11}$$
$$319x \equiv 1 \pmod{19}$$
$$209x \equiv 1 \pmod{29}$$

are satisfied by $x_1 = 1, x_2 = 14$ and $x_3 = 5$ respectively.

A solution of the system is given by

$$\bar{x} = a_1M_1x_1 + a_2M_2x_2 + a_3M_3x_3$$
$$= 3.551.1 + 5.319.14 + 10.209.5$$
$$= 1653 + 22330 + 10450$$
$$= 34433$$
$$= 4128 \pmod{6061}.$$

Thus, we have the unique solution

$$\bar{x} = 4128 \pmod{6061}.$$

Example 10 : Find an integer which leaves remainder 5 when divided by 11 and 2 when divided by 19.

Solution : Let the required number be x. Then we have

$$x \equiv 5 \pmod{11}$$

and $\quad x \equiv 2 \pmod{19}$

Here $m = 11.19 = 209, a_1 = 5, a_2 = 2, m_1 = 11, m_2 = 19$

$$M_1 = \frac{m}{m_1} = 19$$

$$M_2 = \frac{m}{m_2} = 11.$$

Now the linear congruences

$$19x \equiv 1 \pmod{11}$$
$$11x \equiv 1 \pmod{19}$$

are satisfied by $x_1 = 7$ and $x_2 = 7$.

A solution of the system is given by

$$\bar{x} = a_1M_1x_1 + a_2M_2x_2$$
$$= 5.19.7 + 2.11.7$$
$$= 665 + 154$$
$$= 819$$
$$= 192 \bmod (209).$$

Thus, we have

$$x = 192 \pmod{209}.$$

Example 11 : Solve the system

$$x \equiv 3 \pmod{6}$$
$$x \equiv 5 \pmod{7}$$
$$x \equiv 2 \pmod{11}$$

Solution : Here we have

$$m_1 = 6, m_2 = 7 \text{ and } m_3 = 11$$

$$m = m_1 m_2 m_3$$
$$= 6 \times 7 \times 11$$
$$= 462$$

Now $$M_1 = \frac{m}{m_1} = \frac{462}{6} = 77$$

$$M_2 = \frac{m}{m_2} = \frac{462}{7} = 66$$

$$M_3 = \frac{m}{m_3} = \frac{462}{11} = 42.$$

Now the linear congruences

$$77x \equiv 1 \pmod{6}$$
$$66x \equiv 1 \pmod{7}$$
$$42x \equiv 1 \pmod{11}$$

are satisfied by $x_1 = -1$, $x_2 = -2$, $x_3 = 5$

A solution of the given system is given by

$$\bar{x} = a_1 M_1 x_1 + a_2 M_2 x_2 + a_3 M_3 x_3$$
$$= 3 \times 77 \times (-1) + 5 \times 66 \times (-2) + 2 \times 42 \times 5$$
$$= 231 - 660 + 420 = -471$$
$$\equiv 453 \pmod{462}.$$

4.7 Solvability Condition of a System of Linear Congruences

A system of linear congruences

$$x \equiv a_1 \pmod{m_1}$$
$$x \equiv a_2 \pmod{m_2}$$
$$\vdots$$
$$x = a_n \pmod{m_n}$$

is solvable iff (m_i, m_j) divides $(a_i - a_j)$.

Example 1 : Is the following system solvable ?

$$x \equiv 2 \pmod 5$$
$$x \equiv 4 \pmod{21}$$
$$x \equiv 3 \pmod{14}.$$

Solution : Here we have

$4 - 2$ is divisible by $(21, 5) = 1$.

$3 - 2 = 1$ is divisible by $(14, 5) = 1$

but $4 - 3 = 1$ is not divisible by $(21, 14) = 7$.

Hence, the given system is not solvable.

Example 2 : Is the system of linear congruences given below is solvable ?

$$x \equiv 5 \pmod 8$$
$$x \equiv 9 \pmod{12}$$
$$x \equiv 3 \pmod{18}.$$

Solution : Here we have

$(8, 12) = 4$ divides $5 - 9 = 4$

$(8, 18) = 2$ divides $5 - 3 = 2$

$(12, 18) = 6$ divides $9 - 3 = 6$.

Therefore, the given system of linear congruences is solvable.

4.8 Congruences of Higher Degree

Let $\quad f(x) = a_0x^n + a_1x^{n-1} + ... + a_n \equiv 0 \pmod p,\ a_0 \neq 0$ ....(1)

p is a prime and p ... a_0, be a congruence of nth degree. We have to solve this higher degree congruence.

If some coefficients of $f(x)$ in (1) are greater than p, we reduce them to less than p. If the degree of $f(x)$ is not less than p, we get remainder $r(x)$ such that

$$f(x) = (x^p - x)\, q(x) + r(x)$$

where degree $[r(x)] < p$

Now the problem (1) reduces to

$$r(x) \equiv 0 \pmod p$$

Also if $f(x) = f_1(x) f_2(x) \pmod p$ then to solve (1), we have to solve

$$f_1(x) \equiv 0 (\text{mod } p) \text{ and } f_2(x) \equiv 0 \ (\text{mod } p)$$

Futher if $x = a(\text{mod } p)$ is a solution of (1) then $f(x) \equiv (x - a)\, q(x) + r(x)$.

Since $r(x) \equiv 0(\text{mod } p)$, we have to solve

$$q(x) \equiv 0(\text{mod } p)$$

Example 1 : Show that $x^2 \equiv 1(\text{mod } p)$ has only two solutions 1 and $p-1$, p is a prime.

Solution : If a is a solution of the given congruence then we have

$$a^2 - 1 \equiv 0(\text{mod } p)$$

$$\Rightarrow \quad p \mid (a-1)(a+1)$$

$$\Rightarrow \quad p \mid a-1 \text{ or } p \mid (a+1) \qquad [\because p \text{ is a prime}]$$

$$\Rightarrow \quad a - 1 \equiv 0(\text{mod } p) \text{ or } a + 1 \equiv 0(\text{mod } p)$$

Now taking a for the least positive residues, we have

$$a = 1 \quad \text{or} \quad a = p - 1.$$

∎

EXERCISE

1. Find the remainder when 11^{35} is divided by 13.
2. Find the remainder when 2^{14} is divided by 17.
3. Prove that $53^{103} + 103^{53}$ is divisible by 39.
4. Show that $13 \mid (3^{n+2} + 4^{2n+1})$.
5. If a is odd then show that
   $$a^{2^n} \equiv 1 \pmod{2^{n+2}},\ n \geqslant 1.$$
6. Solve the linear congruences
   $30x \equiv 52 \pmod{49}$
7. Solve the linear congruence
   $5x \equiv 2 \pmod{26}$
8. Solve the linear congruence
   $17x \equiv 9 \pmod{276}$
9. Solve the system of linear congruences
   $$x \equiv 5 \pmod{6}$$
   $$x \equiv 4 \ ((\text{mod } 11)$$
   $$x \equiv 3 \pmod{17}$$
10. Using congruences solve the Diophantine equation $4x + 51y = 9$
11. Show that the congruence
    $f(x) = x^3 + x^2 + 4x + 29 \equiv 0 \pmod{125}$ is satisfied by $x = 109$.

(C.C.S.U. 2004)

◆

Answers to Exercise	
1. 6 2. 13 6. 5 7. 16	8. $x = 33$ (Mod 276) 9. $x = 785$ (Mod 1122) 10. ($x = 15, 15t$; $y = -1 + 4t$, $t \in Z$)

❑

CHAPTER 5

Fermat's Theorem

5.1 Introduction

Pierre de Fermat (1601-1665) had no particular training of mathematics. By profession he was a lawyer and magistrate attached to the provincial parliament at Toulouse. To do research work in mathematics was merely a hobby for him to be done in leisure time. In this chapter, we shall discuss some Fermat's work and related topics. We shall discuss Fermat's Factorization Method, Fermat's Little Theorem, Wilson's Theorem and Euler's Factorization Method.

5.2 Fermat's Factorization Method

Let n be an odd positive integer which is the difference of squares of two integers *i.e.*,

$$n = x^2 - y^2$$
$$= (x + y)(x - y)$$

Conversely if $n = ab$, $a \geqslant b \geqslant 1$ then we can write

$$n = \left(\frac{a+b}{2}\right)^2 - \left(\frac{a-b}{2}\right)^2$$

Since n is an odd integer, we have a and b will be odd integers and consequently $\left(\frac{a+b}{2}\right)$ and $\left(\frac{a-b}{2}\right)$ will be non-negative integers.

We have to find the value (integral) of x and y.

satisfying $$n = x^2 - y^2.$$

or $$x^2 - n = y^2.$$

For this we observe the numbers

$$k^2 - n, (k + 1)^2 - n, (k + 2)^2 - n, \ldots\ldots$$

Let $m \geqslant \sqrt{n}$ such that $m^2 - n$ is a square. If in this case n can be factorize n is not expressible as difference of squares of two numbers then n has no factor other than n and 1. In this case n is a prime number.

Example 1 : Use Fermat's method to factor 10541. **(C.C.S.U. 2004)**

Solution : From the table of squares we see that $102^2 < 10541 < 103^2$. Therefore, we have to consider the values of $k^2 - 10541$ for $k \geqslant 103$. Taking $k = 103, 104, \ldots$ we have

$$103^2 - 10541 = 10609 - 10541 = 68$$

$$104^2 - 10541 = 10816 - 10541 = 275$$

$$105^2 - 10541 = 11025 - 10541 = 484 = 22^2.$$

Last relation gives

$$\begin{aligned} 10541 &= 150^2 - 22^2 \\ &= (105 + 22)(105 - 22) \\ &= 127 \times 83. \end{aligned}$$

These are the required factors.

Example 2 : Use Fermat's method to factor 23449.

Solution : From the table of squares we see that $153^2 < 23449 < 154^2$. Therefore, we have to consider the value of $k^2 - 23449$ for $k \geqslant 154$. Taking $k = 154, 155, \ldots$ we have

$$154^2 - 23449 = 23716 - 23449 = 267$$

$$155^2 - 23449 = 24025 - 23449 = 576 = 24^2.$$

The last relation can be written as

$$\begin{aligned} 23449 &= 155^2 - 24^2 \\ &= (155 + 24)(155 - 24) \\ &= 179 \times 131. \end{aligned}$$

Thus, 179 and 131 are the required factors.

Example 3 : Factorize $2^{11} - 1$ by Fermat's factorization method.

Solution : We have

$$\begin{aligned} 2^{11} - 1 &= 2048 - 1 \\ &= 2047. \end{aligned}$$

From the table of squares we see that $45^2 < 2047 < 46^2$. Therefore we have to consider the values $k^2 - 2047$ for $k \geqslant 46$. Taking $k = 46, 47, \ldots$ we have

$$46^2 - 2047 = 2116 - 2047 = 69$$

$$47^2 - 2047 = 2209 - 2047 = 162$$

$$48^2 - 2047 = 2304 - 2047 = 257$$

$$49^2 - 2047 = 2401 - 2047 = 354$$

$$50^2 - 2047 = 2500 - 2047 = 453$$

$$51^2 - 2047 = 2601 - 2047 = 554$$

$$52^2 - 2047 = 2704 - 2047 = 657$$

$$53^2 - 2047 = 2809 - 2047 = 762$$

$$54^2 - 2047 = 2916 = 2047 = 869$$

$$55^2 - 2047 = 3025 - 2047 = 978$$

$$56^2 - 2047 = 3136 - 2047 = 1089 = 33^2.$$

The last relation can be written as

$$\begin{aligned} 2047 &= 56^2 - 33^2 \\ &= (56 + 33)(56 - 33) \\ &= 89 \times 23. \end{aligned}$$

Thus, 89 and 23 are the required factors.

5.3 Fermat's Little Theorem

If p is a prime and $(a, p) = 1$ then $a^{p-1} - 1$ is divisible by p *i.e.*, $a^{p-1} \equiv 1 (\text{mod } p)$.

(C.C.S.U. 2003)

Proof : We have

$$(x_1 + x_2)^p = x_1^p + \binom{p}{1} x_1^{p-1} x_2 + \binom{p}{2} x_1^{p-2} x_2^2 + ... + \binom{p}{p-1} x_1 x_2^{p-1} + x_2^p.$$

$$= x_1^p + x_2^p + \text{terms divisible by } p$$

$$\equiv (x_1^p + x_2^p) (\text{mod } p).$$

Similarly, we can show that

$$(x_1 + x_2 + ... x_a)^p \equiv (x_1^p + x_2^p + ... x_a^p) (\text{mod } p). \qquad ....(1)$$

Putting $x_1 = x_2 .... = x_a = 1$ in (1), we get

$$a^p \equiv a (\text{mod } p). \qquad ....(2)$$

But $(a, p) = 1$. Therefore, we can cancel the common factor a in (2). Thus, we have

$$a^{p-1} \equiv 1 (\text{mod } p).$$

$$\Rightarrow a^{p-1} - 1 \equiv 0 (\text{mod } p)$$

$$\Rightarrow (a^{p-1} - 1) \text{ is divisible by } p.$$

Another Proof : We consider the integers $a, 2a, 3a, ..., (p - 1)a$

None of these integers is congruent mod p to another. Also none of them is congruent to zero. If it is so *i.e.*,

$$r_1 a \equiv r_2 a \pmod{p},\ 1 \leqslant r_1 < r_2 \leqslant p-1$$

then, $$r_1 \equiv r_2 \pmod{p}$$

This is impossible. Therefore, the above integers should be congruent mod p to $1, 2, 3 \ldots, p-1$ in order. Multiplying these congruences together, we have

$$a.2a.3a. \ldots (p-1)a \equiv 1.2.3 \ldots (p-1) \pmod{p}$$

$$\Rightarrow a^{p-1}(p-1)! \equiv (p-1)! \pmod{p}$$

$$\Rightarrow \quad a^{p-1} \equiv 1 \pmod{p}. \qquad [\because p \nmid (p-1)!]$$

The converse of Fermat's little theorem need not be true *i.e.*, if $a^{p-1} \equiv a \pmod{p}$ for some integers a and p then p need not be a prime. For example

$$2^{340} \equiv 1 \pmod{341}$$

341 is not a prime.

Corollary 1 : If p is a prime then $a^p \equiv a \pmod{p}$ for any integer a.

Pseudo prime : An integer n is called a pseudo prime if $2^n \equiv 2 \pmod{n}$.

The number 341 is a pseudo prime because the relation can be written as $2^{341} \equiv 2 \pmod{341}$.

Lemma : If p and q are distinct primes such that $a^p \equiv a \pmod{q}$ and $a^q \equiv a \pmod{p}$.

Then $$a^{pq} \equiv a \pmod{pq}$$

Proof : By the last corollary, we have

$$(a^p)^q \equiv a^p \pmod{q}$$

and $$a^p \equiv a \pmod{q}$$

$$\Rightarrow \quad a^{pq} \equiv a \pmod{q}$$

$$\Rightarrow q \text{ divides } a^{pq} - a. \qquad \ldots\ldots.(1)$$

Similarly, $$(a^q)^p = a^q \pmod{p}$$

and $$a^q \equiv a \pmod{p}$$

$$\Rightarrow \quad a^{pq} = a \pmod{p}$$

$$\Rightarrow p \text{ divides } a^{pq} - a. \qquad \ldots\ldots.(2)$$

Since p and q are distinct primes. We have from (1) and (2) that

$$pq \text{ divides } a^{pq} - a$$

or $$a^{pq} \equiv a \pmod{pq}.$$

For example $341 = 11.31$ is not a prime.

Now $2^{11} = 2^{10+1}$

$= (2^5)^2.2$

$= 32^2.2$

$\equiv 2(\text{mod } 31)$

and $2^{31} = 2^{30+1}$

$= (2^5)^6.2$

$= (32)^6.2$

$\equiv (-1)^6.2 \ (\text{mod } 11)$

$\equiv 2(\text{mod } 11)$

Here 31 and 11 are distinct primes such that

$$2^{11} = 2(\text{mod } 31) \quad \text{and} \quad 2^{31} \equiv 2(\text{mod } 11) \Rightarrow 2^{11.31} = 2^{341} = 2 \ (\text{mod } 341).$$

Example 1 : Show that $8^{30} - 1$ is divisible by 31.

Solution : We have (8, 31) = 1 and 31 is a prime. Therefore, by Fermat's theorem

$$8^{31-1} - 1 = 8^{30} - 1$$

is divisible by 31.

Example 2 : Find the remainder when 72^{1001} is divided by 31.

Solution : We have

$$72 \equiv 10(\text{mod } 31)$$

Therefore, $72^{1001} \equiv 10^{1001} \ (\text{mod } 31)$

Now (10, 31) = 1 and 31 is a prime. Hence, by Fermat's theorem we have

$$10^{30} \equiv 1 \ (\text{mod } 31)$$

$$\Rightarrow \quad 10^{990} \equiv 1 \ (\text{mod } 31)$$

Also $10^2 \equiv 7(\text{mod } 31)$

$10^4 \equiv -13(\text{mod } 31)$

$10^8 \equiv 14(\text{mod } 31)$

Now $72^{1001} \equiv 10^{1001} \ (\text{mod } 31)$

$\equiv 10^{990} \times 10^8 \times 10^2 \times 10(\text{mod } 31)$

$\equiv 1 \times 14 \times 7 \times 10(\text{mod } 31)$

$\equiv 5 \times 10(\text{mod } 31)$

$\equiv 19(\text{mod } 31)$

This shows that the remainder is 19 when 72^{1001} is divided by 31.

Example 3 : If $7 \nmid a$, prove that either $a^3 + 1$ or $a^3 - 1$ is divisible by 7.

Solution : Since 7 is a prime and $(7, a) = 1$ by Fermat's theorem we have

$$a^{7-1} \equiv 1 \pmod 7$$

$$\Rightarrow \quad a^6 \equiv 1 \pmod 7$$

$$\Rightarrow a^6 - 1 \text{ is divisible by } 7$$

$$\Rightarrow (a^3 + 1)(a^3 - 1) \text{ is divisible by } 7$$

This shows that either $a^3 + 1$ or $a^3 - 1$ is divisible by 7.

Example 4 : Show that $5^{38} \equiv 4 \pmod{11}$ **[C.C.S. (B.P.) 2006]**

Solution : Since 11 is a prime and $(5, 11) = 1$ by the corollary 1 we have

$$5^{11} \equiv 5 \pmod{11}$$

$$\therefore \quad 5^{33} \equiv 5^3 \pmod{11}.$$

Now

$$\begin{aligned} 5^{38} &= 5^{33} \times 5^5 \\ &\equiv 5^3 \times 5^5 \pmod{11} \\ &\equiv 5^8 \pmod{11} \\ &\equiv (5^2)^4 \pmod{11} \\ &\equiv 3^4 \pmod{11} \\ &\equiv 81 \pmod{11} \\ &\equiv 4 \pmod{11}. \end{aligned}$$

Example 5 : Find the remainder when 41^{75} is divided by 3.

Solution : We have

$$41 \equiv 2 \pmod 3$$

$$\therefore \quad 41^{75} \equiv 2^{75} \pmod 3$$

Now $(2, 3) = 1$ and 3 is a prime. Therefore, by Fermat's theorem we have

$$2^2 \equiv 1 \pmod 3$$

$$\Rightarrow 2^{74} \equiv 1 \pmod 3$$

Now

$$\begin{aligned} 41^{75} &\equiv 2^{75} \pmod 3 \\ &\equiv 2^{74} \times 2 \pmod 3 \\ &\equiv 1 \times 2 \pmod 3 \\ &\equiv 2 \pmod 3 \end{aligned}$$

This shows that the remainder is 2 when 41^{75} is divided by 3.

Example 6 : Find the remainder when $2^{1000000}$ is divided by 7.

Solution : We have (2, 7) = 1 and 7 is a prime. Therefore, by Fermat's theorem we have

$$2^6 \equiv 1 \pmod 7$$

$$\Rightarrow (2^6)^{166666} \equiv 1 \pmod 7$$

$$\Rightarrow \quad 2^{999996} \equiv 1 \pmod 7$$

Now $$2^{1000000} = 2^{999996} \times 2^4 \pmod 7$$

$$= 1 \times 16 \pmod 7$$

$$= 2 \pmod 7.$$

This shows that the remainder will be 2 when $2^{1000000}$ is divided by 7.

Example 7 : What is the remainder when 3^{287} is divided by 23 ?

Solution : Here (3, 23) = 1 and 23 is a prime.

Therefore,

$$3^{22} \equiv 1 \pmod{23}$$

$$\Rightarrow (3^{22})^{13} \equiv 1 \pmod{23}$$

$$\Rightarrow \quad 3^{286} \equiv 1 \pmod{23}.$$

Now, $$3^{287} \equiv 3^{286} \times 3 \pmod{23}$$

$$\equiv 1 \times 3 \pmod{23}$$

$$\equiv 3 \pmod{23}.$$

This shows that the remainder will be 3 when 3^{287} is divided by 23.

Example 8 : Find the remainder when 5^{11} is divided by 7. (C.C.S. 2001, 2003)

Solution : We have (5, 7) = 1 and 7 is a prime. Therefore,

$$5^6 \equiv 1 \pmod 7$$

Also $$5^4 \equiv 2 \pmod 7$$

Now, $$5^{11} \equiv 5^6 \times 5^4 \times 5 \pmod 7$$

$$\equiv 1 \times 2 \times 5 \pmod 7$$

$$\equiv 10 \pmod 7$$

$$\equiv 3 \pmod 7.$$

$\therefore$ The required remainder is 3.

Absolute Pseudo primes (Carmichael Numbers)

A composite number n is called an absolute pseudo prime if $a^n \equiv a \pmod n$ for all integers a. The least absolute pseudo prime is 561.

Theorem : Let n be a composite square free integer let $n = p_1p_2 \ldots p_r$, p_i are distinct primes. If $(p_i - 1)/(n - 1)$ for $i = 1, 2, \ldots, r$ then n is an absolute pseudo prime.

Proof : Let a be an integer such that $(a, n) = 1$. Then $(a, p_i) = 1$ for each i. By Fermat's theorem we have $p_i/(a^{p_i - 1} - 1)$. Since $(p_i - 1)/(n - 1)$ we have $p_i/(a^{n-1} - 1)$. Therefore, $p_i/(a^n - a)$ for all a and $i = 1, 2, \ldots, r$. Hence, $n/(a^n - a) \Rightarrow a^n \equiv a(\text{mod } n)$. Thus, n is an absolute pseudo prime.

Example 1 : Show that 561 is an absolute pseudo prime.

Solution : We have $561 = 3.11.17$. If $(a, 561) = 1$ then $(a, 3) = 1$, $(a, 11) = 1$ and $(a, 17) = 1$. Therefore, by Fermat's theorem we have,

$$a^2 \equiv 1(\text{mod } 3),\ a^{10} \equiv 1(\text{mod } 11),\ a^{16} \equiv 1(\text{mod } 17)$$

$$\Rightarrow \quad a^{560} = (a^2)^{280} \equiv 1(\text{mod } 3)$$

$$a^{560} = (a^{10})^{56} \equiv 1(\text{mod } 11)$$

$$a^{560} = (a^{16})^{35} \equiv 1(\text{mod } 17)$$

$$\Rightarrow \quad a^{560} \equiv 1(\text{mod } 3.11.17)$$

$$\equiv 1(\text{mod } 561)$$

$$\Rightarrow \quad a^{561} \equiv a(\text{mod } 561).$$

This shows that 561 is an absolute pseudo prime.

Example 2 : Show that 1729 is an absolute pseudo prime.

Solution : We have

$1729 = 7.13.19$. If $(a, 1729) = 1$ then

$$(a, 7) = 1,\ (a, 13) = 1 \text{ and } (a, 19) = 1.$$

Therefore, by Fermat's theorem we have

$$a^6 \equiv 1(\text{mod } 7),\ a^{12} \equiv 1(\text{mod } 13),\ a^{18} \equiv 1(\text{mod } 17)$$

$$\Rightarrow \quad a^{1728} = (a^6)^{288} \equiv 1(\text{mod } 7)$$

$$a^{1728} = (a^{12})^{144} \equiv 1(\text{mod } 13)$$

$$a^{1728} = (a^{18})^{96} \equiv 1(\text{mod } 19)$$

$$\Rightarrow \quad a^{1728} \equiv 1(\text{mod } 7.13.19)$$

$$\equiv 1(\text{mod } 1729)$$

$$\Rightarrow \quad a^{1729} \equiv a(\text{mod } 1729).$$

This shows that 1729 is an absolute pseudo prime.

5.4 Wilson's Theorem

Theorem 1 : If p is a prime then $(p-1)! \equiv -1 \pmod{p}$.

(C.C.S.U. 2000, 2003, 2004)

Proof : Let p be a prime and let a be an integer such that $1 \leqslant a \leqslant p-1$. Then $(a, p) = 1$. Therefore, the congruence $ax \equiv 1 \pmod{p}$ has a unique solution (mod p). Let this solution be b.

Then $\quad ab \equiv 1 \pmod{p}$.

If $\quad b \equiv a \pmod{p}$ then

$$a^2 \equiv 1 \pmod{p}$$

$$\Rightarrow \quad p \mid (a^2 - 1)$$

$$\Rightarrow \quad p(a-1) \text{ or } \quad p/(a+1)$$

$$\Rightarrow \quad a \equiv 1 \pmod{p} \quad \text{or} \quad a \equiv p-1 \pmod{p}.$$

This shows that for each integer $b \in \{2, 3, \ldots. p-2)\}$ there is an integer $b' \in \{2, 3, \ldots., (p-2)\}$ such that

$$bb' \equiv 1 \pmod{p}.$$

Thus, making pairs of b's, $1 < b < p-1$ with b''s, $1 < b' < p-1$ such that $bb' \equiv 1 \pmod{p}$ we get

$$2.3.4 \ldots. (p-2) \equiv 1 \pmod{p}$$

$$\Rightarrow \quad (p-2)! \equiv 1 \pmod{p}$$

$$\Rightarrow \quad (p-1)(p-2)! \equiv (p-1) \pmod{p}$$

$$\Rightarrow \quad (p-1)! \equiv -1 \pmod{p}.$$

Proved

Theorem 2 : (Converse of Wilson's Theorem)

If $(m-1)! + 1$ is divisible by m then m is a prime. **(C.C.S.U. 2000)**

Proof : Let $(m-1)! + 1$ be divisible by m. Then we have to show that m is a prime. Suppose if possible m is a composite number and it has a divisor $d > 1$. Therefore, $1 \leqslant d \leqslant m-1 \Rightarrow d$ divides $(m-1)!$ but d does not divide $(m-1)! + 1$.

$\Rightarrow m$ does not divide $(m-1)! + 1$

This is contradiction. Hence, m must be a prime. This theorem provides a theoretical test to determine whether a given number is a prime but practically it is useless because there is no known fast method to find $m!$

Theorem 3 : The quadratic congruence $x^2 \equiv -1 \pmod{p}$, p is a prime, has a solution iff $p \equiv 1 \pmod{4}$.

Proof : Suppose a is any solution of the given quadratic congruence $x^2 \equiv -1 \pmod{p}$.

Therefore, $a^2 \equiv -1 \pmod{p}$ and $(a, p) = 1$.

By Fermat's theorem, we have

$$a^{p-1} \equiv 1 \pmod{p}$$

$$\therefore \quad 1 \equiv a^{p-1} \equiv (a^2)^{(p-1)/2} \pmod{p}.$$

Since p is odd, $\left(\frac{p-1}{2}\right)$ is an integer and $a^2 \equiv -1 \pmod{p}$

$$\therefore \quad 1 \equiv (-1)^{(p-1)/2} \pmod{p}.$$

This is true only when $\frac{p-1}{2} = 2k$ (even). This gives $p = 4k + 1$. This implies

$$p \equiv 1 \pmod{4}.$$

Conversely suppose $p \equiv 1 \pmod{4}$ then $p = 4k + 1$, k is an integer.

By Wilson's theorem we have

$$(p-1)! \equiv -1 \pmod{p}$$

$$\Rightarrow 1.2.\left(\frac{p-1}{2}\right).\left(\frac{p+1}{2}\right) \ldots\ldots (p-1) \equiv -1 \pmod{p} \qquad \ldots\ldots.(1)$$

But

$$\left.\begin{aligned} \frac{p+1}{2} &\equiv -\left(\frac{p-1}{2}\right) \pmod{p} \\ \frac{p+3}{2} &\equiv -\left(\frac{p-3}{2}\right) \pmod{p} \\ &\vdots \qquad \vdots \\ p-1 &\equiv -1 \pmod{p} \end{aligned}\right\} \qquad \ldots\ldots\ldots (2)$$

Using (2) in (1) we get

$$(-1)^{\frac{(p-1)}{2}}\left[1.2\ldots\ldots\left(\frac{p-1}{2}\right)\right]^2 \equiv -1 \pmod{p}$$

$$\Rightarrow \quad (-)^{2k}\left[\left(\frac{p-1}{2}\right)!\right]^2 \equiv -1 \pmod{p}$$

$$\Rightarrow \quad \left[\left(\frac{p-1}{2}\right)!\right]^2 \equiv -1 \pmod{p}.$$

This shows that $\left(\frac{p-1}{2}\right)!$ is a solution of the congruence $x^2 \equiv -1 \pmod{p}$.

Proved

Example 1 : Show that 17 is a prime by showing that $16! \equiv -1 \pmod{17}$

Solution : We have

$$2.9 \equiv 1 \pmod{17}$$
$$3.6 \equiv 1 \pmod{17}$$
$$4.13 \equiv 1 \pmod{17}$$
$$5.7 \equiv 1 \pmod{17}$$
$$8.15 \equiv 1 \pmod{17}$$
$$10.12 \equiv 1 \pmod{17}$$
$$11.14 \equiv 1 \pmod{17}.$$

Multiplying these relations we have

$$15! = (2.9)(3.6)(4.13)(5.7)(8.15)(10.12)(11.14)$$
$$\equiv 1 \pmod{17}.$$
$$\therefore \quad 16! = 16.15!$$
$$\equiv 16 \pmod{17}$$
$$\equiv -1 \pmod{17}.$$

Thus, $(p-1)! \equiv -1 \pmod{p}$ for $p = 17$. Therefore, by Wilson's theorem we have that 17 is a prime.

Example 2 : Find the remainder when 2(28!) is divided by 31.

Solution : By Wilson's theorem we have

$$(p-1)! \equiv -1 \pmod{p}$$
$$\Rightarrow \quad (p-2)! \equiv 1 \pmod{p}$$
$$\Rightarrow 2(p-2)! \equiv 2 \pmod{p}$$
$$\Rightarrow 2(p-2)(p-3)! = 2 \pmod{p}$$
$$\Rightarrow 2(p-3)! \equiv -1 \pmod{p}.$$

Putting $p = 31$ we get

$$2(28!) \equiv -1 \pmod{31}$$
$$\equiv 30 \pmod{31}.$$

Therefore, the required remainder is 30.

Example 3 : For any prime p show that

$$p / a^p + (p-1)!\, a, \text{ a is any integer.}$$

Solution : By Fermat's theorem, we have

$$p / (a^{p-1} - 1) \qquad \text{.......(1)}$$

By Wilson's theorem, we have

$$p/(p-1)!+1. \quad \text{.......(2)}$$

From (1) and (2) we see that

$$p/(a^{p-1}-1+(p-1)!+1)$$

$$\Rightarrow \quad p/a^{p-1}+(p-1)!$$

$$\Rightarrow \quad p/a^p+(p-1)!\,a.$$ **Proved.**

Example 4 : For any prime p show that $p/(p-1)!\ a^p+a$.

Solution : By Wilson's theorem, we have

$$p/[(p-1)!+1]$$

$$\Rightarrow \quad p/[a^p(p-1)!+a^p)$$

$$\Rightarrow \quad p/(a^p(p-1)!+a+a^p-a]$$

$$\Rightarrow \quad p/[a^p(p-1)!+a].$$

[$\because$ By Fermat's theorem we have $a^p \equiv a(\text{mod } p)$] **Proved.**

5.5 Euler's Factorization Method

Let n be an odd integer to be factorized.

Let $n = a^2 + b^2$ where a is even and b is odd

and $n = c^2 + d^2$ where c is even and d is odd

Then $a^2 + b^2 = c^2 + d^2$

or $a^2 - c^2 = d^2 - b^2$

or $(a-c)(a+c) = (d-b)(d+b).$ ....(1)

Let $k = (a - c, d - b)$. Then k is an even integer greater than equal to 2.

Now if $a - c = kr_1$ and $d - b = kr_2$ then $(r_1, r_2) = 1$

$$\left.\begin{aligned} &\text{and} \quad (a-c)(a+c) = kr_1(a+c) \\ &\text{and} \quad (d-b)(d+b) = kr_2(d+b) \end{aligned}\right\} \quad \text{.......(2)}$$

From (1) and (2) we have

$$r_1(a+c) = r_2(d+b) \quad \text{.......(3)}$$

$$\Rightarrow \quad r_1/s(d+b)$$

$$\Rightarrow \quad r_1/(d+b)$$

Suppose $d + b = r_i t$ then from (3) we have

$$a + c = r_2 t$$

Obviously $t = (a + c, d + b)$ is an even integer.

Thus, $a - c = kr_1$, $a + c = r_2 t$, $d - b = kr_2$ and $d + b = tr_1$

This gives $a = \frac{kr_1 + tr_2}{2}$, $c = \frac{tr_2 - kr_1}{2}$, $d = \frac{kr_2 + tr_1}{2}$ and $b = \frac{tr_1 + kr_2}{2}$

Hence,

$$n = a^2 + b^2$$

$$= \left(\frac{k r_1 + tr_2}{2}\right)^2 + \left(\frac{t r_1 + kr_2}{2}\right)^2$$

$$= \frac{k^2 r_1^2 + t^2 r_2^2 + t^2 r_1^2 + k^2 r_2^2}{4}$$

$$= (r_1^2 + r_2^2)\left(\frac{k^2}{4} + \frac{t^2}{4}\right).$$

This is the required factorization of n.

Example 1 : Factorize 493 by Eulers factorization method.

Solution : We have

$$493 = 13^2 + 18^2$$

Also $493 = 3^2 + 22^2.$

Thus, $13^2 + 18^2 = 3^2 + 22^2$

or $13^2 - 3^2 = 22^2 - 18^2$

or $(13 - 3)(13 + 3) = (22 - 18)(22 + 18)$

or $10.16 = 4.40.$

Now $(16, 40) = 8$, $(10, 4) = 2$ and

$$16 = 2.8$$

$$40 = 5.8$$

$$10 = 5.2$$

$$4 = 2.2.$$

This gives $r_1 = 5$, $r_2 = 2$, $k = 2$ and $t = 8$.

Therefore,

$$n = (r_1^2 + r_2^2)\left(\frac{k^2 + t^2}{4}\right)$$

$$= (5^2 + 2^2)\left(\frac{2^2 + 8^2}{4}\right)$$

$$= (25 + 4)\left(\frac{4 + 64}{4}\right)$$

$$= 29.17.$$

Thus, the required factors are 29 and 17.

Example 2 : Factorize 38025 by Euler's factorization method.

Solution : We have

$$38025 = 168^2 + 99^2$$

and $$38025 = 156^2 + 117^2$$

This gives $$168^2 + 99^2 = 156^2 + 117^2.$$

or $$117^2 - 99^2 = 168^2 - 156^2.$$

or $$(117 - 99)(117 + 99) = (168 - 156)(168 + 156)$$

or $$18.216 = 12.324.$$

Now $(216, 324) = 108$, $(18, 12) = 6$ and

$$216 = 2 \times 108$$

$$324 = 3 \times 108$$

$$18 = 3 \times 6$$

$$12 = 2 \times 6.$$

This gives $r_1 = 3$, $r_2 = 2$, $k = 6$ and $t = 108$

Therefore $$38025 = (r_1^2 + r_2^2)\left(\frac{k^2 + t^2}{4}\right)$$

$$= (3^2 + 2^2)\left(\frac{6^2 + 108^2}{4}\right)$$

$$= (9 + 4)\left(\frac{36 + 11664}{4}\right)$$

$$= 13.\left[\frac{11700}{4}\right]$$

$$= 13.2925.$$

Mersenne's Result

If $n = a^2 + b^2 = c^2 + d^2$ then

$$n = (ac + bd)\,(ac - bd)/(a + d)(a - d).$$

Example 1 : Factorize 10441 by Mersenne's result.

Solution : We have

$$10441 = 35^2 + 96^2 = 21^2 + 100^2.$$

Thus, $a = 35$, $b = 96$, $c = 21$, $d = 100$

Now by Mersenne's result, we have

$$10441 = (ac + bd)(ac - bd)/(a + d)(a - d)$$

$$= \frac{(35.21 + 96.100)(35.21 - 96.100)}{(35 + 100)(35 - 100)}$$

$$= \frac{10335.(-8865)}{-135.65}$$

$$= \frac{10385 \times 8865}{135 \times 65}$$

$$= 53.197.$$

EXERCISE

1. Factorize 8927.
2. Factorize 2279.
3. Factorize 340663.
4. Find the remainder when 15! is divided by 17.
5. Show that 4 (29!) + 5! is divisible by 31.
6. If p and q are distinct primes, show that

$$pq / a^{pq} - a^p - a^q + a$$

for any integer a.

7. Show that $18! \equiv -1 \pmod{437}$
8. If $(a, 42) = 1$ then show that $a^6 \equiv 1 \pmod{168}$.
9. Prove that $a^7 \equiv a \pmod{42}$ for each integer a.
10. What is the remainder when 3^{287} is divided by 23 ?

Answers to Exercise

1. 113.79
2. 127.83
3. 691.493

10. 3

CHAPTER 6

NUMBER THEORETIC FUNCTION

6.1 Introduction

A function whose domain is the set of positive integers is called a number theoretic (or arithmetic) function. Its value may be integral, real or complex. Arithmetic functions have special importance in the study of divisors of integers. In this chapter, we shall discuss τ-function, σ-function, the mobius inversion formula, the greatest integer function and Euler's function.

6.2 The Function τ and σ (C.C.S.U. 2003)

For each positive integer n, $\tau(n)$ is the number of positive divisors of n including 1 and n and $\sigma(n)$ is the sum of these divisors. Thus, these functions are defined as

$\tau : N \to N$ such that

$\tau(n) = \sum_{\substack{d/n \\ d \geq 1}} 1$ where $\sum_{d/n} 1$ denotes the sum of as many 1's as there are positive divisors of n.

and $\sigma : N \to N$ such that

$\sigma(n) = \sum_{\substack{d/n \\ d \geq 1}} d$ where $\sum_{d/n} d$ is the sum of positive divisors of n.

Example 1 : Find $\tau(15)$ and $\sigma(15)$.

Solution : The divisors of 15 are 1, 3, 5 and 15.

Therefore,
$$\tau(15) = 4 \text{ and}$$
$$\sigma(15) = 1 + 3 + 5 + 15 = 24.$$

Example 2 : Find $\tau(18)$ and $\sigma(18)$.

Solution : The divisors of 18 are 1, 2, 3, 6, 9, 18.

Therefore,
$$\tau(18) = 6 \text{ and}$$
$$\sigma(18) = 1 + 2 + 3 + 6 + 9 + 18 = 39.$$

Example 3 : If p is a prime then find $\tau(p)$ and $\sigma(p)$.

Solution : Prime p has only two factors 1 and p itself. Therefore, $\tau(p) = 2$ and $\sigma(p) = p + 1$.

Theorem 1 : If $n = p_1^{a_1}.p_2^{a_2} .... p_k^{a_k}$ is the prime factorization of $n > 1$ then the divisors of n are the various terms of the expansion of

$$P = (1 + p_1 + p_1^2 + ... p_1^{a_1}).(1 + p_2 + p_2^2 + ... p_2^{a_2}) .... (1 + p_k + ... p_k^{a_k}).$$

Proof : From P we see that every divisor d of P is of the form $p_1^{b_1} p_2^{b_2} .... p_k^{b_k}$ where $0 \leqslant b_1 \leqslant a_1, 0 \leqslant b_2 \leqslant a_2, ... 0 \leqslant b_k \leqslant a_k$. Thus, d appears among the terms of the expansion of P. Also every term in the expansion of P is of the form $p_1^{b_1} p_2^{b_2} .... q_k^{b_k}$. Therefore, it is divisor of n. Obviously all the terms in the expansion of P are distinct. This shows that the divisors of n are the various terms of the expansion of P.

Theorem 2 : If $n = p_1^{a_1}.p_2^{a_2} .... p_k^{a_k}$ is the prime factorization then

(*i*) $\tau(n) = (a_1 + 1)(a_2 + 1) .... (a_k + 1)$ and

(*ii*) $$\sigma(n) = \left(\frac{p_1^{a_1+1} - 1}{p_1 - 1}\right).\left(\frac{p_2^{a_2+1} - 1}{p_2 - 1}\right)...\left(\frac{p_k^{a_k+1} - 1}{p_k - 1}\right).$$

Proof :

(*i*) It is obvious that

$$\tau(n) = \text{Number of terms in the expansion of } P \text{ in theorem 1.}$$
$$= (a_1 + 1)(a_2 + 1) .... (a_k + 1).$$

(*ii*) It is also quite obvious that

$$\sigma(n) = \text{sum of terms in the expansion of } P \text{ in theorem 1.}$$
$$= P$$
$$= \left(\frac{p_1^{a_1+1} - 1}{p_1 - 1}\right).\left(\frac{p_2^{a_2+1} - 1}{p_2 - 1}\right)...\left(\frac{p_k^{a_k+1} - 1}{p_k - 1}\right).$$

Theorem 3 : For any integer $n > 1$

$\tau(n)$ is odd iff n is a perfect square.

Proof : Let $n = p_1^{a_1}.p_2^{a_2}. .... p_k^{a_k}$ be square of an integer.

Then $a_1, a_2, ... a_k$ are all even.

Therefore, $(a_1 + 1), (a_2 + 1), ... (a_k + 1)$ are all odd

Now $\tau(n) = (a_1 + 1)(a_2 + 1) .... (a_k + 1)$

$= \text{an odd integer.}$

[$\because$ product of odd integers is an odd integer]

Conversely let $\tau(n) = (a_1 + 1)(a_2 + 1) .... (a_k + 1)$ is an odd integer. Then each $a_i + 1$, $i = 1, 2, ... k$ is an odd integer. This implies each a_i is even *i.e.*,

$$a_i = 2m_i.$$

$$\therefore \quad n = p_1^{2m_1}.p_2^{2m_2} .... p_k^{2m_k}$$
$$= (p_1^{m_1}.\ p_2^{m_2} .... p_k^{m_k})^2$$

This shows that n is a perfect square.

Theorem 4 : For any integer $n > 1$, $\sigma(n)$ is odd iff n is a perfect square or twice of a perfect square.

Proof : For any integer $n = p_1^{a_1}.p_2^{a_2} .... p_k^{a_k}$ we have

$$\sigma(n) = \left(\frac{p_1^{a_1+1} - 1}{p_1 - 1}\right).\left(\frac{p_2^{a_2+1} - 1}{p_2 - 1}\right) \cdots \left(\frac{p_k^{a_k+1} - 1}{p_k - 1}\right)$$

$$= (1 + p_1 + ... p_1^{a_1})(1 + p_2 + ... p_2^{a_2}) .... (1 + p_r + ... p_r^{a_k}).$$

Now $\sigma(n)$ is odd $\Leftrightarrow (1 + p_1 + ... p_1^{a_1})(1 + p_2 + ... p_2^{a_2}) .... (1 + p_r + ... p_k^{a_k})$

$\Leftrightarrow (1 + p_i + ... p_i^{a_i})$ is odd $\forall\ i = 1, 2, ... r$

$\Leftrightarrow a_i$ is even $\forall\ i = 1, 2, ... r$ and a_1 and if one p_i say $p_1 = 2$ then a_1 is any integer

$\Leftrightarrow a_i = 2m_i \ \forall\ i = 1, 2, ... r.$

$\Leftrightarrow n = p_1^{2m_1}.p_2^{2m_2}. .... p_r^{2m_r}$ or

$$= 2^{a_1}(p_2^{2m_2}.p_2^{2m_3}. .... p_r^{2m_r}) \text{ if } p_1 = 2$$

$$= 2^{a_1}(p_2^{m_1}.p_3. .... p_r)$$

$$= \left(2^{\frac{a_1}{2}}\ p_2^{m_2} \ldots\ldots p_r^{m_r}\right)^2.$$

If a_1 is even then

$$n = \left(2^{\frac{a_1}{2}}\ p_2^{m_2} \ldots\ldots p_r^{m_r}\right)^2.$$

and if a_1 is odd say $a_1 = 2m + 1$ then

$$n = 2(2^{m_1}.p_2^{m_2} .... p_r^{m_r})^2.$$

Thus $\sigma(n)$ is odd $\Leftrightarrow n$ is a perfect square or twice of a perfect square.

Theorem 5 : If n is an integer greater than 1 then

$$\prod_{d/n} d = n^{\frac{\tau(n)}{2}}$$

Proof : If d is any divisor of n then $\frac{n}{d}$ is also a divisor of n. Thus, divisors of n are in pair $\left(d, \frac{n}{d}\right)$.

Therefore, product of all divisors of n

$$\prod_{d/n} d = n^{\frac{\tau(n)}{2}}, \quad \tau(n) \text{ is the number of divisors.}$$

Lattice Point : The points whose coordinates are integers are called the lattice points.

Multiplicative Function

An arithmetic function f is said to be multiplicative if

$$f(mn) = f(m)f(n)$$

where $(m, n) = 1$.

Theorem 1 : The arithmetic functions τ and σ are multiplicative.

(C.C.S.U. 2004, B.P. 2006)

Proof : For $m = n = 1$ the result is trivially true. Let $m > 1$ and $n > 1$ be two relatively prime integers *i.e.*, $(m, n) = 1$. Let $m = p_1^{a_1} p_2^{a_2} \ldots p_r^{a_r}$ and $n = q_1^{b_1} q_2^{b_2} \ldots q_s^{b_s}$ be prime factorizations of m and n. Since $(m, n) = 1$ no p_i will be among q_j and vice-versa. Therefore, the prime factorization of mn will be given by

$$mn = p_1^{a_1} p_2^{a_2} \ldots p_r^{a_r} . q_1^{b_1} \ldots q_s^{b_s}.$$

Hence $\tau(mn) = [(a_1+1)(a_2+1) \ldots (a_r+1)][b_1+1)(b_2+1) \ldots (b_s+1)]$

$$= \tau(m)\tau(n) \quad \text{.......(1)}$$

Similarly

$$\sigma(mn) = \left[\left(\frac{p_1^{a_1+1}-1}{p_1-1}\right) \cdots \left(\frac{p_r^{a_r+1}-1}{p_r-1}\right)\right]\left[\left(\frac{q_1^{b_1+1}-1}{q_1-1}\right) \cdots \left(\frac{q_s^{b_s+1}-1}{q_s-1}\right)\right]$$

$$= \sigma(m)\sigma(n) \quad \text{.......(2)}$$

Expressions (1) and (2) show that τ and σ are multiplicative functions.

Lemma : If $(m, n) = 1$ and $d_1|m$ and $d_2|n$ then the set of positive divisors of mn has all products $d_1 d_2$.

Proof : Let $m > 1$ and $n > 1$ be two relatively prime integers *i.e.*, $(m, n) = 1$. Let $m = p_1^{a_1}.p_2^{a_2} \ldots p_r^{a_r}$ and $n = q_1^{b_1}.q_2^{b_2} \ldots q_s^{b_s}$ be the prime factorization of m and n. Then primes $p_1, p_2, \ldots. p_r, q_1, q_2, \ldots. q_s$ are all distinct. Therefore the prime factorization of mn is given by

$$mn = p_1^{a_1}.p_2^{a_2}. \ldots. p_r^{a_r}. q_1^{b_1}. \ldots. q_s^{b_s}.$$

So any positive divisor d of mn can be uniquely represented as

$$d = p_1^{c_1}.p_2^{c_2}. \ldots. .p_r^{c_r} q_1^{e_1} \ldots. q_s^{e_s} \text{ where } 0 \leqslant c_i \leqslant a_i \text{ and } 0 \leqslant e_i \leqslant b_i.$$

Thus we can write $d = d_1 d_2$ where $d_1 = p_1^{c_1}. \ldots. p_r^{c_r}$ divides m and $d_2 = q_1^{e_1} \ldots. q_s^{e_s}$ divides n as no. p_i is equal q_i and vice-versa. Therefore $(d_1, d_2) = 1$.

Theorem 3 : If f is a multiplicative function and

$$S(n) = \sum_{d/n} f(d)$$

then $S(n)$ is also multiplicative

Proof : Let m, n be relatively prime integers. Then

$$S(mn) = \sum_{d|mn} f(d)$$

$$= \sum_{\substack{d_1|m \\ d_2|n}} f(d_1 d_2)$$

$$= \sum_{\substack{d_1|m \\ d_2|n}} f(d_1) f(d_2)$$

$$= \left(\sum_{d_1/m} f(d_1)\right)\left(\sum_{d_2/n} f(d_2)\right)$$

$$= S(m)\, S(n).$$

Example 1 : Evaluate τ and σ for $n = 3655$.

Solution : We have

$$3655 = 5^1 \cdot 17^1 \cdot 43^1.$$

$$\therefore \quad \tau(3655) = (1+1)(1+1)(1+1)$$

$$= 8$$

and $$\sigma(3655) = \left(\frac{5^2-1}{5-1}\right)\left(\frac{17^2-1}{17-1}\right)\left(\frac{43^2-1}{43-1}\right)$$

$$= \frac{(25-1)(289-1)(1849-1)}{4.16.42}$$

$$= \frac{24.288.1848}{4.16.42}$$

$$= 18 \cdot 264 = 4752.$$

Example 2 : Evaluate τ and σ for $n = 3000$.

Solution : We have

$$3000 = 2^3.3^1.5^3.$$

Therefore, $\tau(3000) = (3 + 1).(1 + 1).(3 + 1)$

$$= 4 \cdot 2 \cdot 4$$

$$= 32$$

and $\sigma(3000) = \frac{(2^4 - 1)}{2 - 1} \cdot \frac{(3^2 - 1)}{3 - 1} \cdot \frac{(5^4 - 1)}{5 - 1}$

$$= \frac{(16 - 1)}{1} \cdot \frac{(9 - 1)}{2} \cdot \frac{(625 - 1)}{4}$$

$$= 15 \cdot 4 \cdot 156$$

$$= 9360.$$

Example 3 : If $f(n) = n^2 + 2$ and $n = 6$ then show that $\sum_{d|6} f(d) = \sum_{d|6} f\left(\frac{6}{d}\right)$.

Solution : Here divisors of 6 are given by

$$d = 1, 2, 3, 6$$

$$\therefore \quad \frac{6}{d} = 6, 3, 2, 1.$$

Now $\sum_{d/6} f(d) = (1^2 + 2) + (2^2 + 2) + (3^2 + 2) + (6^2 + 2)$

$$= 58$$

and $\sum_{d/6} f\left(\frac{6}{d}\right) = (6^2 + 2) + (3^2 + 2) + (2^2 + 2) + (1^2 + 2)$

$$= 58.$$

Thus, $\sum_{d/6} f(d) = \sum_{d/6} f\left(\frac{6}{d}\right).$

Example 4 : Verify that $\tau(n) = \tau(n + 1) = \tau(n + 2)$ holds for $n = 4503$.

Solution : We have

$$n = 4503 = 3 \cdot 19 \cdot 79.$$

$$\tau(n) = \tau(4503) = (1+1)\cdot(1+1)\cdot(1+1) = 8.$$

Further $\quad n + 1 = 4504 = 2^3.563$

$\therefore \quad \tau(n+1) = (3+1)\cdot(1+1) = 8.$

Finally $\quad n + 2 = 4505 = 5\cdot 17\cdot 53$

$\therefore \quad \tau(n+2) = (1+1)\cdot(1+1)\cdot(1+1) = 8.$

Thus, $\quad \tau(n) = \tau(n+1) = \tau(n+2).$

Example 5 : Show that $\tau(n)$ is equal to the lattice points on the hyperbola $xy = n$ lying in the first quadrant.

Solution : Suppose $d_1, d_2, ... d_r$ be the divisors of n. Then the lattice points $\left(d_1, \frac{n}{d_1}\right)$, $\left(d_2, \frac{n}{d_2}\right), ..., \left(d_r, \frac{n}{d_r}\right)$ lies on the hyperbola $xy = n$ in the first quadrant. Also if $\left(d, \frac{n}{d}\right)$ be any lattice point on the hyperbola $xy = n$ then it belongs to the above lattice points as $\frac{n}{d}$ is an integer. Therefore, $\tau(n)$ is equal to the number of lattice points on the hyperbola $xy = n$.

Behaviour of $\tau(n)$ as $n \to \infty$ (C.C.S.U. 2004)

For every prime p we have $\tau(p) = 2$. For any integer n there are at least two divisors 1 and n. Therefore, $\tau(n) \geqslant 2$ for all n. For any integer of the form $n = p^a$, p is a prime, we have $\tau(n) = a + 1$. This depends on a. For large a, $\tau(n)$ is also sufficiently large. Therefore, $\lim_{n\to\infty} \tau(n) = \infty$. The behaviour of $\tau(n)$ is irregular.

Behaviour of $\sigma(n)$ as $n \to \infty$ (C.C.S.U. 2004)

We know that $\sigma(n) > n$. Therefore, $\sigma(n)$ takes values larger than any given sufficiently large number n. Hence, $\lim_{n\to\infty} \sigma(n) = \infty$. But it is not an increasing function as shown below :

Let $p = 2^r + 1, r > 1$ be a prime > 3 then

$$\begin{aligned}\sigma(p-1) &= \sigma(2^r)\\ &= 2^r + 2^{r-1} + ... + 2 + 1\\ &> 2^r + 2\\ &= p + 1\\ &= \sigma(p).\end{aligned}$$

If $p-1 = p_1^{r_1}.p_2^{r_2}. \ldots. p_k^{r_k}$ then

$$\begin{aligned}\sigma(p-1) &= \sigma(p_1^{r_1})\,\sigma(p_2^{r_2}) \ldots.\ \sigma(p_k^{r_k})\\ &= (p_1^{r_1}+1)(p_2^{r_2}+1) \ldots.\ (p_k^{r_k}+1)\\ &\geqslant p_1^{r_1}p_2^{r_2} \ldots.\ p_k^{r_k} + (p_1^{r_1}+p_2^{r_2}+ \ldots.\ p_k^{r_k})\\ &= p-1+k+1\\ &> p+1 \qquad [\because k>1]\\ &= \sigma(p).\end{aligned}$$

$\sigma(n)$ is also an irregular function.

6.3 The Mobius Function (or The Mobius Inversion Formula)

For a positive integer n the Mobius function μ is defined as

$$\mu(n) = \begin{cases} 1 & \text{if} \quad n = 1 \\ 0 & \text{if} \quad p^2/n \quad \text{for some prime } p \\ (-1)^k & \text{if} \quad n = p_1p_2 \ldots.\ p_k \text{ is the product of } k \text{ distinct primes.} \end{cases}$$

For example

$$\begin{aligned}\mu(6) &= \mu(2\cdot3)\\ &= (-1)^2\\ &= 1\\ \mu(9) &= \mu(3^2)\\ &= 0.\end{aligned}$$

Theorem 1 : Mobius function $\mu(n)$ is multiplicative *i.e.*, $\mu(mn) = \mu(m)\,\mu(n)$, m and n are relatively prime. **(C.C.S.U. 2003)**

Proof : We consider the following three conditions :

(*i*) $m = 1$ then
$$\begin{aligned}\mu(mn) &= \mu(1.n)\\ &= \mu(n)\\ &= 1.\mu(n)\\ &= \mu(m)\mu(n).\end{aligned}$$

Thus, the given result is true for $m = 1$.

(*ii*) m is divisible by p^2, p is a prime. In this case $\mu(m) = 0$ and $\mu(mn) = 0$. Therefore

$$\mu(mn) = \mu(m)\cdot\mu(n)$$

(*iii*) $m = p_1p_2 \ldots.\ p_{k_1}$

$n = q_1q_2 \ldots.\ q_{k_2}$

where p_i's are different from q_i.

In this case $\mu(mn) = (-1)^{k_1+k_2}$

$$= (-1)^{k_1}(-1)^{k_2}$$

$$= \mu(m)\,\mu(n).$$

Theorem 2 : (F. Morten's Lemma) : For each integer $n \geqslant 1$

$$\sum_{d|n} \mu(d) = \begin{cases} 1 & \text{if } n = 1 \\ 0 & \text{if } n > 1 \end{cases}$$

Proof : If $n = 1$ then

$$\sum_{d/n} \mu(d) = \mu(1) = 1$$

If $n > 1$ then we can write

$n = p_1^{k_1}.p_2^{k_2} \ldots. p_r^{k_r}$, p_i are distinct primes and $k_i \geqslant 1\, r$

$$\therefore \quad \sum_{d|n} \mu(d) = \mu(1) + \sum_{i=1} \mu(p_i) + \sum_{\substack{i<j \\ i<j=1}} \mu(p_i\, p_j) + \mu(p_1\, p_2 \ldots p_r) + 0 + \ldots 0$$

[∵ The remaining terms contain square factor]

$$= 1 + r(-1) + \binom{r}{2}(-1)^2 + \ldots. (-1)^r$$

$$= 1 + \binom{r}{1}(-1) + \binom{r}{2}(-1)^2 + \ldots. (-1)^r$$

$$= (1-1)^r$$

$$= 0.$$

Theorem 3 : (Mobius Inversion Formula) : Let

$$F(n) = \sum_{d/n} f(d)$$

then $f(n) = \sum_{d|n} \mu(d) F(n/d) = \sum_{d|n} \mu(n/d) F(d).$ **(C.C.S.U. 2001, 2004)**

Proof : We have

$$\sum_{d|n} \mu(d) F(n/d) = \sum_{d|n}\left[\mu(d) \sum_{c/(n|d)} f(c)\right]$$

$$= \sum_{d|n}\left[\sum_{c/(n|d)} \mu(d) f(c)\right]$$

$$= \sum_{c|n} \left[\sum_{d|(n|c)} f(c)\mu(d) \right]$$

[$\because$ $d|n$ and $c|(n|d) \Leftrightarrow c|n$ and $d|(n|c)$].

$$= \sum_{c|n} \left[f(c) \sum_{d|(n|c)} \mu(d) \right]$$

$$= \sum_{c=n} f(c).1$$

$$= f(n).$$

The second can be shown by replacing the dummy index d by $d^1 = n|d$.

Theorem 4 : If $F(n)$ is a multiplicative function and $F(n) = \sum_{d|n} f(d)$ then f is also multiplicative.

Proof : Let m and n be relatively prime. Then any divisor d of mn can be written uniquely as $d = d_1 d_2$ where d_1/m and d_2/n and $(d_1, d_2) = 1$.

Now by inversion formula we have

$$f(mn) = \sum_{d|mn} \mu(d) F\left(\frac{mn}{d}\right)$$

$$= \sum_{\substack{d_1|m \\ d_2|n}} \mu(d_1 d_2) F\left(\frac{mn}{d_1 d_2}\right)$$

$$= \sum_{\substack{d_1|m \\ d_2|n}} \mu(d_1)\mu(d_2) F\left(\frac{m}{d_1}\right) F\left(\frac{n}{d_2}\right)$$

[$\because$ μ and F are multiplicative].

$$= \sum_{d_1|m} \mu(d_1) F\left(\frac{m}{d_1}\right) \sum_{d_2|n} \mu(d_2) F\left(\frac{n}{d_2}\right)$$

$$= f(m) f(n).$$

Proved

Theorem 5 : If $n = p_1^{a_1} p_2^{a_2} \ldots\ldots p_k^{a_k}$ then $\sum_{d|n} |\mu(d)| = 2^k$.

Proof : For every divisor d for which $\mu(d) \neq 0$ we have $|\mu(d)| = 1$. Therefore, by definition of Mobius function and the number of such divisors is given by

$$1 + \binom{k}{1} + \binom{k}{2} + \ldots + \binom{k}{k} = (1+1)^k = 2^k.$$

Hence, $$\sum_{d/n} |\mu(d)| = 2^k.1$$
$$= 2^k.$$ **Proved.**

Theorem 6 : If $n = p_1^{a_1}.p_2^{a_2}. .... p_k^{a_k}$ then

$$\sum_{d/n} \frac{\mu(d)}{d} = \left(1 - \frac{1}{p_1}\right)\left(1 - \frac{1}{p_2}\right)...\left(1 - \frac{1}{p_k}\right).$$

Proof : Let $f(n) = \frac{1}{n}$. Then we have

$$\sum_{d|n} \mu(d) f(d) = \sum_{d|n} \frac{\mu(d)}{d}.$$

Since $f(n) = \frac{1}{n}$ is a multiplicative function, we have

$$\sum_{d|n} \mu(d) f(d) = [1 - f(p_1)][1 - f(p_2)]....[1 - f(p_k)]$$

$$= \left(1 - \frac{1}{p_1}\right)\left(1 - \frac{1}{p_2}\right)...\left(1 - \frac{1}{p_k}\right)$$

or $$\sum_{d|n} \mu(d).\frac{1}{d} = \left(1 - \frac{1}{p_1}\right)\left(1 - \frac{1}{p_2}\right)...\left(1 - \frac{1}{p_k}\right)$$

or $$\sum_{d|n} \frac{\mu(d)}{d} = \left(1 - \frac{1}{p_1}\right)\left(1 - \frac{1}{p_2}\right)...\left(1 - \frac{1}{p_k}\right).$$ **Proved.**

Example 1 : For each positive integer n, show that

$$\mu(n)\,\mu(n+1)\,\mu(n+2)\,\mu(n+3) = 0.$$

Solution : We have

$$\mu(n)\,\mu(n+1)\,\mu(n+2)\,\mu(n+3) = \mu[n(n+1)(n+2)(n+3)].$$

[By multiplicative property]

Now for each value of n there will be two even numbers and two odd numbers among the four factors of right hand side. Therefore there will be one factor 2^2 in the product. Hence, the Mobius function will be zero because $\mu(2^2) = 0$

Example 2 : Find a positive integer n such that $\mu(n) + \mu(n+1) + \mu(n+2) = 3$.

Solution : We have

$$\mu(33) = \mu(3 \cdot 11) = (-1)^2 = 1$$
$$\mu(34) = \mu(2 \cdot 17) = (-1)^2 = 1$$
$$\mu(35) = \mu(5 \cdot 7) = (-1)^2 = 1$$

Thus, $\mu(33) + \mu(34) + \mu(35) = 3.$

Therefore n should be equal to 33.

Similarly,

$$\mu(85) = \mu(5.17) = (-1)^2 = 1$$

$$\mu(86) = \mu(2.43) = (-1)^2 = 1$$

$$\mu(87) = \mu(3.29) = (-1)^2 = 1.$$

Thus, $\mu(85) + \mu(86) + \mu(87) = 3$. Therefore $n = 85$.

Also $$\mu(93) = \mu(3.31) = (-1)^2 = 1$$

$$\mu(94) = \mu(2.47) = (-1)^2 = 1$$

$$\mu(95) = \mu(5.19) = (-1)^2 = 1.$$

Thus, $\mu(93) + \mu(94) + \mu(95) = 3$. Therefore, $n = 93$.

Example 3 : If n is a positive integer such that $n \geqslant 3$ then $\sum_{k=1}^{n}(k!) = 1$.

Solution : For $n = 3$ we have

$$\sum_{k=1}^{3}\mu(k!) = \mu(1!) + \mu(2!) + \mu(3!)$$

$$= \mu(1) + \mu(2) + \mu(6)$$
$$= 1 + (-1) + \mu(2\cdot 3)$$
$$= (-1)^2$$
$$= 1.$$

Let the result be true for $n = m$ *i.e.*,

$$\sum_{k=1}^{m}\mu(k!) = 1.$$

We shall show that the result is true for $n = m + 1$

i.e., $$\sum_{k=1}^{m+1}\mu(k!) = 1.$$

We have

$$\sum_{k=1}^{m+1}\mu(k!) = \sum_{k=1}^{m}\mu(k!) + \mu[(m+1)!]$$

$$= 1 + 0 \quad [\because \mu\,(m+1)! \text{ there will be one factor } 2^2]$$

$$= 1.$$

Thus the result is true for $n = m + 1$. Hence, by mathematical induction the result will be true for all values of $n \geqslant 3$.

6.4 The Greatest Integer Function

If x is any real number then the largest integer less than or equal to x denoted by $[x]$ is the unique integer such that

$$x - 1 < [x] \leqslant x.$$

For example

$$[5] = 5$$

$$\left[\frac{20}{3}\right] = 6$$

$$\left[-\frac{5}{2}\right] = -3$$

$$[\pi] = 3$$

$$\left[\frac{2}{3}\right] = 0$$

$$[e] = 2.$$

We can write

$$x = [x] + (x)$$

where (x) is the fractional part of x.

Theorem 1 : For any real number x, prove that

(i) $[x] \leqslant x \leqslant [x] + 1$

(ii) $[x + n] = [x] + n$, **n is any integer.**

(iii) $[x] + [y] \leqslant [x + y] \leqslant [x] + [y] + 1$

(iv) $[x] + [-x] = \begin{cases} 0 & \text{if } x \text{ is an integer} \\ -1 & \text{otherwise} \end{cases}$

(v) $\left[\frac{[x]}{n}\right] = \left[\frac{x}{n}\right]$, **$n$ is a positive integer.**

(vi) $[x - y] = [x] - [y]$ **or** $[x] - [y] - 1$

Proof : For any real number, we have

$$x = [x] + \theta, \text{ where } 0 \leqslant \theta < 1. \qquad ....(1)$$

(i) From (1), we have

$$x + n = [x] + \theta + n$$

$$\Rightarrow [x + n] = [x] + n. \quad [\because [x] + n \text{ is an integer}] \qquad ....(2)$$

(ii) From (1), we have

$$[x] \leqslant x < [x] + 1. \qquad ....(3)$$

(*iii*) Let $x = [x] + \theta_1, \quad 0 \leqslant \theta_1 < 1$

and $y = [y] + \theta_2, \quad 0 \leqslant \theta_2 < 1.$

Therefore,

$$x + y = [x] + [y] + \theta_1 + \theta_2$$

$$\Rightarrow [x+y] = \begin{cases} [x] + [y] & \text{when} \quad \theta_1 + \theta_2 < 1 \\ [x] + [y] + 1 & \text{when} \quad \theta_1 + \theta_2 \geqslant 1 \end{cases}$$

$$\Rightarrow [x + y] \leqslant [x] + [y] + 1. \qquad \text{.......(4)}$$

(*iv*) If x is an integer then

$$[x] = x \text{ and } [-x] = -x.$$

Therefore, $[x] + [-x] = 0.$

If x is not an integer then

$$x = [x] + \theta, 0 \leqslant \theta < 1$$

and $[-x] = [-[x] - \theta]$

$$= -[x] - 1.$$

Therefore, $[x] + [-x] = -1. \qquad$ ....(5)

(*v*) By division algorithm, we have

$$[x] = nq + r, 0 \leqslant r < n.$$

By (1) we have:

$$x = [x] + \theta, 0 \leqslant \theta < 1.$$

Therefore, $\left[\frac{x}{n}\right] = \left[\frac{[x] + \theta}{n}\right]$

$$= \left[\frac{nq + r + \theta}{n}\right]$$

$$= \left[q + \frac{r + \theta}{n}\right]$$

$$= q. \qquad [\because r < n \Rightarrow r \leqslant n - 1 \Rightarrow r + \theta < n]$$

Also $\left[\frac{[x]}{n}\right] = \left[q + \frac{r}{n}\right] = q.$

Thus, we have $\left[\frac{[x]}{n}\right] = \left[\frac{x}{n}\right].$

(*vi*) We have

$$[x] = [(x - y) + y]$$

$$= [x - y] + [y] \qquad \text{.......(1)}$$

or $$[x] = [x-y] + [y] + 1. \qquad \text{.......(2)}$$

From (1) and (2) we have

$$[x-y] = [x] - [y]$$

or $$[x-y] = [x] - [y] - 1.$$

Theorem 2 : **The highest power of a prime p which divides $n!$ is $\sum_{i=1}^{k}\left[\frac{n}{p}\right]$ where $p^k \leqslant n \leqslant p^{k+1}$.**

Proof : Let $S = \{1, 2, ..., n\}$ and p is a prime. Then S has

$\left[\frac{n}{p}\right]$ integers divisible by p ....(1)

$\left[\frac{n}{p^2}\right]$ integers divisible by p^2 ....(2)

$\left[\frac{n}{p^3}\right]$ integers divisible by p^3 ....(3)

$\left[\frac{n}{p^k}\right]$ integers divisible by p^k. ....(4)

Since $p^k \leqslant n < p^{k+1}$ there will be no integer in S divisible by higher powers of p than p^k. Moreover, p is a prime there will be no more integers of S the product of which is divisible by p.

Now every number of (1) gives a factor p of $n!$. Every number of (2) is included in (1) and gives an additional factor p to $n!$.

In the same way every number of (3) is included in (2) and gives one additional factor p to $n!$ and so on. Therefore, the total number of factors p in $n!$ will be

$$\left[\frac{n}{p}\right] + \left[\frac{n}{p^2}\right] + \cdots \left[\frac{n}{p^k}\right].$$

Proved.

Corollary : The highest power of a prime p dividing $n!$ is $\sum_{k=1}^{\infty}\left[\frac{n}{p^k}\right]$.

Proof : Since $\left[\frac{n}{p^{k+r}}\right] = 0$ for $r > 0$. We have the highest power of a prime p dividing $n!$

$$= \sum_{k=1}^{\infty}\left[\frac{n}{p^k}\right].$$

Theorem 3 : The number of integers of

$$S = \{1, 2, ... n\}$$

divisible by a positive integer a is $\left[\frac{n}{a}\right]$.

Proof : The numbers of S divisible by a will be $a, 2a, ... ka$ where ka is the largest multiple of a not greater than n. Then $n = ka + r$, where $0 \leqslant r < a$. This gives

$$\frac{n}{a} = k + \frac{r}{a}, \quad 0 \leqslant \frac{r}{a} < 1$$

$$\Rightarrow \left[\frac{n}{a}\right] = \left[k + \frac{r}{a}\right] = k.$$

Proved.

Theorem 4 : The highest power of a prime contained in $n!$ is $h_1 + h_2 + ... h_k$ where

$$h_1 = \left[\frac{n}{p}\right], \; h_2 = \left[\frac{h_1}{p}\right], \; .... h_k = \left[\frac{h_{k-1}}{p}\right].$$

Proof : The highest power of p in $n!$ is

$$\left[\frac{n}{p}\right] + \left[\frac{n}{p^2}\right] + \left[\frac{n}{p^3}\right] + ... \left[\frac{n}{p^k}\right].$$

Now $\left[\frac{n}{p}\right] = h_1$

$$\left[\frac{n}{p^2}\right] = \left[\frac{1}{p}.\left[\frac{n}{p}\right]\right] = \left[\frac{h_1}{p}\right] = h_2$$

$$\left[\frac{n}{p^3}\right] = \left[\frac{1}{p}.\left[\frac{n}{p^2}\right]\right] = \left[\frac{h_2}{p}\right] = h_3$$

$$\left[\frac{n}{p^k}\right] = \left[\frac{1}{p}\left[\frac{n}{p^{k-1}}\right]\right] = \left[\frac{h_{k-1}}{p}\right] = h_k.$$

Therefore, the highest power of a prime p contained in $n!$ is given by

$$h_1 + h_2 + ... h_k.$$

Example 1 : Find the highest power of 3 contained in 40!.

Solution : The highest power of a prime p dividing $n!$ is given by

$$\left[\frac{n}{p}\right] + \left[\frac{n}{p^2}\right] + ... + \left[\frac{n}{p^k}\right]$$

where $p^k \leqslant n < p^{k+1}$.

Therefore, the highest power of 3 dividing 40! will be

$$\left[\frac{40}{3}\right]+\left[\frac{40}{3^2}\right]+\left[\frac{40}{3^3}\right]=13+4+1$$
$$=18.$$

Example 2 : Find the highest power of 7 contained in 2000!

Solution : The highest power of 7 contained in 2000! is given by

$$H = h_1 + h_2 + h_3$$

$$h_1 = \left[\frac{2000}{7}\right] = 285$$

$$h_2 = \left[\frac{285}{7}\right] = 40$$

$$h_3 = \left[\frac{40}{7}\right] = 5.$$

Therefore,

$$H = h_1 + h_2 + h_3$$
$$= 285 + 40 + 5$$
$$= 330.$$

Example 3 : Find the highest power of 13 contained in 20000!

Solution : The highest power of 13 contained in 20000! is given by

$$H = h_1 + h_2 + h_3$$

where

$$h_1 = \left[\frac{20000}{13}\right] = 1538$$

$$h_2 = \left[\frac{1538}{13}\right] = 118$$

$$h_3 = \left[\frac{118}{13}\right] = 9$$

$$\therefore \quad H = 1538 + 118 + 9$$
$$= 1665.$$

Example 4 : Find the highest power of 18 contained in 500!

Solution : Here 18 is a composite number which can be decomposed into a product of primes as

$$18 = 2 \times 3^2.$$

Therefore, the primes contained in 18 are 2 and 3. Now we calculate the highest powers of these primes in 500!. The highest powers of 2 in 500! is given by

$$H_1 = \left[\frac{500}{2}\right] + \left[\frac{250}{2}\right] + \left[\frac{125}{2}\right] + \left[\frac{62}{2}\right] + \left[\frac{31}{2}\right] + \left[\frac{15}{2}\right] + \left[\frac{7}{2}\right] + \left[\frac{3}{2}\right]$$
$$= 250 + 125 + 62 + 31 + 15 + 7 + 3 + 1$$
$$= 494.$$

Similarly the highest power 3 contained in 500! is given by

$$H_2 = \left[\frac{500}{3}\right] + \left[\frac{166}{3}\right] + \left[\frac{55}{3}\right] + \left[\frac{18}{3}\right] + \left[\frac{6}{3}\right]$$
$$= 166 + 55 + 18 + 6 + 2$$
$$= 247.$$

Therefore,

$$500! = 3^{494} \times 3^{247} \times t \text{ for some } t \text{ such that } (t, 18) = 1$$
$$= (2^2 \times 3)^{247} \times t.$$

Thus, highest power of 18 in 500! is 247.

Example 5 : Show that $\dfrac{n!}{a_1!a_2!a_3!}$ is an integer when

$a_1, a_2, a_3 \geqslant 0$ and $n = a_1 + a_2 + a_3$.

Solution : Let p be prime that divides $n!$. Then the highest power of p which divides $n!$ is given by

$$H = \sum_{k=1}^{\infty} \frac{n}{p^k}.$$

The highest power of p dividing $a_i!$, $i = 1, 2, 3$ is given by

$$H_i = \sum_{k=1}^{\infty} \frac{a_i}{p^k}.$$

Now $$\left[\frac{a_1}{p^k}\right] + \left[\frac{a_2}{p^k}\right] + \left[\frac{a_3}{p^k}\right] \leqslant \left[\frac{a_1 + a_2 + a_3}{p^k}\right] = \left[\frac{n}{p^k}\right] \ \forall\ k$$

$$\therefore \quad \sum_{k=1}^{\infty} \left[\left[\frac{a_1}{p^k}\right] + \left[\frac{a_2}{p^k}\right] + \left[\frac{a_3}{p^k}\right]\right] \leqslant \left[\frac{n}{p^k}\right].$$

This shows that the highest power of a prime dividing the numerator of the given expression is greater than or equal to highest power of that prime dividing the denominator. Hence, $\dfrac{n!}{a_1!\, a_2!\, a_3!}$ is an integer.

Example 6 : Show that $\dfrac{(2n)!}{(n!)^2}$ is an even integer.

Solution : Let $f(n) \equiv \dfrac{(2n)!}{(n!)^2}$.

For $n = 1$ we have

$$f(1) \equiv \frac{(2.1)!}{(1!)^2}$$

$$= \frac{2}{1}$$

$$= 2, \text{ an even integer.}$$

Thus, the result is true for $n = 1$.

Let the result be true for $n = m$ *i.e.*,

$$f(m) \equiv \frac{(2m)!}{(m!)^2} \text{ is an even integer.}$$

$$= 2k. \text{ (say)}$$

Then

$$f(m+1) \equiv \frac{[2(m+1)]!}{[(m+1)!]^2}$$

$$= \frac{(2m+2)(2m+1)(2m)!}{(m+1)^2 [(m)!]^2}$$

$$= \frac{2[2m+1]2k}{(m+1)}.$$

This is an even integer for any value of m. Hence by mathematical induction $\frac{(2n)!}{(n!)^2}$ is an even integer.

6.5 Euler's Function

For any positive integer n, Euler's function $\phi(n)$ is defined as the number of positive integers relatively prime to n not exceeding n.

For example $\phi(1) = 1$.

$\phi(12) = 4$ [$\because$ The relatively prime integers less than 12 are 1, 5, 7, 11]

$\phi(p) = p - 1$ if p is a prime.

Theorem 1 : For any positive integer n, $\phi(n) = n - 1$ iff n is a prime.

Proof : Suppose n is a prime. Then 1, 2, 3, ... $n - 1$ are all integers $< n$ which are relatively prime to n. Therefore, $\phi(n) = n - 1$.

Conversely if n has a divisor d such that $1 < d < n$ then $\phi(n) \leqslant (n-2) < n - 1$ which is contradiction. Therefore n has no divisor other than 1 and n. Hence, n is a prime.

Theorem 2 : If the n terms of an A.P.

$$r, r+m, r+2m, \ldots, r+(n-1)m \qquad \ldots\ldots(1)$$

with common difference m relatively prime to n then the remainders obtained are 0, 1, 2, ... $(n-1)$ in some order.

Proof : If the terms of (1) are divided by n, we get n remainders belonging to the set

$$\{0, 1, 2, ... n - 1\}.$$

in some order. These remainders will be distinct as shown below :

Suppose two terms of (1) say $r + xm$ and $r + ym$ have the same remainder where x and y are integers such that.

$0 \leqslant x < y \leqslant n - 1$. Then we have

$$(r + ym) - (r + xm) = (y - x)m$$

is divisible by n. But this is not possible as $(m, n) = 1$ and $y - x < n$.

Thus, when we divide the terms of (1) by n then we have n distinct remainders $0, 1, 2, ... (n - 1)$ in some order.

Theorem 3 : An integer a is relatively prime to n iff its remainder with respect to n is relatively prime to n.

Proof : Let r be the remainder when a is divided by n. Thus, we have

$$a = nq + r, \quad 0 \leqslant r < n.$$

Let $(a, n) = 1$ then if d divides r and n, it divides a and n contradicting the fact that $(a, n) = 1$. Therefore $(r, n) = 1$.

Let $(r, n) = 1$ then if d_1 divides a and n, it divides r and n contradicting that $(r, n) = 1$. Therefore $(a, n) = 1$.

Theorem 4 : If $S = \{r, r + m, r + 2m, ... r + (n - 1)m\}$ are n terms of an A.P. whose common difference m relatively by prime to n. Then there are exactly $\phi(n)$ integers prime to n.

Proof : If we divide the integers given in S by n then we get remainders $S_1 = \{0, 1, 2, ... (n - 1)\}$ in some order. We know that there are as many integers prime to n in S as there are in S_1. But there are $\phi(n)$ integers prime to n is S_1. Therefore, the number of integers prime to n in S is $\phi(n)$.

Theorem 5 : If m and n are relatively prime then $\phi(mn) = \phi(m)\,\phi(n)$, *i.e.*, ϕ is multiplicative. **(C.C.S.U. 2005)**

Proof : We have to show that $\phi(mn) = \phi(m)\,\phi(n)$ where $(m, n) = 1$. Since $\phi(1) = 1$, the result is obviously true if either m or n is equal to 1. We consider $m > 1, n > 1$. We arrange the integers $1, 2, ..., mn$ in m columns and n rows as follows :

$$\begin{array}{ccccccc} 1 & 2 & .... & r & .... & m \\ m+1 & m+2 & .... & m+r & .... & 2m \\ \vdots & \vdots & & \vdots & & \vdots \\ (n-1)m+1 & (n-1)m+2 & & (n-1)m+r & & mn \end{array}$$

Now $\phi(mn)$ is equal to the number of entries in the above array which are relatively prime to mn. This is the same as the number of integers which are relatively prime to both m and n.

We take the entries of say rth column given by

$$r, m + r, ... (n - 1)m + r \qquad ....(1)$$

These entires form an A.P. of n terms with common difference m prime to n. Each column in the above array contains exactly $\phi(n)$ integers prime to n. Also it is obvious that each term of (1) is prime to m iff r is prime to m. But r is prime to m for $\phi(m)$ values of r. Thus, there are exactly $\phi(m)$ columns in which every integer is relatively prime to m. Therefore, there are in all $\phi(m)\ \phi(n)$ integers less than mn and prime to both m and n. Hence,

$$\phi(mn) = \phi(m)\ \phi(n).$$

Proved.

Corollary : If $n_1, n_2, ... n_r$ are pairwise prime integers them

$$\phi(n_1 n_2 .... n_r) = \phi(n_1)\ \phi(n_2) .... \phi(n_r).$$

Theorem 6 : If p is a prime and $k > 0$ then

$$\phi(p^k) = p^k\left[1 - \frac{1}{p}\right] = p^k - p^{k-1}.$$

Proof : If $k = 1$ then the integers less than p and relatively prime to it are $1, 2, ...p - 1$. Therefore,

$$\phi(p) = p - 1.$$

If $k > 1$ then $p, 2p, ... p^{k-1}, p^k$ are divisible by p among the integers $1, 2, ... p^k$.

Thus, the set $\{1, 2, ... p^k\}$ contains exactly $p^k - p^{k-1}$ integers which are relatively prime to p^k. This implies that

$$\phi(p^k) = p^k - p^{k-1}$$
$$= p^k\left[1 - \frac{1}{p}\right].$$

Proved.

Corollary : $\phi(p^{k+1}) = p\ \phi(p^k)$.

Proof : We have

$$\phi(p^{k+1}) = p^{k+1} - p^k$$
$$= p(p^k - p^{k-1})$$
$$= p\phi(p^k).$$

Theorem 7 : If $n = p_1^{k_1}.p_2^{k_2}. .... p_r^{k_r}$ is the canonical representation then

$$\phi(n) = n\left(1 - \frac{1}{p_1}\right)\left(1 - \frac{1}{p_2}\right)...\left(1 - \frac{1}{p_r}\right).$$

Proof : Since $p_1, p_2, ... p_r$ are pairwise prime integers,

we have

$$\phi(n) = \phi(p_1^{k_1}.p_2^{k_2} .... p_r^{k_r})$$
$$= \phi(p_1^{k_1})\ \phi(p_2^{k_2}) .... \phi(p_r^{k_r})$$
$$= p_1^{k_1}\left(1 - \frac{1}{p_1}\right) p_2^{k_2}\left(1 - \frac{1}{p_2}\right) ... p_r^{k_r}\left(1 - \frac{1}{p_r}\right)$$

$$= p_1^{k_1} p_2^{k_2} \dots p_r^{k_r} \left(1-\frac{1}{p_1}\right)\left(1-\frac{1}{p_2}\right)\dots\left(1-\frac{1}{p_r}\right)$$

$$= n\left(1-\frac{1}{p_1}\right)\left(1-\frac{1}{p_2}\right)\dots\left(1-\frac{1}{p_r}\right).$$

Example 1 : Evaluate $\phi(900)$

Solution : We have

$$900 = 2^2.3^2.5^2.$$

$$\therefore \quad \phi(900) = \phi(2^2.3^2.5^2)$$
$$= \phi(2^2).\phi(3^2).\phi(5^2)$$
$$= (2^2 - 2).(3^2 - 3).(5^2 - 5)$$
$$= (4 - 2).(9 - 3).(25 - 5)$$
$$= 2.6.20$$
$$= 240.$$

Example 2 : Evaluate $\phi(5186)$.

Solution : We have

$$5186 = 2 \times 2593$$

$$\therefore \quad \phi(5186) = \phi(2 \times 2593)$$
$$= \phi(2).\phi(2593)$$
$$= (2^1 - 2^0).(2593^1 - 2593^0)$$
$$= (2 - 1).(2593 - 1)$$
$$= 2592.$$

Example 3 : Evaluate $\phi(5040)$.

Solution : We have, $\quad 5040 = 2^4 \times 3^2 \times 5 \times 7$

$$\therefore \quad \phi(5040) = \phi(2^4 \times 3^2 \times 5 \times 7)$$
$$= \phi(2^4).\ \phi(3^2).\ \phi(5).\ \phi(7)$$
$$= (2^4 - 2^3).(3^2 - 3^1).(5^1 - 5^0)(7 - 7^0)$$
$$= (16 - 8).\ (9 - 3).(5 - 1)(7 - 1).$$
$$= 8.6.4.6$$
$$= 1152.$$

Example 4 : Show that $\phi(n) = \phi(n + 1) = \phi(n + 2)$ for $n = 5186$.

Solution : We have

$$\phi(n) = \phi(5186)$$
$$= \phi(2 \times 2593)$$
$$= \phi(2).\ \phi(2593)$$
$$= (2^1 - 2^0).(2593^1 - 2593^0)$$
$$= 1.(2593 - 1)$$
$$= 2592.$$

$$\begin{aligned}\phi(n+1) &= \phi(5187)\\ &= \phi(3.7.13.19)\\ &= \phi(3).\phi(7).\phi(13).\phi(19)\\ &= (3-1)(7-1)(13-1)(19-1)\\ &= 2.6.12.18\\ &= 2592.\end{aligned}$$

$$\begin{aligned}\phi(n+2) &= \phi(5188)\\ &= \phi(2^2.1297)\\ &= \phi(2^2).\phi(1297)\\ &= (2^2-2).(1297-1)\\ &= 2.(1296)\\ &= 2592.\end{aligned}$$

Thus, $\phi(n) = \phi(n+1) = \phi(n+2)$.

Example 5 : Prove that $\phi(n) = \phi(n+2)$ is satisfied by $n = 2(2p-1)$ whenever p and $2p-1$ are both odd prime.

Solution : We have

$$\begin{aligned}\phi(n) &= \phi[2.(2p-1)]\\ &= \phi(2).\phi(2p-1)\\ &= (2-1)(2p-1-1) && [\because 2p-1 \text{ is a prime}]\\ &= 2(p-1).\end{aligned}$$

And
$$\begin{aligned}\phi(n+2) &= \phi[2(2p-1)+2)]\\ &= \phi[4p]\\ &= \phi(2^2p)\\ &= \phi(2^2).\phi(p)\\ &= (2^2-2).(p-1)\\ &= 2(p-1).\end{aligned}$$

Thus, $\phi(n) = \phi(n+2)$. **Proved**

Example 6 : If p and $p+2$ are both primes than show that

$$\phi(p+2) = \phi(p) + 2.$$

Solution : We have

$$\begin{aligned}\text{L.H.S.} &= \phi(p+2)\\ &= (p+2-1) && [\because p+2 \text{ is a prime}]\\ &= p+1.\end{aligned}$$

$$\begin{aligned}\text{R.H.S.} &= \phi(p)+2.\\ &= (p-1)+2 && [\because p \text{ is a prime}]\\ &= p+1.\end{aligned}$$

Thus, L.H.S. = R.H.S. **Proved**

Example 7 : If p and $2p + 1$ are both primes and $n = 4p$ then show that

$$\phi(n + 2) = \phi(n) + 2.$$

Solution : We have

$$\begin{aligned}
\text{L.H.S.} &= \phi(n + 2) \\
&= \phi(4p + 2) \\
&= \phi[2(2p + 1)] \\
&= \phi(2).\phi(2p + 1) \\
&= (2 - 1)(2p + 1 - 1) && [\because 2p + 1 \text{ is a prime}] \\
&= 2p. \\
\text{R.H.S.} &= \phi(n) + 2 \\
&= \phi(4p) + 2 \\
&= \phi(2^2 p) + 2 \\
&= \phi(2^2).\phi(p) + 2 \\
&= (2^2 - 2)(p - 1) + 2 && [\because p \text{ is a prime}] \\
&= 2p - 2 + 2 \\
&= 2p.
\end{aligned}$$

Thus, L.H.S. = R.H.S. **Proved.**

Example 8 : If n is an odd integer then

$$\phi(2n) = \phi(n).$$ **(C.C.S.U. 2000)**

Solution : Since n is an odd integer, we have $(2, n) = 1$.

Therefore,

$$\begin{aligned}
\phi(2n) &= \phi(2).\phi(n) \\
&= (2 - 1).\phi(n) \\
&= \phi(n).
\end{aligned}$$ **Proved**

Example 9 : If n is a composite number then $\phi(n) \leqslant n - \sqrt{n}$.

Solution : Let $n = p_1^{k_1}.p_2^{k_2} \ldots. p_r^{k_r}$, p_1 is the smallest prime. Then

$$\begin{aligned}
\phi(n) &= n\left(1 - \frac{1}{p_1}\right)\left(1 - \frac{1}{p_2}\right)\ldots\left(1 - \frac{1}{p_r}\right) \\
&\leqslant n\left(1 - \frac{1}{p_1}\right) \\
&\leqslant n\left(1 - \frac{1}{\sqrt{n}}\right) && [\because p_1 \leqslant \sqrt{n}] \\
&= n - \sqrt{n}.
\end{aligned}$$

Thus, $\phi(n) \leqslant n - \sqrt{n}$. **Proved**

Example 10 : If every prime that divides n also divides m then $\phi(mn) = n\,\phi(m)$ in particular

$$\phi(n^2) = n\,\phi(n)$$

Solution : Since every prime divisor of n is also a prime divisor of m we write n and m as

$$n = p_1^{k_1}.p_2^{k_2}.\ \ldots.\ p_r^{k_r}.$$

and $$m = p_1^{l_1}.p_2^{l_2}.\ \ldots.\ p_r^{l_r}.\ p_{r+1}^{l_r+1}.\ \ldots.\ p_t^{l_t}$$

Here all p_i are prime, k_i, l_i are integers $\geqslant 1$ and $t \geqslant r$.

Therefore,

$$\phi(mn) = \phi(p_1^{k_1+l_1}.p_2^{k_2+l_2}.\ \ldots.\ p_r^{k_r+l_r}.\ p_{r+1}^{l_r+1}\ \ldots.\ p_t^{l_t})$$

$$= \phi(p_1^{k_1+l_1}).\phi(p_2^{k_2+l_2})\ \ldots.\ \phi(p_r^{k_r+l_r}).\phi(p_{r+1}^{l_r+1})\ \ldots.\ \phi(p_t^{l_t})$$

$$= (p_1^{k_1+l_1} - p_1^{k_1+l_1-1}).(p_2^{k_2+l_2} - p_2^{k_2+l_2-1})\ \ldots.$$

$$(p_r^{k_r+l_r} - p_r^{k_r+l_r-1}).\phi(p_{r+1}^{l_r+1})\ \ldots.\ \phi(p_t^{l_t}).$$

$$= p_1^{k_1}.p_2^{k_2}.\ \ldots.\ p_r^{k_r}(p_1^{l_1} - p_1^{l_1-1}).(p_2^{l_2} - p_2^{l_2-1})\ \ldots.\ (p_r^{l_r} - p_r^{l_r-1}).$$

$$\phi(p_{r+1}^{l_r+1})\ \ldots.\ \phi(p_t^{l_t})$$

$$= n.\phi(p_1^{l_1})\ \phi(p_2^{l_2})\ \ \ldots.\ \phi(p_t^{l_t})$$

$$= n\phi(m). \qquad \ldots\ldots(1)$$

Putting $m = n$ in (1) we get

$$\phi(n^2) = n\phi(n).$$

6.6 Euler's Theorem (C.C.S.U 2004)

If a and $n > 0$ are integers such that $(a, n) = 1$ then $a^{\phi(n)} \equiv 1 \pmod{n}$.

Proof : If $n = 1$ then $\phi(1) = 1$ and $a^1 = a \equiv 1 \pmod 1$ $[\because 1|(a-1)]$

Now we assume $n > 1$. Let $a_1, a_2, \ldots.\ a_{\phi(n)}$ be the positive integers less than n which are relatively prime to n *i.e.*, $(a_i, n) = 1$.

We consider $aa_1, aa_2, \ldots.\ aa_{\phi(n)}$. For each i, $1 \leqslant i \leqslant \phi(n)$ $aa_i \not\equiv 0 \pmod n$ because m/aa_i, $(a, n) = 1 \Rightarrow n|a_i$ which is not possible, because $aa_i \equiv aa_j \pmod n$

Also $aa_i \not\equiv aa_j \pmod n$

$$\Rightarrow n/(aa_i - aa_j) = a(a_i - a_j) \text{ and } (a, n) = 1$$

$$\Rightarrow n/(a_i - a_j)$$

$$\Rightarrow a_i \equiv a_j \pmod n \text{ which is again not possible.}$$

Thus, $aa_1, aa_2, \ldots.\ aa_{\phi(n)}$ are $\phi(n)$ mutually congruent integers and therefore

$$aa_1 \equiv aa_1' \pmod n$$

$$aa_2 \equiv aa_2' \pmod n$$

$\vdots$

$aa_{\phi(r)} \equiv aa'_{\phi(n)} \pmod n$ where $a_1', a_2', \ldots.$ are $a_1, a_2 \ldots.$ in some other order.

Multiplying these relations we get

$$aa_1.aa_2 \dots aa_{\phi(n)} \equiv a_1'a_2' \dots a'_{\phi(n)} \pmod n$$

or $$a^{\phi(n)}a_1a_2 \dots a_{\phi(n)} \equiv a_1a_2 \dots a_{\phi(n)} \pmod n.$$

Since each a_i is coprime to n we have

$a_1, a_2, \dots a_{\phi(n)}$ is coprime to n. Therefore,

$a^{\phi(n)} \equiv 1 \pmod n$. [By cancellation law]

6.7 Some Properties of Euler's Function

Theorem 1 (Gauss theorem) : For each positive integer $n \geqslant 1$,

$$n = \phi(d_1) + \phi(d_2) + \dots \phi(d_k)$$

where $d_1, d_2, \dots d_k$ are all divisors of n.

or $$n = \sum_{d/n} \phi(d) \quad \text{where } \Sigma \text{ is carried over all divisors.}$$

Proof : Let d be a positive divisor of n and let

$$S_1 = \{m : (m, n) = d, 1 \leqslant m \leqslant n\}.$$

Now $(m, n) = d \Leftrightarrow \left(\frac{m}{d}, \frac{n}{d}\right) = 1$. Therefore, S_1 contains the positive integers relatively prime to n/d and not exceeding n/d. Since each integer in the set

$$S_2 = \{1, 2, \dots n\}$$

lies in exactly one class S_1, we have

$$n = \sum_{d/n} \phi(n/d).$$

But $$\sum_{d/n} \phi(n/d) = \sum_{d/n} \phi(d)$$

$\therefore$ $$n = \sum_{d/n} \phi(d).$$

Theorem 2 : The sum of the positive integers less than n and relatively prime to n is equal to $\frac{1}{2}n\phi(n)$ *i.e.*

$$\sum_{\substack{(r,n)=1 \\ 1 \leqslant r < n}} r = \frac{1}{2} n\phi(n).$$

Proof : Let $r_1, r_2, \dots r_{\phi(n)}$ be the positive integers less than n and relatively prime to n.

Now $(r, n) = 1 \Leftrightarrow (n - r, n) = 1$. Therefore,

$$r_1 + r_2 + \dots r_{\phi(n)} = (n - r_1) + (n - r_2) + \dots n - r_{\phi(n)}$$

$$= n\phi(n) - (r_1 + r_2 + \dots + r_{\phi(n)})$$

$$\Rightarrow 2(r_1 + r_2 + \dots r_{\phi(n)}) = n\phi(n)$$

$$\Rightarrow r_1 + r_2 + \dots r_{\phi(n)} = \tfrac{1}{2} n_{\phi(n)}.$$

Proved.

Example 1 : Find the last two digits in the decimal representation of 3^{100}.

Solution : The given problem is equivalent to find the smallest non-negative integer to which 3^{100} is congruent modulo 100.

Since 3 and 100 are relatively prime we have

$$\phi(100) = \phi(2^2.5^2)$$

$$= 100\left(1-\frac{1}{2}\right)\left(1-\frac{1}{5}\right)$$

$$= 40 \qquad \text{.......(1)}$$

By Euler's theorem, we have

$$3^{\phi(100)} \equiv 1(\text{mod } 100)$$

or $$3^{40} \equiv 1(\text{mod } 100). \qquad \text{[By (1)]} \qquad \text{.......(2)}$$

Now $$3^{100} = 3^{40.2+20}$$

$$= (3^{40})^2.3^{20}$$

$$\equiv 3^{20} \text{ (mod 100)}$$

$$\equiv (3^5)^4 \text{ (mod 100)}$$

$$\equiv (43)^4 \text{ (mod 100)}$$

$$\equiv [(43)^2]^2 \text{ mod 100}$$

$$\equiv (49)^2 \text{ (mod 100)}$$

$$\equiv 01(\text{mod } 100).$$

Therefore, the last two digits are 01.

Example 2 : Show that if n is the product of twin primes *i.e.*, $n = p(p+2)$ where p and $p+2$ are primes then $\phi(n)\ \sigma(n) = (n+1)(n-3)$.

Solution : Since $n = p(p+2)$ the product of primes p and $p+2$ we have

$$\phi(n) = \phi[p(p+2)]$$

$$= \phi(p)\ \phi(p+2)$$

$$= (p-1)(p+2-1)$$

$$= (p-1)(p+1)$$

$$= p^2 - 1$$

$$\sigma(n) = \sigma[p(p+2)]$$

$$= \sigma(p)\sigma(p+2)$$

$$= (p+1)(p+2+1)$$

$$= (p+1)(p+3)$$

$$= p^2 + 4p + 3.$$

Therefore,

$$\phi(n)\sigma(n) = (p^2-1)(p^2+4p+3)$$

$$= p^4 + 4p^3 + 2p^2 - 4p - 3$$

$$= p^4 + 2p^3 + 2p^3 + 4p^2 - 2p^2 - 4p - 3$$

$$= p^2[p^2+2p] + 2p[p^2+2p] - 2[p^2+2p] - 3$$

$$= (p^2 + 2p)(p^2 + 2p) - 2(p^2 + 2p) - 3$$
$$= n^2 - 2n - 3$$
$$= (n + 1)(n - 3).$$ **Proved.**

6.8 Function *T(n)*

The function $T(n)$ is defined as

$$T(n) = \tau(1) + \tau(2) + \ldots. \tau(n) = \sum_{x=1}^{n} \tau(x).$$

For example

$$T(8) = \tau(1) + \tau(2) + \ldots. + \tau(8)$$
$$= 1 + 2 + 2 + 3 + 2 + 4 + 2 + 4 = 20.$$

Theorem 1 : *T(n)* is equal to the number of lattice points which lie in the region *R* given by $x > 0, y > 0, xy \leqslant n$. *i.e.*, *T(n)* is equal to the number of lattice point lying on or under the hyperbola $xy = n$ in the first quadrant excluding the lattice points on the coordinate axis.

Proof : Since the region, R is given by $x > 0$, $y > 0$, $xy \leqslant n$, the lattice points must be on one of the curves.

$$xy = 1, xy = 2, \ldots., xy = n$$

in the first quadrant which is equal to $\tau(1) + \tau(2) + \ldots. + \tau(n) = T(n)$. **Proved**

Theorem 2 : Show that

$$T(n) = \left[\frac{n}{1}\right] + \left[\frac{n}{2}\right] + \ldots. + \left[\frac{n}{n}\right] = \sum_{x=1}^{n} \left[\frac{n}{x}\right]$$

Proof : By theorem 1 we know that $T(n)$ is equal to the lattice points in the region R given by $x > 0$, $y > 0$, $xy \leqslant n$. This will be equal to the lattice points on the verticals at $x = 1, x = 2, \ldots. x = n$ on the curve $xy = n$. The lengths of these verticals are $\frac{n}{1}, \frac{n}{2}, \ldots., \frac{n}{n}$ respectively. Therefore, the number of lattice points on them are respectively $\left[\frac{n}{1}\right], \left[\frac{n}{2}\right], \ldots., \left[\frac{n}{n}\right]$

So $$T(n) = \left[\frac{n}{1}\right] + \left[\frac{n}{2}\right] + \ldots. + \left[\frac{n}{n}\right].$$

For example $n = 10$ we have

$$T(10) = \left[\frac{10}{1}\right] + \left[\frac{10}{2}\right] + \ldots. + \left[\frac{10}{10}\right]$$
$$= 10 + 5 + 3 + 2 + 2 + 1 + 1 + 1 + 1 + 1$$
$$= 27.$$

Theorem 3 : If n is a positive integer then

$$\sum_{m=1}^{n} \frac{1}{m} = \log n + \gamma + \frac{\theta}{n}$$

where γ is a constant called Euler's constant and $0 < \theta < 1$.

Proof : Let $f(x) = \frac{1}{x}$, $x > 0$ be a decreasing function. Then by the property of definite integral we have

$$\frac{1}{m+1} < \int_m^{m+1} \frac{dx}{x} < \frac{1}{m}, m > 0.$$

This gives

$$0 < \frac{1}{m} - \int_m^{m+1} \frac{dx}{x} < \frac{1}{m} - \frac{1}{m+1}. \qquad \text{.......(1)}$$

Let $$F(m) = \frac{1}{m} - \int_m^{m+1} \frac{dx}{x}. \qquad \text{.......(2)}$$

Then (1) can be written as

$$0 < F(m) < \frac{1}{m} - \frac{1}{m+1}. \qquad \text{.......(3)}$$

Let a be a fixed integer such that $r > a$.
Putting $m = a, a+1, a+2, \ldots, r$ in (3) we get

$$0 < F(a) < \frac{1}{a} - \frac{1}{a+1}$$

$$0 < F(a+1) < \frac{1}{a+1} - \frac{1}{a+2}$$

$$\vdots \qquad \vdots$$

$$0 < F(r) < \frac{1}{r} - \frac{1}{r+1}.$$

By adding these results column-wise, we get

$$0 < \sum_{m=a}^{r} F(m) < \frac{1}{a} - \frac{1}{r+1}. \qquad \text{.......(4)}$$

Sum function $\sum_{m=a}^{r} F(m)$ is an increasing functions of r and is bounded above by $\frac{1}{a}$. This sum function tends to a finite limit as $r \to \infty$.

Therefore,

$$\sum_{m=a}^{\infty} F(m) = \text{a finite number} \leqslant \frac{1}{a}. \qquad \text{.......(5)}$$

Let, $\gamma = \sum_{m=1}^{\infty} F(m)$ (taking $a = 1$) be a constant.

Then $\gamma = \sum_{m=1}^{n} F(m) + \sum_{m=n+1}^{\infty} F(m)$

$$= \sum_{m=1}^{n} \frac{1}{m} - \int_1^{n+1} \frac{dx}{x} + \sum_{m=n+1}^{\infty} F(m)$$

$$\left[\because \sum_{m=a}^{r} F(m) = \frac{1}{a} - \int_a^{a+1} \frac{dx}{x} + \frac{1}{a+1} - \int_{a+1}^{a+2} \frac{dx}{x} \ldots + \frac{1}{r} - \int_r^{r+1} \frac{dx}{x} \right.$$
$$\left. = \sum_{m=a}^{r} \frac{1}{m} - \int_a^{r+1} \frac{dx}{x} \right]$$

$$= \sum_{m=1}^{n} \frac{1}{m} - \int_1^{n} \frac{dx}{x} - \int_n^{n+1} \frac{dx}{x} + \sum_{m=n+1}^{\infty} F(m)$$

$$= \sum_{m=1}^{n} \frac{1}{m} - \log n - \left(\int_n^{n+1} \frac{dx}{x} - \sum_{m=n+1}^{\infty} F(m) \right). \qquad \ldots\ldots.(6)$$

But $\frac{1}{n+1} < \int_n^{n+1} \frac{dx}{x} < \frac{1}{n}.$

From (5) we have

$$0 < \sum_{m=(n+1)}^{\infty} F(m) \leqslant \frac{1}{n+1}.$$

Consequently

$$0 < \int_n^{n+1} \frac{dx}{x} - \sum_{m=n+1}^{\infty} F(m) < \frac{1}{n}.$$

This gives $\int_n^{n+1} \frac{dx}{x} - \sum_{m=n+1}^{\infty} = \frac{\theta}{n}$ $\qquad \ldots\ldots.(7)$

for some θ, a function of n such that $0 < \theta < 1$.

Now from (6) and (7) we get

$$\gamma = \sum_{m=1}^{n} \frac{1}{m} - \log n - \frac{\theta}{n}$$

$$\Rightarrow \sum_{m=1}^{n} \frac{1}{m} = \gamma + \log n + \frac{\theta}{n}. \qquad \ldots\ldots.(8)$$

Proved

Note : Taking limit $n \to \infty$ in (8) we get

$$\gamma = \lim_{n \to \infty} \left(1 + \frac{1}{2} + ... + \frac{1}{n} - \log n\right)$$

This value of γ is known as Euler's constant.

Theorem 4 : If α is real number $\geqslant 1$, then

$$\sum_{n=1}^{[\alpha]} = \log \alpha + \gamma + \frac{\theta_1}{\alpha}, \; -1 < \theta_1 < 1. \qquad \text{(C.C.S.U. 2004)}$$

Proof : We have

$$\gamma = \sum_{m=1}^{\infty} F(m)$$

$$= \sum_{m=1}^{[\alpha]} F(m) + \sum_{m=[\alpha]+1}^{\infty} F(m)$$

$$= \sum_{m=1}^{[\alpha]} \frac{1}{m} - \int_1^{[\alpha]+1} \frac{dx}{x} + \sum_{m=[\alpha]+1}^{\infty} F(m)$$

$$= \sum_{m=1}^{[\alpha]} \frac{1}{m} - \int_1^{\alpha} \frac{dx}{x} - \int_1^{[\alpha]+1} \frac{dx}{x} + \sum_{m=[\alpha]+1}^{\infty} F(m)$$

$$= \sum_{m=1}^{[\alpha]} \frac{1}{m} - \log \alpha - \left[\int_1^{[\alpha]+1} \frac{dx}{x} + \sum_{m=[\alpha]+1}^{\infty} F(m)\right]. \qquad ....(1)$$

Also from theorem 3 we have

$$\theta < \sum_{m=[\alpha]+1}^{\infty} F(m) < \frac{1}{[\alpha]+1} < \frac{1}{\alpha}.$$

Also by the property of definite integral we have

$$0 < \int_{\alpha}^{[\alpha]+1} \frac{dx}{x} < \frac{1}{\alpha}.$$

Therefore,

$$0 \leqslant \left| \int_{\alpha}^{[\alpha]+1} \frac{dx}{x} - \sum_{m=[\alpha]+1}^{\infty} F(m) \right| < \frac{1}{\alpha}.$$

This gives

$$\int_{\alpha}^{[\alpha]+1} \frac{dx}{x} - \sum_{m=[\alpha]+1}^{\infty} F(m) = \frac{\theta_1}{\alpha}, \; -1 < \theta_1 < 1. \qquad ....(2)$$

From (1) and (2), we have

$$\gamma = \sum_{m=1}^{[\alpha]} \frac{1}{m} - \log n - \frac{\theta_1}{\alpha}.$$ **Proved.**

6.9 Function *S*(*n*)

The function $S(n)$ is defined as

$$S(n) = \sigma(1) + \sigma(2) + ... + \sigma(n) = \sum_{x=1}^{n} \sigma(x).$$

For example

$$\begin{aligned} S(8) &= \sigma(1) + \sigma(2) + ... + \sigma(8) \\ &= 1 + (1+2) + (1+8) + (1+2+n) + (1+5) + (1+2+6) \\ &\quad + (1+7) + (1+2+4+8) \\ &= 1 + 3 + 4 + 7 + 6 + 9 + 8 + 15 \\ &= 53. \end{aligned}$$

Theorem 1 : If k is a given positive integer then

$$\sum_{x=k+1}^{\infty} \frac{1}{x^2} = 0\left(\frac{1}{k}\right).$$

Proof : We know that $\frac{1}{x^2}$ is a strictly decreasing function. Therefore,

$$0 < \frac{1}{(k+1)^2} < \int_{k}^{k+1} \frac{dx}{x^2}$$

$$0 < \frac{1}{(k+2)^2} < \int_{k+1}^{k+2} \frac{dx}{x^2}$$

$$\vdots \qquad\qquad \vdots$$

$$0 < \frac{1}{(k+r)^2} < \int_{k+r-1}^{k+r} \frac{dx}{x^2}.$$

Adding these relations column-wise we get

$$0 < \sum_{x=k+1}^{k+r} \frac{1}{x^2} < \int_{k}^{k+r} \frac{dx}{x^2}$$

$$= \frac{1}{k} - \frac{1}{k+r}.$$

Taking limit $r \to \infty$, *i.e.*, $k + r \to \infty$, we get

$$\sum_{k+1}^{\infty} \frac{1}{x^2} < \frac{1}{k} = 0\left(\frac{1}{k}\right)$$ **Proved**

Theorem 2 : For any positive integer *n*

$$\sum_{x=1}^{n}\frac{1}{x^2}=\frac{\pi^2}{6}+0\left(\frac{1}{n}\right).$$ **(C.C.S.U. 2004)**

Proof : By theorem 1, we have

$$\sum_{x=1}^{n}\frac{1}{x^2}=\sum_{x=1}^{\infty}\frac{1}{x^2}-\sum_{x=n+1}^{\infty}\frac{1}{x^2}$$

$$=\frac{\pi^2}{6}+0\left(\frac{1}{n}\right). \qquad \left[\because \sum_{x=1}^{\infty}\frac{1}{x^2}=\frac{\pi^2}{6}\right]$$

6.10 Function $\zeta(s)$

If s is a real number greater than 1 then the function ζ (zeta) is defined as

$$\zeta(s)=\sum_{m=1}^{\infty}\frac{1}{m^s},\ s>1$$

$$=\frac{1}{s-1}+L,\ L \text{ is a constant} \leqslant 1$$

$$=\frac{1}{s-1}+0(1).$$

For example

$$\zeta(2)=1+\frac{1}{2^2}+\frac{1}{3^2}+\ldots.=\frac{\pi^2}{6}.$$

$$\zeta(4)=1+\frac{1}{2^4}+\frac{1}{3^4}+\ldots.=\frac{\pi^4}{90}.$$

If $f(n)$ be multiplicative function such that $\sum_{n=1}^{\infty}f(n)$ is absolutely convergent then

$$\sum_{n=1}^{\infty}f(n)=\prod_{p}\left[1+f(p)+f(p^2)+\ldots.\right].$$

Theorem 1 : (Euler) : If s is greater than 1 then

$$\zeta(s)=\prod_{p}\left[1-\frac{1}{p^s}\right]^{-1}.$$

Proof : Let $f(n)=\frac{1}{n^s}$. This function is multiplicative and $\sum_{n=1}^{\infty}\frac{1}{n^s}$ is absolutely convergent.

Therefore,

$$\sum_{n=1}^{\infty}\frac{1}{n^s}=\prod_p\left[1+f(p)+f(p^2)+....\right].$$

Hence,

$$\zeta(s)=\prod_p\left[1+\frac{1}{p^s}+\frac{1}{p^{2s}}+....\right]$$

$$=\prod_p\left[1-\frac{1}{p^s}\right]^{-1}.$$

Theorem 2 : If s is greater then 1 then

$$\sum\frac{\mu(n)}{n^s}=\prod_p\left[1-\frac{1}{p^s}\right]=\frac{1}{\zeta(s)}.$$ **(C.C.S.U. 2004)**

Proof : Since $\mu(n)$ and $\frac{1}{n^s}$ both are multiplication functions, their product is also multiplicative. Also $\frac{\mu(n)}{n^s}$ is absolutely convergent. Therefore,

$$\sum\frac{\mu(n)}{n^s}=\prod\left[1+\frac{\mu(p)}{p^s}+\frac{\mu(p^2)}{p^{2s}}+....\right]$$

$$=\prod_p\left[1-\frac{1}{p^s}\right]\quad [\because \mu(p)=-1,\ \mu(p^2)=\mu(p^3)=....=0]$$

$$=\frac{1}{\zeta(s)}.$$

Proved

6.11 Function $\overline{\phi}(n)$

The function $\overline{\phi}(n)$ is defined as

$$\overline{\phi}(n)=\phi(1)+\phi(2)+....+\phi(n)$$

$$=\sum_{x=1}^{n}\phi(x).$$

is called the summatory function of $\phi(n)$.

For example,

$$\overline{\phi}(8)=\phi(1)+\phi(2)+....+\phi(8)$$
$$=1+1+2+2+4+2+6+4$$
$$=22.$$

Theorem 1 : Show that $\bar{\phi}(n)=\frac{1}{2}\sum_{x=1}^{n}\mu(x)\left[\left[\frac{n}{x}\right]^2+\left[\frac{n}{x}\right]\right]$

Proof : We have

$$\bar{\phi}(n)=\phi(1)+\phi(2)+\ldots.\ \phi(n)$$

$$=1\sum_{d|1}\frac{\mu(d)}{d}+2\sum_{d|2}\frac{\mu(d)}{d}+\ldots+n\sum_{d|n}\frac{\mu(d)}{d}.$$

These terms can be rearranged as

$$\bar{\phi}(n)=a_1\mu(1)+a_2\mu(2)+\ldots.+a_n\,\mu(n) \qquad \ldots\ldots.(1)$$

$$=\sum_{x=1}^{n}a_x\,\mu(x).$$

We see that $\mu(x)$ appears once in the following terms of (1)

$$x\sum_{d|x}\frac{\mu(d)}{d},\ 2x\sum_{d|2x}\frac{\mu(d)}{d},\ \ldots.,\ \left[\frac{n}{x}\right]x\sum_{d|[n/x]x}\frac{\mu(d)}{d}.$$

Therefore,

$$a_x=x.\frac{1}{x}+2x.\frac{1}{x}+\ldots.+\left[\frac{n}{x}\right]x.\frac{1}{x}$$

$$=1+2+\ldots.+\left[\frac{n}{x}\right]$$

$$=\frac{1}{2}\left[\left[\frac{n}{x}\right]^2+\left[\frac{n}{x}\right]\right].$$

Hence,

$$\bar{\phi}(n)=\frac{1}{2}\sum_{x=1}^{n}\mu(x)\left[\left[\frac{n}{x}\right]^2+\left[\frac{n}{x}\right]\right].$$

Theorem 2 : Show that $\bar{\phi}(n)=\frac{3n^2}{\pi^2}+0(n\log n)$.

Proof : By theorem 1 we have

$$\bar{\phi}(n)=\frac{1}{2}\sum_{x=1}^{n}\mu(x)\left[\left[\frac{n}{x}\right]^2+\left[\frac{n}{x}\right]\right]$$

$$=\frac{1}{2}\sum_{x=1}^{n}\mu(x)\left[\left(\frac{n}{x}+0(1)\right)^2+\left(\frac{n}{x}+0(1)\right)\right]$$

$$=\frac{1}{2}\sum_{x=1}^{n}\mu(x)\left[\frac{n^2}{x^2}+\frac{n}{x}(20(1)+1)+(0(1))^2+0(1)\right]$$

$$= \frac{1}{2}\sum_{x=1}^{n} \mu(x)\left[\frac{n^2}{x^2} + \frac{n}{x}\,0(1) + 0(1)\right]$$

$$= \frac{1}{2}\sum_{x=1}^{n} \mu(x)\left[\frac{n^2}{x^2} + \frac{0(n)}{x}\right]$$

$$= \frac{n^2}{2}\sum_{x=1}^{n} \frac{\mu(x)}{x^2} + 0(n)\sum_{x=1}^{n}\frac{\mu(x)}{x}. \qquad \text{.......(1)}$$

Now $\frac{n^2}{2}\sum_{x=1}^{n}\frac{\mu(x)}{x^2} = \frac{n^2}{2}\cdot\left[\frac{6}{\pi^2} + 0\left(\frac{1}{n}\right)\right]$ $\left[\because \sum \frac{\mu(x)}{x^2} = \frac{6}{\pi^2} + 0\left(\frac{1}{n}\right)\right]$

$$= \frac{3n^2}{\pi^2} + 0(n). \qquad \text{.......(2)}$$

Also, $\left|\sum_{x=1}^{n}\frac{\mu(x)}{x}\right| < \sum_{x=1}^{n}\frac{1}{x} = \log n + 0(n).$

$$\therefore \quad \sum_{x=1}^{n}\frac{\mu(x)}{x} = 0[\log n + 0(1)]$$

$$= 0(\log n).$$

$$\therefore \quad 0(n)\sum_{x=1}^{n}\frac{\mu(x)}{x} = 0(n)\,0(\log n)$$

$$= 0(n \log n). \qquad \text{.......(3)}$$

From (1), (2) and (3) we have

$$\bar{\phi}(n) = \frac{3n^2}{\pi^2} + 0(n) + 0(n\log n)$$

$$= \frac{3n^2}{\pi^2} + 0(n\log n)$$

6.12 Square Free Integer

An integer n is called a square free integer if it is positive and not divisible by any square integer > 1.

The general form of a square free integer is $p_1 p_2 \dots p_r$ where $p_1, p_2, \dots, p_r$ are distinct primes.

For example 105 is a square free integer as $105 = 3 \times 5 \times 7$ is a product of three distinct primes.

6.13 Application to Cryptography

Few decades back the number theory was not applicable to ordinary human activities. Now it has been used successfully for information transmission and cryptography. Cryptography is the only known practical means for protecting information transmitted through public communications networks. With the availability of computer power a new branch of the number theory, known as the computational number theory has been developed. In cryptography, we study the methods of transmitting messages in secret codes form, so that only that person can understand it for which it is meant.

In cryptography, the codes are called ciphers the message to be transmitted is called plaintext and the message in hidden form is called ciphertext. The process of converting plaintext to ciphertext is called enciphering and the reverse process is called deciphering.

If P is the set of all plaintext messages and C that of ciphertext messages. Then a mapping $f: P \to C$ is called enciphering function and the function $f^{-1}: C \to P$ is called deciphering function. The set up

$$P \xrightarrow{f} C \xrightarrow{f^{-1}} P \text{ is called cryptosystem.}$$

One of the earliest cryptographic system was applied by Julius Caesar around 50 B.C. Caesar's cryptosystem is given by

P : A B C D E F G H I J K L M N O P Q R S T U V W X Y Z

C : D E F G H I J K L M N O P Q R S T U V W X Y Z A B C

For example the plaintext message

WORK HARD

is transformed into the ciphertext

ZRUH KDUG

The Cesar cipher can be described by using the congruence theory. For this the plaintext is first expressed numerically by converting the text into digits by means of correspondence as given below :

A	B	C	D	E	F	G	H	I	J	K	L	M
01	02	03	04	05	06	07	08	09	10	11	12	13
N	O	P	Q	R	S	T	U	V	W	X	Y	Z
14	15	16	17	18	19	20	21	22	23	24	25	26

The plaintext letter and the ciphertext letter digital equivalent P and C are related as

$$C \equiv P + 3 \pmod{26}.$$

The digital equivalent P of plaintext 'WORK HARD' is

23151811 08011804.

The corresponding cipher text digital equivalent

$$C \equiv P + 3 \pmod{26} \text{ is given by}$$

$$2618211411042107.$$

The plaintext is recovered by the congruence

$$P \equiv C + 23 \pmod{26}.$$

Caesar's cryptosystem being very simple is insecure.

Affine map is a better improvement which is defined as

$$C = aP + b \pmod{n}.$$

Here a, b are fixed integers

R. Rivest, A. Shamir and L. Adleman in 1977 proposed a public key cryptosystem. This enciphering system is called RSA. Its effectiveness depends upon the speed and time for factorization of composite numbers into products of primes.

In RSA system one chooses a pair of distinct primes p and q so large that the factorization of their product $n = pq$ called the enciphering modulus, is beyond the current computational capabilities. For example if one chooses p and q of 100 digits than n has roughly 200 digits. After selecting n the user chooses an arbitrary positive integer k such that $(k, \phi(n)) = 1$, k is called enciphering exponent. The pair (n, k) is placed in a public file but the factors of n are kept secret.

The encryption process is done by converting the message to be sent into an integer N by means of a digital alphabet in which each letter or number of the plaintext is assigned a two digit integer. One such procedure is given below :

A	B	C	D	E	F	G	H	I	J	K	L
01	02	03	04	05	06	07	08	09	10	11	12
M	N	O	P	Q	R	S	T	U	V	W	X
13	14	15	16	17	18	19	20	21	22	23	24
Y	Z	,		?	0	1	2	3	4	5	6
25	26	27	28	29	30	31	32	33	34	35	36
7	8	9	!								
37	38	39	40								

Besides these 00 indicates space between two words.

For example the plaintext message 'NUMBER THEORY' transform to

$$N\text{- }1421130205180020080515 1825.$$

The plaintext message N is assumed to be less than n the enciphering modulus so that it would be possible to distinguish N from any larger integer congruent to it modulo

n. In case the message is very lengthy and it is not possible to handle it as a single integer $N < n$ then N can be broken into blocks of digits $N_1, N_2, \ldots, N_t$ of appropriate size. Each block is encrypted separately.

The numeric form N of the plaintext is converted into ciphertext r as a number such that

$$N^k \equiv r \pmod{n}.$$

On receiving the transmitted message the authorised person deciphers it by first determining the integer j called the deciphering exponent such that

$$kj \equiv 1 \ [\text{mod } \phi(n)].$$

The recipient can retrieve N from r by calculating r^j modulo n.

Since $kj = 1 + \phi(n)t$ for some integer t, we have

$$\begin{aligned} r^j &\equiv (N^k)^j \\ &\equiv N^{1 + \phi(n)t} \\ &\equiv N.N^{\phi(n)t} \\ &\equiv N(1)^t \\ &\equiv N \pmod{n}. \end{aligned}$$

Example 1 : Encrypt the message No using RSA system.

Solution : First we convert plaintext number of the message which is given by

$$N = 1415$$

Let, $p = 19$ and $q = 23$.

Then $n = 19.23 = 437$.

Also $\phi(n) = (19 - 1)(23 - 1)$

$= 18.22$

$= 396$.

Since we require

$N < n$ we split N into blocks of two digits each given by $N_1 = 14$ and $N_2 = 15$

Now selecting $k = 29$ we have

$$kj \equiv 1 \ [\text{mod } \phi(n)]$$

or $$29j \equiv 1 \pmod{396}.$$

This gives $j = 41$.

Now N_1 encrypts as

$$14^{29} \equiv 203 \pmod{437}$$

$$(203)^{41} \equiv 14 \pmod{437}.$$

Thus, the secret transmission of N_1 is 203 and the authorised recipient recovers it by calculating $(203)^{41} \pmod{437}$

Further for $N_2 = 15$ we have

$$15^{29} \equiv -35 \pmod{437}$$
$$\equiv 402 \pmod{437}.$$

Thus, secret transmission of N_2 is 402. Therefore, ciphertext is 203402.

RSA system to be safe it must not be computationally feasible to recover the plaintext from the public key $(n > k)$. the larger is the enciphering modulus the safer is the message coded from deciphering.

◆

EXERCISE

1. Find $\tau(n)$ and $\sigma(n)$ for $n = 7056$
2. Prove that $\sum_{d/n} [\tau(d)]^3 = \left[\sum_{d/n} \tau(d)\right]^2$ for $n \geqslant 1$.
3. For $n = 957$ show that $\sigma(n) = \sigma(n+1)$
4. Prove that $\sigma(2^{k-1}) = 2^k - 1$.
5. If $2^k - 1$ is a prime and $n = 2^{k-1}(2^k - 1)$ then show that $\sigma(n) = 2n$.
6. Prove that $\dfrac{\phi(n)}{n} = \sum \dfrac{\mu(d)}{d}$.
7. Find $\phi(1896)$
8. If $(r, n) = (r-1, n) = 1$, prove that
$$1 + r + r^2 + ... r^{\phi(n)-1} \equiv 0 (\text{mod } n)$$
9. If $n = 2^k$ or $n = 2^k 3^l$, $k, l \geqslant 0$ then prove that $\phi(n)/n$.

◆

Answers to Exercise

1. 45, 204321
7. 624

❑

CHAPTER 7

PRIMITIVE ROOTS AND INDICES

7.1 Introduction

In this chapter, we shall discuss the primitive roots for primes, composite numbers having primitive roots and theory of indices.

7.2 The Order of an Integer Modulo *n*

If $n > 1$ is any integer and a is another integer such that $(a, n) = 1$. Then the order of a modulo n is the smallest positive integer k such that $a^k \equiv 1 \pmod{n}$.

Example 1 : Show that order of 2 modulo 7 is 3.

Solution : We have

$$2^1 \equiv 2 \pmod 7$$
$$2^2 \equiv 4 \pmod 7$$
$$2^3 \equiv 1 \pmod 7.$$

This shows that order of 2 modulo 7 is 3.

Example 2 : Show that order of 3 mod 8 is 2.

Solution : We have

$$3^1 \equiv 3 \pmod 8$$
$$3^2 \equiv 1 \pmod 8.$$

This shows that order of 3 modulo 8 is 2.

Example 3 : Show that order of 3 modulo 9 is not defined.

Solution : We have

$$3^1 \equiv 3 \pmod 9$$
$$3^2 \equiv 0 \pmod 9$$
$$3^3 \equiv 0 \pmod 9$$
$$\vdots$$
$$3^n \equiv 0 \pmod 9 \qquad \forall\, n \geqslant 2$$

This shows that order of 3 modulo 9 is not defined.

These examples show that some integers have order modulo a given integer while some integers have not. The following theorem will explain the reason of this fact.

Theorem 1 : If a is an integer having order k modulo n i.e., $a^k \equiv 1 \pmod n$ then,

(i) $a^h \equiv 1$ (mod) n) for some integer $h \Rightarrow k | h$

(ii) $a \equiv b \pmod n \Rightarrow b$ has order k modulo n.

(iii) $a^i \equiv a^j \pmod n \Leftrightarrow i \equiv j \pmod k$

Proof : (i) If $a^h \equiv 1 \pmod n$ then by definition of order we have $h \geqslant k$. By division algorithm we have

$$h = kq + r, \qquad 0 \leqslant r < k$$

Therefore,

$$a^h = a^{kq+r}$$
$$= a^{kq}.a^r$$
$$\equiv 1^q.a^r \pmod n$$

or $$1 \pmod n \equiv a^r \pmod n$$

or $$a^r \equiv 1 \pmod n. \qquad ....(1)$$

But $r < k$ (the order of a), therefore (1) holds only when $r = 0$. So $h = kq$ or $\frac{h}{k} = q$.

Thus, $k | h$.

(ii) If $$a \equiv b \pmod n \text{ then}$$
$$a^k \equiv b^k \pmod n$$
$$\Rightarrow 1 \pmod n \equiv b^k \pmod n \qquad [\because k \text{ is the order of } a]$$
$$\Rightarrow \qquad b^k \equiv 1 \pmod n.$$

This shows that order of b is k modulo n.

(iii) We have,

$$a^i \equiv a^j \pmod n \Leftrightarrow a^{|i-j|} \equiv 1 \pmod n$$
$$\Leftrightarrow h \,|\, |i-j|$$
$$\Leftrightarrow i \equiv j \pmod h).$$

Proved.

Theorem 2 : If a has order k mod n then a^h has order $\frac{k}{d}$ where $d = (k, h)$

Proof : Let a^h has order t modulo n. Then

$$(a^h)^t \equiv 1 \pmod n$$

or $$a^{ht} \equiv 1 \pmod n.$$

Also a has order k modulo n.

Therefore, $k \mid ht$

Now since $d = (k, h)$ we have integers k_1, h_1

such that $k = dk_1$, $h = dh_1$, $(k_1, h_1) = 1$.

So, $k \mid ht \Rightarrow k_1 d \mid h_1 dt$

$\Rightarrow k_1 | t$ $[\because (k_1, h_1) = 1]$

$\Rightarrow \frac{k}{d} \Big| t.$ ....(1)

Now $(a^h)^{k/d} = (a^h)^{k_1}$

$= (a^{dh_1})^{k_1}$

$= (a^{dk_1})^{h_1}$

$= (a^k)^{h_1}$

$\equiv 1 \pmod{n}.$

Therefore, $t \Big| \frac{k}{d}.$ ....(2)

From (1) and (2) we have

$$t = \frac{k}{d}.$$ **Proved.**

Corollary 1 : If a has order h modulo n. Then a^h has order k modulo n iff $(h, k) = 1$.

Theorem 3 : If the orders of a_1 and a_2 modulo n be k_1 and k_2 respectively and $(k_1, k_2) = 1$. Then the order of $a_1 a_2 \pmod{n}$ is $k_1 k_2$.

Proof : Let the order of $a_1 a_2 \pmod{n} = k$. Then

$(a_1 a_2)^k \equiv 1 \pmod{n}$

$\Rightarrow [(a_1 a_2)^k]^{k_2} \equiv 1 \pmod{n}$

$\Rightarrow a_1^{kk_2} . a_2^{kk_2} \equiv 1 \pmod{n}$

$\Rightarrow a_1^{kk_2} \equiv 1 \pmod{n}$ $[\because a_2^{k_2} \equiv 1 \pmod{n}]$

$\Rightarrow k_1 \mid k k_2.$

But $(k_1, k_2) = 1$. Therefore, $k_1 | k$. ....(1)

Similarly, we can show that, $k_2 | k$. ....(2)

From (1) and (2) we have

$k_1 k_2 | k.$ ....(3)

Now $a_1^{k_1 k_2} \equiv 1 \pmod{n}$ and $a_2^{k_1 k_2} \equiv 1 \pmod{n}$

$\Rightarrow (a_1 a_2)^{k_1 k_2} \equiv 1 \pmod{n}$

$$\Rightarrow k \mid k_1 k_2. \quad ....(4)$$

From (3) and (4) we have

$$k = k_1 k_2.$$

Example 1 : Find the order of 5(mod 29)

Solution : We have

$$\phi(29) = 29 - 1 = 28 = 2^2 \times 7$$

The divisors of ϕ (29) are 2, 4, 7, 14, 28.

Now
$$5^2 \equiv -4 \pmod{29}$$
$$5^4 \equiv 16 \pmod{29}$$
$$5^7 = 5^4 \times 5^2 \times 5$$
$$\equiv 16 \times (-4) \times 5 \pmod{29}$$
$$\equiv -1 \pmod{29}$$
$$5^{14} \equiv 1 \pmod{29}.$$

This gives that order 5 modulo 29 is 14.

7.3 Primitive Roots

If an integer a has order ϕ (n) modulo n (a positive integer) and $(a, n) = 1$ then a is a primitive root of n.

Thus, n has a primitive root a if

$$a^{\phi(n)} \equiv 1 \text{ ((mod } n) \text{ and } a^k \equiv 1 \pmod{n} \ \forall\, k < \phi(n).$$

Example 1 : Show that 3 is a primitive root of 7.

Solution : We have $\phi(7) = 6$

$$3^1 \equiv 3 \pmod 7$$
$$3^2 \equiv 2 \pmod 7$$
$$3^3 \equiv 6 \pmod 7$$
$$3^4 \equiv 2 \pmod 7$$
$$3^5 \equiv 5 \pmod 7$$
$$3^6 \equiv 1 \pmod 7.$$

Thus, $3^{\phi(7)} \equiv 1 \pmod 7$. Therefore, 3 is a primitive root of 7.

Example 2 : List the primitive roots of 6.

Solution : We have $\phi(6) = 2$.

Now
$$2^2 \equiv 4 \pmod 6$$
$$3^2 \equiv 3 \pmod 6$$

$$4^2 \equiv 4 \pmod 6$$
$$5^2 \equiv 1 \pmod 6.$$

Thus, we see that 5 is the only primitive root (mod 6).

Example 3 : Find the primitive roots of 15.

Solution : We have $\phi(15) = \phi(3.5)$

$$= \phi(3).\phi(5) = (3-1)(5-1) = 8 = 2^3.$$

Therefore 2 is the only prime divisor of $\phi(15)$.

The possible coprimes to 15 are 1, 2, 4, 7, 8, 11, 13, 14. Therefore, possible primitive roots may be 2, 7, 11, 13.

Now $2^4 \equiv 1 \pmod{15}$, $4^2 \equiv 1 \pmod{15}$

$7^4 \equiv 1 \pmod{15}$ $11^2 \equiv 1 \pmod{15}$

$13^4 \equiv 1 \pmod{15}$.

This shows that there exists no primitive root of 15.

Example 4 : Find the primitive roots of 10.

Solution : We have

$$\phi(10) = \phi(2.5)$$
$$= \phi(2).\phi(5) = (2-1)(5-1) = 4$$

3, 5, 7 are coprime to 10. Therefore, possible primitive roots are 3, 5 and 7.

Now $3^2 \equiv 9 \pmod{10}$

$$3^3 \equiv 7 \pmod{10}$$
$$3^4 \equiv 1 \pmod{10}.$$

Therefore, 3 is a primitive root of modulo 10.

$$5^2 \equiv 5 \pmod{10}$$
$$5^3 \equiv 5 \pmod{10}$$
$$\vdots$$
$$5^n \equiv 5 \pmod{10}.$$

This shows that 5 is not a primitive root of modulo 10.

$$7^2 \equiv 9 \pmod{10}$$
$$7^3 \equiv 3 \pmod{10}$$
$$7^4 \equiv 1 \pmod{10}.$$

Therefore, 7 is a primitive root of modulo 10. Thus, 3 and 7 are two primitive roots of modulo 10.

Theorem 4 : If a is a primitive root modulo n then $a, a^2, \ldots a^{\phi(n)}$ is a reduced system (mod n).

Proof : Since a is a primitive root mod n, we have $(a, n) = 1$

$$\Rightarrow (a^k, n) = 1, \qquad 1 \leqslant k \leqslant \phi(n)$$

The integers $a, a^2, \ldots a^{\phi(n)}$ are in congruent (mod h).

Let r be an integer coprime to n. We have to show that

$$r \equiv a^n \pmod{n} \text{ for some } h$$

satisfying $1 \leqslant h \leqslant \phi(n) - 1$. Let $a_1, a_2, \ldots a_{\phi(n)}$ be the reduced system (mod n) having all integers less than or equal to n. Then $r \equiv a_i \pmod{n}$ for some unique i satisfying $1 \leqslant i \leqslant \phi(n)$.

For k satisfying $1 \leqslant k \leqslant \phi(n) - 1$ there exists a unique j such that

$$a^k \equiv a_j \pmod{n}$$

Therefore, if $a_j \equiv a^h \pmod{n}$, $1 \leqslant h \leqslant \phi(n) - 1$

then $r \equiv a^h \pmod{n}$. Hence, $a, a^2, \ldots a^{\phi(n)}$ is a reduced system (mod n).

7.4 Primitive Roots for Primes

Theorem 1 : (Lagrange Theorem) : If p is a prime and

$$f(x) = a_n x^n + a_{n-1} x^{n-1} + \ldots a_1 x + a_0, \; a_n \equiv 0 \pmod{p}$$

is a polynomial of degree $n \geqslant 1$ with integral coefficient then $f(x) \equiv 0 \pmod{p}$ has at least n in congruent solutions mod p.

Proof : For, $n = 1$ the given polynomial takes the form

$$f(x) = a_1 x + a_0 \qquad \ldots\ldots(1)$$

Since $(a_1, p) = 1$ we have $a_1 x \equiv -a_0 \pmod{p}$ has a unique solution modulo p. This shows that the theorem holds for $n = 1$.

Let the theorem be true for $n = m - 1$ solutions *i.e.*, $f(x) \equiv 0 \pmod{p}$ has $m - 1$ in congruent solutions. Let $f(x)$ be a function of degree m. Then either $f(x) \equiv 0$ (mod p) has no solution and we have nothing to do or it has at least one solution (say a). In this case we can write

$$f(x) = (x - a)\, q(x) + r \qquad \ldots\ldots(2)$$

where $q(x)$ is a polynomial of degree $(m - 1)$ with integral coefficients and r is an integer.

Putting $x = a$ in (2) we get

$x^{p-1} - 1 \equiv 0 \pmod{p}$ which is not a solution of $f(x) \equiv 0 \pmod{p}$ should satisfy $x^d - 1 \equiv 0 \pmod{p}$.

Now, $0 \equiv a^{p-1} - 1 \equiv (a^d - 1) f(a) \pmod{p}$ with $p \nmid f(a)$ gives that $p \mid a^d - 1$. Therefore, $x^d - 1 \equiv 0 \pmod{p}$ should have at least $p - 1 - (p - 1 - d) = d$ solutions. The above congruence will possess at most d solutions. Thus, the given congruence has exactly d solutions.

Theorem 2 : If p is a prime and $d \mid (p-1)$ then the congruence $x^d - 1 \equiv 0 \pmod p$ has exactly d solutions.

Proof : Since $d \mid (p-1)$ we have $(p-1) = dr$ for some r. Therefore,

$$x^{p-1} - 1 = (x^d - 1) f(x)$$

where $f(x) = x^{d(r-1)} + \ldots\ x^d + 1$ has integral coefficients

and its degree $= d(r-1) = dr - d = p - 1 - d$. By Lagrange theorem the congruence $f(x) \equiv 0 \pmod p$ has at most $p - 1 - d$ solutions. Also by Fermat's theorem we have that $x^{p-1} - 1 \equiv 0 \pmod p$ has $(p-1)$ incongruence solutions $1, 2, \ldots, p-1$.

Any solution $x = a$ of $x^{p-1} - 1 \equiv 0 \pmod p$ which is not a solution of $f(x) \equiv 0 \pmod p$ should satisfy

$$x^d - 1 \equiv 0 \pmod p.$$

Now, $0 \equiv a^{p-1} - 1 = (a^d - 1) f(a) \pmod p$ with $p \nmid f(a)$ gives that $p \mid a^d - 1$. Therefore, $x^d - 1 \equiv 0 \pmod p$ should have at least.

$(p-1) - (p-1-d) = d$ solutions. The last congruence possesses d solutions.

Hence, the given congruence has exactly d solutions.

Theorem 3 : If p is a prime and $d \mid p-1$ then there are exactly $\phi(d)$ incongruent integers having d modulo p.

Proof : Let $d \mid p-1$ (p is a prime) and $\phi_1(d)$ denotes the number of integers m, $1 \leqslant m \leqslant p-1$ having order d modulo p. Now since each integer between 1 and $p-1$ has order d for some $d \mid p-1$ we have

$$p - 1 = \sum_{d \mid p-1} \phi_1(d) \qquad \text{.......(1)}$$

Also by Gauss theorem, we have

$$p - 1 = \sum_{d \mid p-1} \phi(d) \qquad \text{.......(2)}$$

From (1) and (2) we have

$$\sum_{d \mid p-1} \phi_1(d) = \sum_{d \mid p-1} \phi(d) \qquad \text{.......(3)}$$

For an arbitrary divisor d of $p-1$ either $\phi_1(d) = 0$ or $\phi_1(d) > 0$. If $\phi_1(d) = 0$ then $\phi_1(d) \leqslant \phi(d)$. If $\phi_1(d) > 0$ there exists an integer a of order d. Then integers $a, a^2, \ldots\ a^d$ incongruent modulo p satisfying the polynomial congruence

$$x^d - 1 \equiv 0 \pmod p \qquad \text{.......(4)}$$

By theorem 2 there will be no other solutions of (4). Therefore, any integer that has order d modulo p should be congruent to one of $a, a^2 \ldots\ a^d$. But $\phi(d)$ of these powers have order d. Therefore, $\psi(d) = \phi(d)$. Hence, the number of integers having order d modulo p is equal to $\phi(d)$.

Theorem 4 : If $(a, m) = 1$ then a is a primitive root of m iff $a^{\frac{\phi(m)}{p}} \not\equiv 1 \pmod{m}$ for every prime divisor p of $\phi(m)$.

Proof : Let a be an integer such that

$$a^{\frac{\phi(m)}{p}} \not\equiv 1 \pmod{m}$$

for every prime divisor p of $\phi(m)$. We have to show that a is a primitive root of m. Suppose if possible a is not a primitive root of m. Then the order of $a \pmod{m}$ is some integer r less than $\phi(m)$. This gives that r divides $\phi(m)$. Thus, we have that $\frac{\phi(m)}{r}$ is an integer and so it is divisible by some prime divisor p of $\phi(m)$. Therefore,

$$a^{\frac{\phi(m)}{p}} = (a^r)^{\frac{\phi(m)}{rp}} \equiv 1 \pmod{m}. \qquad [\because a^r \equiv 1 \pmod{m}]$$

This contradicts the given condition. Hence, a is a primitive root of m.

Conversely, let a be a primitive root of m. Then we have that,

$$a^{\phi(m)} \equiv 1 \pmod{m} \text{ and } a^k \not\equiv 1 \pmod{m}$$

$$\text{for } \quad 0 < k < \phi(m)$$

This gives that

$$a^{\frac{\phi(m)}{p}} \not\equiv 1 \pmod{m}$$

for every prime divisor p of $\phi(m)$. **Proved.**

Example 1 : Find a primitive root mod 5^2.

Solution : We have that 2 is a primitive root of 5.

Also $2^2 \equiv 4 \pmod{5}$, $2^3 \equiv 3 \pmod{5}$, $2^4 \equiv 1 \pmod{5}$

Further $2^4 \not\equiv 1 \pmod{5^2}$.$2^5 \equiv 7 \pmod{5^2}$, $2^6 \equiv 14 \pmod{5^2}$, $2^7 \equiv 3 \pmod{5^2}$ ....., $2^{20} \equiv 1 \pmod{5^2}$. Therefore, 2 is a primitive root $\pmod{5^2}$.

Similarly, we can show that 3 is also a primitive root $\pmod{5^2}$.

Example 2 : Find the primitive roots of 17.

Solution : Here $\phi(17) = 17 - 1 = 16 = 2^4$. Thus, $\phi(17)$ has only one prime factor 2. Also $(16/2) = 8$. Therefore, a is a primitive root of 17 if $a^8 \not\equiv 1 \pmod{17}$.

Now, $2^8 \equiv 1 \pmod{17}$

and $3^8 \not\equiv 1 \pmod{17}$.

Thus, 3 is the smallest primitive root of 17,

Similarly, we can show that

$$5^8 \not\equiv 1 \pmod{17}$$
$$6^8 \not\equiv 1 \pmod{17}$$
$$7^8 \not\equiv 1 \pmod{17}$$
$$10^8 \not\equiv 1 \pmod{17}$$
$$11^8 \not\equiv 1 \pmod{17}$$
$$12^8 \not\equiv 1 \pmod{17}$$
$$14^8 \not\equiv 1 \pmod{17}$$

Thus, the primitive roots of 17 are 3, 5, 6, 7, 10, 11, 12 and 14.

Example 3 : Show that 2 is a primitive root of 11.

Solution : We have $\phi(11) = 10$ whose divisors are 2, 5 and 10. Now

$$2^2 = 4$$
$$2^5 \equiv -1 \pmod{11}$$
$$2^{10} \equiv 1 \pmod{11}$$

This shows that 2 is a primitive root of 11.

7.5 Composite Numbers Having Primitive Roots

In this section we shall discuss the composite numbers which have primitive roots.

Theorem 1 : Show that the integers 2 and 4 possess one primitive root each which are 1 and 3 respectively.

Proof : We have

$$\phi(2) = 2 - 1 = 1$$

and $\quad 1^1 \equiv 1 \pmod{2}$.

This shows that 1 is the primitive root of 2.

Similarly, $\quad \phi(4) = \phi(2^2)$

$$= 2^2 - 2^1$$
$$= 4 - 2 = 2$$

and $\quad 1^2 \equiv 1 \pmod{4}$

$$3^2 \equiv 1 \pmod{4}.$$

This shows that 3 is the primitive root of 4. Thus, 2 and 4 possess one primitive root each which are 1 and 3 respectively.

Theorem 2 : The integer 2^n has no primitive root for $n \geqslant 3$.

Proof : Let a be an odd integer. We will show that

$$a^{2^{n-2}} \equiv 1 \pmod{2^n} \text{ for } n \geqslant 3$$

For $\quad n = 3$ we have

$$a^2 \equiv 1 \pmod 8$$

Since a is odd, it is congruent to 1, 3, 5 or 7 (mod 8). Thus, $a^2 \equiv 1 \pmod 8$

Suppose the statement holds for $n = m \geqslant 3$ *i.e.*,

$$a^{2^{m-2}} \equiv 1 \pmod{2^m}$$

Now $\quad a^{2^{(m+1)-2}} = a^{2^{m-1}}$

$$= (a^{2^{m-2}})^2$$

$$= (1 + \lambda 2^m)^2 \qquad [\lambda \text{ is an integer}]$$

$$= 1 + 2\lambda 2^m + \lambda^2 2^{2m}$$

Therefore, $\quad a^{2^{(m-1)}} = 1 + \lambda 2^{m+1} + \lambda^2 2^{2m}$

$$= 1 + \lambda.2^{m+1} + \lambda^2 2^{m-1}.2^{m+1}$$

Now $n \geqslant 3 \Rightarrow n > 2 \Rightarrow n - 1 > 1$

Therefore, $\quad a^{2^{(m-1)}} \equiv 1 \pmod{2^{m+1}}$

or $\quad a^{2^{(m+1)-2}} \equiv 1 \pmod{2^{m+1}}$.

This shows that the result is true for $n = m + 1$.

Hence, by mathematical induction the result is true for all values of n.

Also, the integers relatively prime to 2^m are the odd integers and $\phi(2^m) = 2^{m-1}$.

Therefore

$$a^{\phi(2^m/2)} \equiv 1 \pmod{2^m}$$

and hence there is no primitive root of 2^n.

Theorem 3 : If $m, n > 2$ and $(m, n) = 1$ then there exists no primitive root (mod mn).

Proof : Suppose if possible a is a primitive root to mn. Then $(a, mn) = 1$ and a has order $\phi(mn)$ mod (mn).

Now $(a, mn) = 1 \Rightarrow (a, m) = 1$ and $(a, n) = 1$.

Therefore, $\quad a^{\phi(m)} \equiv 1 \pmod m$

and $\quad a^{\phi(n)} \equiv 1 \pmod n$.

Let
$$h = \frac{\phi(m)\phi(n)}{[\phi(m), \phi(n)]}. \qquad \text{.......(1)}$$

Since $m, n > 2$ we have

$$(\phi(m), \phi(n)) \geqslant 2. \quad [\because \phi(m), \phi(n) \text{ both are even}] \qquad \text{.......(2)}$$

From (1) and (2) we have

$$h \leqslant \frac{\phi(m)\phi(n)}{2} = \frac{\phi(mn)}{2}$$

$< \phi(mn).$

Now $$a^h = \left(a^{\phi(m)}\right)^{\frac{\phi(n)}{(\phi(m),\phi(n))}} \equiv 1 \pmod m \qquad \text{.......(3)}$$

and $$a^h = \left(a^{\phi(n)}\right)^{\frac{\phi(m)}{(\phi(m),\phi(n))}} \equiv 1 \pmod n \qquad \text{.......(4)}$$

From (3) and (4), we have

$$a^h \equiv 1 \pmod{mn} \qquad [\because (m, n) = 1]$$

This contradicts the assumption that order of a is $\phi(mn)$.

Theorem 4 : If p is an odd prime then there exists a primitive root r of p such that $r^{p-1} \not\equiv 1 \pmod{p^2}$.

Proof : Since p is an odd prime it has a primitive root. Let r be the primitive root of p. If $r^{p-1} \not\equiv 1 \pmod{p^2}$ then the proof is complete. If $r^{p-1} \equiv 1 \pmod{p^2}$ we replace r by r_1 given by $r_1 = r + p$ which is also a primitive root of p.

Now $$r_1^{p-1} \equiv (r+p)^{p-1}$$
$$\equiv r^{p-1} + (p-1)pr^{p-2} \pmod{p^2}$$
$$\equiv (1 - pr^{p-2}) \pmod{p^2}. \qquad [\because r^{p-1} \equiv 1 \pmod{p^2})$$

Since r is a primitive root of p we have $(r, p) = 1$

Therefore, $p \nmid r^{p-1}$. Hence, $r_1^{p-1} \not\equiv 1 \pmod{p^2}$. Proved

Corollary : If p is an odd prime then p^2 has a primitive root. In other words for a primitive root r of p, either r or $r + p$ is a primitive root of p^2.

Theorem 5 : If p is an odd prime and r a primitive root of p such that $r^{p-1} \not\equiv 1 \pmod{p^2}$ then for each positive integer $k \geqslant 2$,

$$r^{p^{k-2}(p-1)} \not\equiv 1 \pmod{p^k}.$$

Proof : For $k = 2$ the result is true by the hypothesis. Let the result be true for $k \geqslant 2$. We shall how that the result is true for $k + 1$.

Since $(r, p^{k-1}) = (r, p^k) = 1$, by Euler's theorem we have,

$$r^{p^{k-2}(p-1)} = r^{\phi(p^{k-1})} \equiv 1 \pmod{p^{k-1}}$$

Therefore, there exists an integer a such that

$$r^{p^{k-2}(p-1)} = 1 + ap^{k-1}, \; p \nmid a$$

$$\Rightarrow r^{p^{k-1}(p-1)} = (1 + ap^{k-1})^p$$

$$\equiv 1 + ap^k \pmod{p^{k+1}}$$

Since $p \nmid a$ we have

$$r^{p^{k-1}(p-1)} \not\equiv 1 \pmod{p^{k+1}}$$

This shows that the result is true for $k + 1$. Hence, by mathematical induction the given result will be true for all values of $k \geqslant 2$.

Theorem 6 : There exists a primitive root for p^k when p is an odd prime and $k \geqslant 1$.

Proof : Let p be an odd prime. If $k = 1$ then these exists a primitive root (mod p). For $k > 1$ let r be a primitive root (mod p). Then as shown in theorem 5. We have

$$r^{p^{k-2}(p-1)} \not\equiv 1 \pmod{p^k}.$$

Also $$r^{p-1} \not\equiv 1 \pmod{p^2}.$$

We will show that r is a primitive root for all powers of p.

Let n be the order of r mod p^k. Then n must divide $\phi(p^k) = p^{k-1}(p-1)$. Also $r^n \equiv 1 \pmod{p^k}$ implies $r^n \equiv 1 \pmod p$ and $(p-1) \mid n$. Therefore, n takes the form $n = p^{n_1}(p-1)$, $0 \leqslant n_1 \leqslant k-1$.

Now, if $n \neq p^{k-1}(p-1)$ then $p^{k-2}(p-1)$ will be divisible by n and we can write

$$r^{p^{k-2}(p-1)} \equiv 1 \pmod{p^k}.$$

This contradicts the earlier assumed value of r. Therefore, $n = p^{k-1}(p-1)$ and r is a primitive root of p^k.

Corollary : There are primitive roots for $2p^k$ where p is an odd prime and $k \geqslant 1$.

Proof : Let r be an odd primitive root for p^k. Then $(r, 2p^k) = 1$. The order n of r modulo $2p^k$ should divide

$$\phi(2p^k) = \phi(2)\,\phi(p^k) = \phi(p^k).$$

Now, $r^n \equiv 1 \pmod{2p^k} \Rightarrow r^n = 1 \pmod{p^k}$. Therefore, $\phi(p^k) \mid n$ so $n = \phi(2p^k)$. Hence r is a primitive root of $2p^k$.

Example 1 : Show that the congruence $x^{18} \equiv 5 \pmod{73}$ is not solvable.

Solution : Here $\phi(m) = \phi(73) = 72$

$$d = (n, \phi(m)) = (18, 72) = 18$$

Therefore, $a^{\frac{\phi(m)}{d}} = 5^4 \not\equiv 1 \pmod{73}$

Hence, the given congruence is not solvable.

Example 2 : Solve $x^{15} \equiv 7 \pmod{19}$

Solution : Here $\phi(m) = \phi(19) = 18 = 2 \times 3^2$.

$$d = (n, \phi(m)) = (15, 18) = 3$$

Therefore, $a^{\frac{\phi(m)}{d}} = 7^{\frac{18}{3}}$

$$= 7^6$$

$$\equiv 1 \pmod{19}.$$

Hence, the given congruence is solvable.

Obviously 2 and 3 are the only prime divisors of $\phi(19)$. Also

$$2^6 \equiv 7 \pmod{19}$$

$$\not\equiv 1 \pmod{19}.$$

Therefore, 2 is the smallest primitive root of 19. Now we will find an integer h such that

$$2^h \equiv 7 \pmod{19},\ 0 \leqslant h < 18.$$

This gives $h = 6$. We consider the congruence

$$ny \equiv h\ [\text{mod } \phi(m)]$$

$\therefore$ $$15y \equiv 6 \pmod{18}.$$

This gives $$y \equiv 4, 10, 16 \pmod{18}.$$

Therefore, the solution of the given congruence are given by

$$x \equiv 2^4, 2^{10}, 2^{16} \pmod{19}$$

$$\equiv 16, 7, 5 \pmod{19}.$$

Example 3 : Find the primitive root of 15.

Solution : The relatively primes to 15 are 2, 4, 7, 8, 11, 13, 14.

Also $$\phi(15) = \phi(3.5)$$

$$= (3-1)(5-1)$$

$$= 2.4 = 8 = 2^3.$$

Thus, 2 is the only prime divisor of $\phi(15)$.

$$\frac{\phi(m)}{p} = \frac{\phi(15)}{2}$$

$$= \frac{8}{2} = 4.$$

Now a is a primitive root of 15 if

$$a^4 \not\equiv 1 \pmod{15}.$$

We have $$2^4 \equiv 1 \pmod{15}$$

$$4^4 \equiv 1 \pmod{15}$$

$$7^4 \equiv 1 \pmod{15}$$

$$8^4 \equiv 1 \pmod{15}$$

$$11^4 \equiv 1 \pmod{15}$$
$$13^4 \equiv 1 \pmod{15}$$
$$14^4 \equiv 1 \pmod{15}.$$

This shows that there exists no primitive root of 15.

7.6 The Theory of Indices

If r is a primitive root of n and $(a, n) = 1$ then the smallest positive integer h such that $a \equiv r^h \pmod{n}$ is called the index of a relative to r. It is denoted by ind. a. This can also be written as $r^{\text{ind. } a} \equiv a \pmod{n}$.

Example 1 : Find the index of 9 (mod 19).

Solution : The smallest primitive root of 19 is 2 and $2^8 \equiv 9 \pmod{19}$.

Therefore, ind. $9 = 8$.

Example 2 : Find the index of 5 (mod 13).

Solution : The smallest primitive root of 13 is 2. and $2^9 \equiv 5 \pmod{13}$.

Therefore, $\text{ind.}_2\, 5 = 9$, 6, 7 and 11 are the other primitive roots of 13.

Also, $6^9 \equiv 5 \pmod{13}$

$\therefore$ $\text{ind.}_6\, 5 \equiv 9$

$7^3 \equiv 5 \pmod{13}$

$\therefore$ $\text{ind.}_7\, 5 = 3$

$11^3 \equiv 5 \pmod{13}$

$\therefore$ $\text{ind.}_{11}\, 5 = 3$.

Example 3 : Obtain the index of 17 (mod 18).

Solution : We can show that 5 is the smallest primitive root of 18. Now

$$5^3 \equiv 17 \pmod{18}.$$

Therefore, ind. $17 = 3$.

Theorem 1 : Let a be a primitive root modulo n and b, c and k are any integers then

(*i*) $b \equiv c \pmod{n} \Rightarrow \text{ind.}b \equiv \text{ind.}c \pmod{\phi(n)}$]

(*ii*) $\text{ind.}(bc) \equiv \text{ind.}b + \text{ind.}c \pmod{\phi(n)}$]

(iii) $\text{ind.}b^k \equiv k\, \text{ind.}b \pmod{\phi(n)}$]

(iv) $\text{ind.}1 \equiv 0 \pmod{\phi(n)}$].

Proof : Let ind.$b = r_1$ and ind.$c = r_2$. Then

$$b \equiv a^{r_1} \pmod{n} \text{ and } c = a^{r_2} \pmod{n}.$$

(*i*) Now $b \equiv c \pmod{n}$

$$\Rightarrow \quad a^{r_1} \equiv a^{r_2} \pmod{n}$$

$$\Rightarrow \quad a^{r_1 - r_2} \equiv 1 \pmod{n}.$$

By definition, $\phi(n) \mid r_1 - r_2$

$$\therefore \quad r_1 \equiv r_2 \; [\text{mod } \phi(n)] \quad i.e.$$

$$\text{ind.}b \equiv \text{ind.}c \; [\text{mod } \phi(n)].$$

(ii) We have

$$bc \equiv a^{r_1}.a^{r_2} \pmod{n}$$

$$\equiv a^{r_1 + r_2} \pmod{n}.$$

Now, if $r = \text{ind.}bc$ then $bc = a^r \pmod{n}$

$$\therefore \quad r_1 + r_2 \equiv r \;(\text{mod} \,.\, \phi(n))$$

$$i.e., \quad \text{ind.}(bc) = \text{ind.}b + 1 \text{ ind.}c \;(\text{mod } \phi(n)].$$

(iii) We have

$$\text{ind.}b^k = \text{ind.}(b.b \; .... \; k \text{ times})$$

$$= \text{ind.}b + \text{ind. } b + ... \text{ upto } k \text{ times } (\text{mod } \phi(n)) \quad [\text{Using } (ii)]$$

$$= k \text{ ind.}b \;(\text{mod } \phi(n)).$$

(iv) Putting $k = 0$ in *(iii)*, we have

$$\text{ind.}1 = 0 \;(\text{mod } \phi(n)).$$

Theorem 2 : If r is the smallest primitive root of n and $r^h \equiv a \pmod{n}$ then $h \equiv \text{ind. } a \pmod{n}$.

Proof : We have

$$r^h \equiv a \pmod{n}$$

$$\equiv r^{\text{ind.}a} \pmod{n}.$$

Now the order of $r \pmod{n}$ is $\phi(n)$.

Therefore, $\quad h = \text{ind.}\,a \;[\text{mod } \phi(n)].$

Theorem 3 : If $a_1, a_2, ... a_k$ are all primes to n [mod $\phi(n)$]

then, $\text{ind.}a_1 + \text{ind.}a_2 + ... + \text{ind.}a_k \equiv \text{ind.}a_1 a_2 .... a_k$.

Proof : If r is the smallest primitive root of n then we have

$$r^{\text{ind.}a_1} \equiv a_1 \pmod{n}$$

$$r^{\text{ind.}a_2} \equiv a_2 \pmod{n}$$

$$\vdots \qquad \vdots$$

$$r^{\text{ind.}a_k} \equiv a_k \pmod{n}.$$

Therefore,

$$r^{\text{ind.}a_1 + ind.a_2 + ... \text{ind.}a_k} = a_1 a_2 \; .... \; a_k \pmod{n}.$$

Hence,

$$\text{ind}.a_1 + \text{ind}.a_2 + \ldots.\ \text{ind}.a_k \equiv a_1a_2 \ldots.\ a_k \pmod{\phi(n)}.$$

The theory of indices is applicable for the modulii having primitive roots. However, the table of indices may be prepared for each modulus. The theory of indices can be used to solve the congruences.

Example 1 : Construct the index (mod 18).

Solution : We have $\phi(18) = \phi(2.3^2) = \phi(2).\phi(3^2) = 6$ and 5 is the smallest primitive root of 18.

Now,
$$5^0 = 1$$
$$5^1 = 5$$
$$5^2 \equiv 7 \pmod{18}$$
$$5^3 \equiv 17 \pmod{18}$$
$$5^4 \equiv 13 \pmod{18}$$
$$5^5 \equiv 11 \pmod{18}.$$

Therefore, the required index table for primitive root 5 is

a	1	5	7	11	13	17
$\text{ind}_5\ a$	0	1	2	5	4	3

Example 2 : Solve the linear congruence : $7x \equiv 2 \pmod 9$

Solution : We know that 2 is a primitive root modulo 9.

Now
$$2^1 = 2$$
$$2^2 = 4$$
$$2^3 = 8$$
$$2^4 \equiv 7 \pmod 9$$
$$2^5 \equiv 5 \pmod 9$$
and
$$2^6 \equiv 1 \pmod 9.$$

This gives that index of 2 is 1 and 7 is 4.

The given congruence $7x \equiv 2 \pmod 9$ is equivalent to

$$\text{ind}.7 + \text{ind}.x \equiv \text{ind}.2 \pmod{\phi(9)}$$
$$\Rightarrow 4 + \text{ind}.x \equiv 1 \pmod 6 \qquad [\because\ \phi(9) = 6]$$
$$\Rightarrow \text{ind}.x \equiv -3 \pmod 6$$
$$\equiv 3 \pmod 6$$

$$\Rightarrow \quad x \equiv 2^3 \pmod 9$$
$$\equiv 8 \pmod 9.$$

This gives that the solution of the given congruence are of the form $9t + 8$ where $t = 0, \pm 1, \ldots$.

Example 3 : Solve the congruence : $x^3 \equiv 5 \pmod{13}$.

Solution : We know that 2 is a primitive root modulo 13.

Now,

$$2^1 = 2$$
$$2^2 = 4$$
$$2^3 = 8$$
$$2^4 \equiv 3 \pmod{13}$$
$$2^5 \equiv 6 \pmod{13}$$
$$2^6 \equiv 12 \pmod{13}$$
$$2^7 \equiv 11 \pmod{13}$$
$$2^8 \equiv 9 \pmod{13}$$
$$2^9 \equiv 5 \pmod{13}.$$

This gives that index number of 2 is 1 and 5 is 9.

The given congruence $x^3 = 5 \pmod{13}$ is equivalent to

$$\equiv \text{ind. } 5 \pmod{\phi(13)}$$
$$3 \text{ ind.}_2\, x \equiv 9 \pmod{\phi(13)}$$
$$\equiv 9 \pmod{12} \qquad [\because \phi(13) = 12]$$
$$\Rightarrow \text{ind.}_2\, x \equiv 3 \pmod 4$$
$$= 3, 7, 11.$$

The integers corresponding to these indices will be 8, 11 and 7. Therefore, the required solution are

$$x \equiv 7, 8 \text{ and } 11 \pmod{13}.$$

Example 4 : Solve the congruence $17x^{20} \equiv 19 \pmod{37}$.

Solution : The given congruence is equivalent

$$\text{ind. } 17 + 20 \text{ ind. } x \equiv \text{ind. } 19 \pmod{\phi(37)}$$
$$\Rightarrow \quad 7 + 20 \text{ ind. } x \equiv 35 \pmod{36} \qquad [\because \phi(37) = 36]$$
$$\Rightarrow \quad 20 \text{ ind. } x \equiv 28 \pmod{36}$$
$$\Rightarrow \quad \text{ind. } x = 5, 14, 23., 32 \pmod{36}.$$

The integers corresponding to these indices are 32, 30, 5, 7. Therefore, the solution of the given congruence is given by

$$x = 5, 7, 30, 32 \pmod{37}.$$

Example 5 : Construct the index table for 17 with primitive root 5.

Solution : We have, $\phi(17) = 16$

5 is the primitive root.

Now, we have, $5^0 = 1$, $5^1 = 5$, $5^2 \equiv 8 \pmod{17}$, $5^3 \equiv 6 \pmod{17}$

$5^4 \equiv 13 \pmod{17}$, $5^5 \equiv 14 \pmod{17}$, $5^6 \equiv 2 \pmod{17}$

$5^7 \equiv 10 \pmod{17}$, $5^8 \equiv 16 \pmod{17}$, $5^9 \equiv 12 \pmod{17}$

$5^{10} \equiv 9 \pmod{17}$, $5^{11} \equiv 11 \pmod{17}$, $5^{12} \equiv 4 \pmod{17}$

$5^{13} \equiv 3 \pmod{17}$, $5^{14} \equiv 15 \pmod{17}$, $5^{15} \equiv 7 \pmod{17}$.

Thus, we have the following index $5^{16} \equiv 1 \pmod{17}$ table

a	1	2	3	4	5	6	7	8	9	10	11	12	13	14	15	16
ind. *a*	0	6	13	12	1	3	15	2	10	7	11	9	4	5	14	8

∎

EXERCISE

1. Find the order of 3 modulo 19.
2. Show that $\phi(2^n - 1)$ is a multiple of n for any $n > 1$.
3. Show that 2 is not a primitive root of 17.
4. Show that every odd prime divisor of $n^2 + 1$ is of the form like $hk + 1$.
5. Find the order of 5 (mod 7^2)
6. Find two primitive roots of 10.
7. Find primitive roots of 3^3.
8. Find all primitive roots of 82.
9. Find the index of 5 relative to each of the primitive roots of 13.
10. Show that $x^5 \equiv 13$ (mod 23) is solvable.

Answers to Exercise			
1. 18	**5.** 42	**6.** 3, 4	**7.** 2
8. 7, 11, 13, 15, 17, 19, 29, 35, 47, 53, 63, 65, 67, 69, 71, 75.			
9. $\text{ind}_2\, 5 = 9$; $\text{ind}_6\, 5 = 9$; $\text{ind}_7\, 5 = 3$; $\text{ind}_{11}\, 5 = 3$			

CHAPTER 8

QUADRATIC CONGRUENCE AND QUADRATIC RECIPROCITY LAW

8.1 Introduction

In this chapter, we shall discuss the quadratic congruence and quadratic reciprocity law. The general form of a quadratic congruence in one variable is given by

$$ax^2 + bx + c \equiv 0 \pmod{n} \qquad \text{.......(1)}$$

where a is not divisible by n. There exists no general and direct method to solve a quadratic congruence. The quadratic reciprocity law has long exerted a fascination for mathematicians. Since Gauss time so many proofs of it have been published. Eminent contributors for its proof are Cauchy, Jacobi, Dirichlet, Eienstein, Kronecker and Dedikind.

8.2 Quadratic Congruence

The quadratic congruence in one variable is given by

$$ax^2 + bx + c \equiv 0 \pmod{p}$$

where a, b, c are integers, p is an odd prime and $p \nmid a$.

Theorem 1 : The quadratic congruence

$$ax^2 + bx + c \equiv 0 \pmod{p}$$

can be reduced to the form $y^2 \equiv d \pmod{p}$

where $y = 2ax + b$ and $d = b^2 - 4ac$.

Proof : Multiplying the given quadratic congruence by $4a$, we get

$$4a^2x^2 + 4abx + 4ac = 0 \pmod{p}$$

which can be written as

$$(2ax + b)^2 \equiv (b^2 - 4ac) \pmod{p}.$$

Putting $2ax + b = y$ and $b^2 - 4ac = d$, we get

$$y^2 \equiv d \pmod{p}.$$

Theorem 2 : If the congruence

$$x^2 \equiv a \pmod{p}$$

is solvable then it has exactly two solutions.

Proof : Let x_0 be a solution of the given congruence. Then

$$x_0^2 \equiv a \pmod{p}. \qquad ....(1)$$

Obviously $(p - x_0)$ also satisfies the given congruence

$$\therefore \quad (p - x_0)^2 \equiv a \pmod{p} \quad [\because (p - x_0)^2 \equiv (-x_0)^2 \pmod{p}] \qquad ....(2)$$

Thus, x_0 and $(p - x_0)$ are two solutions of the given congruence.

Suppose if possible x_1 be a third solution of the given congruence. Then

$$x_1^2 \equiv a \pmod{p}. \qquad ....(3)$$

With the help of (1) and (3) we have

$$x_1^2 \equiv x_0^2 \pmod{p}$$

This gives that p divides $(x_1 - x_0)(x_1 + x_0)$. This implies that either p divides $x_1 - x_0$ or p divides $(x_1 + x_0)$. In the first case we have $x_1 \equiv x_0 \pmod{p}$ and in the second case we have $x_1 \equiv p - x_0 \pmod{p}$. This shows that x_1 is not a distinct solution. Thus, the congruence $x^2 \equiv a \pmod{p}$ has exactly two solutions.

Theorem 3 : The congruence

$$x^{(p-1)/2} \equiv 1 \pmod{p}$$

has exactly $\frac{p-1}{2}$ solutions given by, $1^2, 2^2, \ldots, \left(\frac{p-1}{2}\right)^2 \pmod{p}$.

Proof : Let

$$A = \left\{1^2, 2^2, \ldots, \left(\frac{p-1}{2}\right)^2\right\}.$$

Now if $r^2 \in A$ then $(r, p) = 1$. By Fermat's theorem we have

$$r^{p-1} \equiv 1 \pmod{p}$$

$$\Rightarrow (r^2)^{\left(\frac{p-1}{2}\right)} \equiv 1 \pmod{p}.$$

This shows that every number of A is a solution of the given congruence.

Further if $r_1^2 \equiv r_2^2 \pmod{p}$ such that $1 \leqslant r_1 \leqslant r_2 \leqslant \frac{p-1}{2}$, then $(r_1 - r_2)(r_1 + r_2)$, will be divisible by p. But this is not possible because $r_1 - r_2$ and $r_1 + r_2$ both are numerically less than p. Also $\frac{p-1}{2}$ divides $p - 1$. Therefore, the given congruence has exactly $\left(\frac{p-1}{2}\right)$ solutions given by A.

Example 1 : Find the solution of the congruence

$$x^{11} \equiv 1 \pmod{23}$$

Solution : Here 23 is a prime and $\frac{23-1}{2} = 11$. Therefore $x^{11} \equiv 1 \pmod{23}$ has exactly 11 solutions given by

$$x \equiv 1^2, 2^2, \ldots, 11^2 \text{ (mod) } 23)$$
$$\equiv 1, 4, 9, 16, 2, 13, 3, 18, 12, 8, 6 \pmod{23}. \qquad \textbf{Ans.}$$

Example 2 : Solve the congruence

$$x^2 + 3x + 11 \equiv 0 \pmod{13}.$$

Solution : We have

$$x^2 + 3x + 11 \equiv 0 \pmod{13}$$
$$\Rightarrow \quad 4x^2 + 12x + 44 \equiv 0 \pmod{13}$$
$$\Rightarrow \quad (2x+3)^2 \equiv 4 \pmod{13}$$

or $\quad y^2 \equiv 4 \pmod{13}$, where $y = 2x + 3$

$$y \equiv 2 \pmod{13}$$
$$y \equiv 11 \pmod{13}.$$

Thus, $2x + 3 \equiv 2 \pmod{13}$ and $2x + 3 \equiv 11 \pmod{13}$

or $\quad 2x = 12 \pmod{13}$ and $2x \equiv 8 \pmod{13}$

or $\quad x = 6 \pmod{13}$ and $x \equiv 4 \pmod{13}$. **Ans.**

Problem 3 : Solve the congruence

$$x^2 \equiv 5 \pmod{29}.$$

Solution : We have

$$x^2 \equiv 5 \pmod{29}$$
$$\equiv (5 + 29) \pmod{29}$$
$$\equiv (34 + 29) \pmod{29}$$
$$\equiv (63 + 29) \pmod{29}$$
$$\equiv (92 + 29) \pmod{29}$$
$$\equiv 121 \pmod{29}$$
$$\equiv 11^2 \pmod{29}.$$

Therefore the required solutions are

$$x \equiv 11, (29 - 11) \pmod{29}$$
$$\equiv 11, 18 \pmod{29}. \qquad \textbf{Ans.}$$

Example 4 : Solve the congruence

$$3x^2 + 5x + 9 \equiv 0 \pmod{11}$$ **[C.C.S. (B.P.) 2006]**

Solution : We have

$$3x^2 + 5x + 9 \equiv 0 \pmod{11}. \quad \text{.......(1)}$$

Multiplying (1) by $3 \times 4 = 12$, we get

$$36x^2 + 60x + 108 \equiv 0 \pmod{11}.$$

This can be written as

$$(6x + 5)^2 \equiv 5 \pmod{11}. \quad \text{.......(2)}$$

Putting $y \equiv (6x + 5)$ in (2), we get

$$y^2 \equiv 5 \pmod{11}$$
$$\equiv (5 + 11) \pmod{11}$$
$$\equiv 4^2 \pmod{11}$$

This gives, $y \equiv \pm 4 \pmod{11}$

or $6x + 5 \equiv \pm 4 \pmod{11}$

or $6x \equiv (2, 10) \pmod{11}$

or $x = 4, 9 \pmod{11}$.

8.3 Quadratic Residue

If p is a prime and a is an integer coprime to p then a is called a quadratic residue (mod p) iff $x^2 \equiv a \pmod{p}$ has a solution otherwise a is called quadratic non-residue (mod p).

For example $x^2 = 4 \pmod{5}$ has solutions 2, 3 (mod 5). Therefore 4 is a quadratic residue (mod 5).

8.4 Euler's Criterion

Theorem 1 : If p is an odd prime and a is any integer such that $(a, p) = 1$ then a is a quadratic residue (mod p) iff $a^{\frac{p-1}{2}} \equiv 1 \pmod{p}$. **(C.C.S.U. 2004)**

Proof : Let a be a quadratic residue (mod p) and $(a, p) = 1$. Then the quadratic congruence $x^2 \equiv a \pmod{p}$ has a solution (say x_0).

Thus, $x_0^2 \equiv a \pmod{p}, (x_0, p) = 1$. ....(1)

By Fermat's Little Theorem, we have

$$x_0^{p-1} \equiv 1 \pmod{p}. \quad \text{.......(2)}$$

Therefore,

$$a^{\frac{p-1}{2}} = (x_0^2)^{\frac{p-1}{2}}$$

$$\equiv x_0^{p-1} \pmod p)$$

$$= 1 \pmod p. \qquad \text{[By (2)].}$$

Conversely, suppose $a^{\frac{p-1}{2}} \equiv 1 \pmod p$.

Let r be a primitive root (mod p). Then 1, r, r^2, ... r^{p-2} form a reduced residue system (mod p) and $a = r^k$ (mod p) for some integer k such that, $1 \leqslant k \leqslant p-1$.

Now we have,

$$1 = a^{\frac{p-1}{2}} \equiv (r^k)^{\frac{p-1}{2}} \pmod p$$

$$\equiv r^{\frac{k(p-1)}{2}} \pmod p.$$

As r is a primitive root (mod p) it has exponent (order) $(p-1)$ (mod p). This implies $(p-1) \left| \frac{k(p-1)}{2} \right.$. This gives that k must be an even integer say $2t$.

Therefore $a = r^{2t}$ (mod p). This shows that r^t is a solution of the congruence

$$x^2 \equiv a \pmod p$$

Corollary 1 : If r is a primitive root (mod p) then r^k is a quadratic residue (mod p) iff k is even.

Theorem 2 : If $(a, p) = 1$ then either

$$a^{\frac{p-1}{2}} \equiv 1 \pmod p \quad \text{or} \quad a^{\frac{p-1}{2}} \equiv -1 \pmod p.$$

Proof : By Fermat's theorem, we have

$$a^{p-1} \equiv 1 \pmod p.$$

This gives

$$\left(a^{\frac{p-1}{2}} - 1\right)\left(a^{\frac{p-1}{2}} + 1\right) \equiv 0 \pmod p.$$

Therefore, p divides either $\left(a^{\frac{p-1}{2}} - 1\right)$ or $\left(a^{\frac{p-1}{2}} + 1\right)$. It cannot divide both because in that case $\left(a^{\frac{p-1}{2}} + 1\right) - \left(a^{\frac{p-1}{2}} - 1\right) = 2$ will be divisible by p which is not possible.

Example 1 : Find the quadratic residue and non-quadratic of 13.

Solution : We have (2, 13) = 1 and

$$2^{\frac{13-1}{2}} = 2^6 = 64 \equiv 12 \pmod{13}$$
$$\equiv -1 \pmod{13}.$$

Therefore, 2 is a quadratic non-residue of 13.

Also, (3, 13) = 1 and

$$3^{\frac{13-1}{2}} = 3^6$$
$$= (27)^2$$
$$\equiv 1^2 \pmod{13}$$
$$\equiv 1 \pmod{13}.$$

Therefore, 3 is a quadratic residue of 13.

Example 2 : Show that 3 is a quadratic residue of 23, but a non-residue of 31.

Solution : We have (3, 23) = 1 and

$$3^{\frac{23-1}{2}} = 3^{11},\ 7^2 \equiv 3 \pmod{23}.$$

Therefore, 3 is a quadratic residue of 23. Further (3, 31) = 1 and the quadratic congruence

$$x^2 \equiv 3 \pmod{31}$$

has no solution. Therefore, 3 is a non-residue of 31.

Example 3 : Find all the quadratic residue of 23.

Solution : Here $\frac{p-1}{2} = \frac{23-1}{2} = 11$. Therefore, there are 11 quadratic residue. Since 1, 4, 9 and 16 are square integers less than 23. Therefore 1, 4, 9, 16 are quadratic residue of 23.

Further, we have

$$4 \times 9 \equiv 13 \pmod{23}$$
$$4 \times 16 \equiv 18 \pmod{23}$$
$$9 \times 16 \equiv 6 \pmod{23}.$$

Therefore, 13, 18 and 6 are also quadratic residue of 23.

Finally, we have

$$9 \times 13 = 2 \pmod{23}$$
$$4 \times 18 \equiv 3 \pmod{23}$$
$$6 \times 9 \equiv 8 \pmod{23}$$
$$4 \times 3 = 12.$$

Therefore, 2, 3, 8 and 12 are also quadratic residue of 23.

Thus, 1, 2, 3, 4, 6, 8, 9, 12, 13, 16 and 18 are quadratic residue of 23.

8.5 Legendre Symbol and Its Properties

Definition : If p is an odd prime and a is any integer such that $(a, p) = 1$ then Legendre symbol (a/p) is defined as

$$\left(\frac{a}{p}\right) = \begin{cases} 1 & \text{if } a \text{ is a quadratic residue (mod } p) \\ -1 & \text{If } a \text{ is a quadratic non-residue (mod } p) \end{cases}$$

For example, $\left(\frac{3}{13}\right) = 1$ because 3 is a quadratic residue (mod 13) and $\left(\frac{5}{17}\right) = -1$ because 5 is a quadratic non-residue (mod 17).

Theorem 1 : If p is an odd prime and a and b are any integers coprime to p then the Legendre symbol has the following properties :

(i) $a \equiv b \pmod{p} \Rightarrow \left(\frac{a}{p}\right) = \left(\frac{b}{p}\right)$

(ii) $\left(\frac{a^2}{p}\right) = 1$

(iii) $\left(\frac{ab}{p}\right) = \left(\frac{a}{p}\right)\left(\frac{b}{p}\right)$

(iv) $\left(\frac{1}{p}\right) = 1$ and $\left(-\frac{1}{p}\right) = (-1)^{\frac{(p-1)}{2}}$

(v) $\left(\frac{ab^2}{p}\right) = \left(\frac{a}{p}\right)$.

Proof :

(*i*) We have

$a \equiv b \pmod{p} \Rightarrow$ the congruences $x^2 \equiv a \pmod{p}$

and $x^2 \equiv b \pmod{p}$ have the same solutions.

Thus, $x^2 \equiv a \pmod{p}$ and $x^2 \equiv b \pmod{p}$ are either both solvable or both are not solvable. Therefore, in both the cases we have

$$\left(\frac{a}{p}\right) = \left(\frac{b}{p}\right).$$

(*ii*) Since integer a trivially satisfies the congruence $x^2 \equiv a^2 \pmod{p}$.

Therefore, $\left(\frac{a^2}{p}\right) = 1.$

(*iii*) By Euler's criterion we have

$$\left(\frac{ab}{p}\right) \equiv (ab)^{\frac{(p-1)}{2}} \pmod{p}$$

$$\equiv a^{\frac{(p-1)}{2}} . b^{\frac{(p-1)}{2}} \pmod{p}$$

$$\equiv a^{\frac{(p-1)}{2}} \pmod{p} . b^{\frac{(p-1)}{2}} \pmod{p}$$

$$\equiv \left(\frac{a}{p}\right) \pmod{p} . \left(\frac{b}{p}\right) \pmod{p}$$

$$\equiv \left(\frac{a}{p}\right)\left(\frac{b}{p}\right) \pmod{p}.$$

Since the Legendre symbol takes the values – 1 and 1 we have

$$\left(\frac{ab}{p}\right) = \left(\frac{a}{p}\right)\left(\frac{b}{p}\right).$$

(*iv*) Since 1 is a quadratic residue of every p, we have $\left(\frac{1}{p}\right) = 1$

Further the quantities $-\frac{1}{p}$ and $(-1)^{\left(\frac{p-1}{2}\right)}$ are either 1 or – 1. Therefore,

$$\left(-\frac{1}{p}\right) \equiv (-1)^{\left(\frac{p-1}{2}\right)} \pmod{p}$$

$$\Rightarrow \left(-\frac{1}{p}\right) = (-1)^{\left(\frac{p-1}{2}\right)}.$$

(*v*) We have

$$\left(\frac{ab^2}{p}\right) = \left(\frac{a}{p}\right)\left(\frac{b}{p}\right)\left(\frac{b}{p}\right)$$

$$= \left(\frac{a}{p}\right)\left(\frac{b}{p}\right)^2$$

$$= \left(\frac{a}{p}\right). \qquad \left[\because \left(\frac{b}{p}\right)^2 = 1 \text{ as } p \nmid b\right]$$

Theorem 2 : There are infinitely many primes of the form $4k + 1$ where k is an integer. **(C.C.S.U. 2003)**

Proof : We assume contrarily that there are finitely many primes $p_1, p_2, ..., p_n$ of the form $4k + 1$. We consider an integer

$$N = (2p_1 . p_2 ..... p_n)^2 + 1.$$

Obviously N is an integer of the form $4k + 1$ and is coprime to each $p_1, p_2, ... p_n$. Now by the fundamental theorem of arithmetic N has a prime factor p (say). Now p cannot be one of $p_1, p_2, ..., p_n$. Therefore, it should be a prime of the form $4k + 3$. This gives

$$(2p_1 . p_2 .... p_n)^2 \equiv -1 \pmod{p}.$$

This shows that $2p_1p_2 ... p_n$ is a solution of the congruence $x^2 = -1 \pmod{p}$. Thus, -1 is a quadratic residue (mod p). This is contradiction. Hence, there must be infinitely many primes of the form $4k + 1$.

Theorem 3 : If p is an odd prime then

$$\sum_{n=1}^{p-1} \left(\frac{n}{p}\right) = 0.$$

Proof : Let p be an odd prime and r be a primitive root of p. Then the powers $r, r^2, ... r^{p-1}$ are permutation of the integer $1, 2, ... (p - 1)$. Therefore for any integer n from 1 to $(p - 1)$ there exists a unique positive integer k from 1 to $(p - 1)$ such that $n \equiv r^k \pmod{p}$. Now by the application of Euler's criterion we have

$$\left(\frac{n}{p}\right) = \left(\frac{r^k}{p}\right)$$

$$\equiv (r^k)^{\left(\frac{p-1}{2}\right)}$$

$$\equiv \left[r^{\left(\frac{p-1}{2}\right)}\right]^k$$

$$\equiv (-1)^k \pmod{p}$$

$$\left[\because r \text{ is a primitive root of } p \text{ so } r^{\left(\frac{p-1}{2}\right)} \equiv -1 \pmod{p}\right.$$

But $\left(\frac{n}{p}\right)$ and $(-1)^k$ are equal to 1 or -1.

Therefore, $\sum_{n=1}^{(p-1)} \left(\frac{n}{p}\right) = \sum_{n=1}^{(p-1)} (-1)^k = 0.$ **Proved.**

Theorem 4 : (Gauss Lemma) : If p is an odd integer, a is an integer such that $(a, p) = 1$ and n is number of integers in the set

$$\left\{a, 2a, \ldots, \left(\frac{p-1}{2}\right)a\right\} \qquad \text{.......(1)}$$

then $$\left(\frac{a}{p}\right) = (-1)^n.$$ **(C.C.S.U. 2005)**

Proof : Since $(a, p) = 1$, each integer of (1) is coprime to p and no two of them are congruent to each other (mod p). Let $r_1, r_2, \ldots r_{n_1}$ be the remainder on division by p such that $0 < r_i < p/2$ and $t_1, t_2, \ldots t_n$ be the remainders such that $p/2 < s_i < p$. Then we have $n_1 + n = \dfrac{(p-1)}{2}$ and $r_1, r_2, \ldots, r_{n_1}, p - t_1, \ldots p - t_n$ are positive integers less than $p/2$. Now we shall show that these integers are distinct. Suppose if possible $p - t_i = r_j$ for some i and j. Then there exist integers h and k with $1 \leqslant h, k \leqslant \left(\dfrac{p-1}{2}\right)$ such that

$$t_i \equiv ha \pmod{p} \quad \text{and} \quad r_j \equiv ka \pmod{p}.$$

This gives

$$(h + k)\, a \equiv t_i + r_j \equiv p \equiv 0 \pmod{p}.$$

$$\Rightarrow \qquad (h + k) \equiv 0 \pmod{p}.$$

But this is not possible because $1 < h + k \leqslant p - 1$. Hence $r_1, r_2 \ldots r_{n_1}, p - t_1, \ldots pt_n$ are all distinct. Thus, $r_1, r_2, \ldots r_{n_1}, p - t_1, \ldots p - t_n$ are simply the integers $1, 2, \ldots, \left(\dfrac{p-1}{2}\right)$.

Therefore, there product is

$$\left(\frac{p-1}{2}\right)! = r_1, r_2 \ldots r_{n_1} (p - t_1) \ldots (p - t_n)$$

$$\equiv r_1 . r_2 \ldots r_{n_1} (-t_1) \ldots (-t_n) \pmod{p}$$

$$\equiv (-1)^k\, r_1 r_2 \ldots r_{n_1} t_1 \ldots t_n.$$

But $r_1, r_2, \ldots r_{n_1}, t_1, t_2, \ldots t_n$ are congruent (mod p) to $a, 2a, \ldots, \left(\dfrac{p-1}{2}\right) a$ in some order. Hence,

$$\left(\frac{p-1}{2}\right)! = (-1)^n\, a . 2a \ldots \left(\frac{p-1}{2}\right) a \pmod{p}$$

$$\equiv (-1)^n\, a^{\left(\frac{p-1}{2}\right)} \left(\frac{p-1}{2}\right)! \pmod{p}$$

$$\Rightarrow 1 \equiv (-1)^n\, a^{\left(\frac{p-1}{2}\right)} \pmod{p}. \quad \left[\because \left(\frac{p-1}{2}\right)! \text{ is relatively prime to } p\right]$$

$$\Rightarrow a^{\left(\frac{p-1}{2}\right)} \equiv (-1)^n \pmod{p}.$$

By Euler's criterion we have

$$\left(\frac{a}{p}\right) \equiv a^{\left(\frac{p-1}{2}\right)} \equiv (-1)^n \pmod{p}$$

$$\Rightarrow \left(\frac{a}{p}\right) = (-1)^n.$$

Proved

Theorem 5 : If p is an odd prime then

$$\left(\frac{2}{p}\right) = \begin{cases} 1 & \text{if } p = 1 \pmod 8 \text{ or } p \equiv 7 \pmod 8 \\ -1 & \text{if } p = 3 \pmod 8 \text{ or } p \equiv 5 \pmod 8 \end{cases}$$

Hence, $$\frac{2}{p} = (-1)^{\frac{p^2-1}{8}}$$

Proof : By Gauss Lemma, we have

$$\left(\frac{2}{p}\right) = (-1)^n$$

where n is the number of integers in the set

$$\left\{2.1, 2.2, \ldots. 2.\left(\frac{p-1}{2}\right)\right\}$$

which on division by p have the remainder greater than $\frac{p}{2}$. Also the numbers in the above set are less than p. For $1 \leqslant n \leqslant \frac{p-1}{2}$, $2k < \frac{p}{2}$, we have $k < \frac{p}{4}$. Then there are $\left[\frac{p}{4}\right]$ integers in the above set less than $\frac{p}{2}$. Therefore,

$$n = \frac{p-1}{2} - \left[\frac{p}{4}\right]$$

which are greater than $\frac{p}{2}$.

Since p is an odd prime it must have any one of the form $8k + 1$, $8k + 3$, $8k + 5$ or $8k + 7$.

Now,

if $p = 8k + 1$ then $n = 4k - 2k = 2k$

if $p = 8k + 3$ then $n = 4k - (2k - 1) = 2k + 1$

if $p = 8k + 5$ then $n = 4k + 2 - (2k + 1) = 2k + 1$

and if $p = 8k + 7$ then $n = 4k + 3 - (2k + 1) = 2k + 2$.

Thus, we see that n is even when p is of the form $8k + 1$ or $8k + 7$ and therefore $\left(\frac{2}{p}\right) = 1$ and if p is of the form $8\,k + 3$ or $8k + 5$ then n is odd which gives

$$\left(\frac{2}{p}\right) = -1.$$

Further

$$(-1)^{\frac{p^2-1}{8}} = \begin{cases} (-1)^{\frac{(8k+1)^2-1}{8}} & \text{if} \quad p = 8k+1 \\ (-1)^{\frac{(8k+3)^2-1}{8}} & \text{if} \quad p = 8k+3 \\ (-1)^{\frac{(8k+5)^2-1}{8}} & \text{if} \quad p = 8k+5 \\ (-1)^{\frac{(8k+7)^2-1}{8}} & \text{if} \quad p = 8k+7 \end{cases}$$

$$= \begin{cases} (-1)^{\frac{64k^2+16k}{8}} & \text{if} \quad p = 8k+1 \\ (-1)^{\frac{64k^2+48k+8}{8}} & \text{if} \quad p = 8k+3 \\ (-1)^{\frac{64k^2+80k+24}{8}} & \text{if} \quad p = 8k+5 \\ (-1)^{\frac{64k^2+112k+48}{8}} & \text{if} \quad p = 8k+7 \end{cases}$$

$$= \begin{cases} 1 & \text{if} \quad p \equiv 1 \pmod 8 \\ -1 & \text{if} \quad p \equiv 3 \pmod 8 \\ 1 & \text{if} \quad p \equiv 5 \pmod 8 \\ -1 & \text{if} \quad p \equiv 7 \pmod 8 \end{cases}$$

$$= \begin{cases} 1 & \text{if} \quad p \equiv \pm 1 \pmod p \\ -1 & \text{if} \quad p \equiv \pm 3 \pmod p \end{cases}$$

Hence, $\left(\frac{2}{p}\right) = (-1)^{\frac{p^2-1}{8}}$. **Proved**

Theorem 6 : If p and $2p + 1$ both are odd primes then $(-1)^{\left(\frac{p-1}{2}\right)}.2$ is a primitive root of $2p + 1$.

Proof : We put $q = 2p + 1$. Since p and $2p + 1$ both are odd prime, we have either $p \equiv 1 \pmod 4$ or $p \equiv 3 \pmod 4$

If $p \equiv 1 \pmod 4$ then $(-1)^{\left(\frac{p-1}{2}\right)}.2 = 2$

Now $\phi(q) = q - 1 = 2p$ the order of 2 modulo q is any one of the numbers 1, 2, ... p or $2p$.

Also we have

$$\left(\frac{2}{q}\right) \equiv 2^{\frac{q-1}{2}} \equiv 2^p \pmod q.$$

But $q \equiv 3 \pmod 8$, therefore $\left(\frac{2}{q}\right) = -1.$

Hence, $2^p \equiv -1 \pmod q$. This shows that 2 cannot have order p modulo q. Also 2 cannot have order 1 and 2 because $2^2 \equiv 1 \pmod q$ implies $q/3$ which is impossible. So the order of 2 modulo q is $2p$. This shows that 2 is a primitive root of q.

If $p \equiv 3 \pmod 4$ then $(-1)^{\left(\frac{p-1}{2}\right)}.2 = -2$ and

$$(-2)^p \equiv \left(-\frac{2}{q}\right) = \left(-\frac{1}{q}\right)\left(\frac{2}{q}\right) \pmod q.$$

Since $q \equiv 7 \pmod 8$ we have $\left(-\frac{1}{q}\right) = -1.$

Also $\left(\frac{2}{q}\right) = 1$. Therefore, $(-2)^p \equiv -1 \pmod q$.

This shows that -2 is a primitive root of q.

Theorem 7 : There are infinitely many primes of the form $8k - 1$.

Proof : Suppose there are only finite number of primes of the form $8k - 1$ given as $p_1, p_2, \ldots. p_n$. Let

$$N = (4p_1 p_2 \ldots p_n)^2 - 2.$$

Obviously N is an integer of the form $2\,(8n_1 - 1)$. Therefore it will have an odd prime divisor, say, p. So

$$N \equiv 0 \pmod p.$$

This implies that $x^2 \equiv 2 \pmod p$ has a solution $4p_1, p_2, \ldots, p_n \pmod p$. Therefore,

$$\left(\frac{2}{p}\right) = 1$$

Hence, p must be of the forms $8n_1 + 1$ or $(8m_1 - 1)$. Since p and 2, $p_1, p_2 \ldots p_n$ are coprime p cannot be of the form $8n_1 - 1$. So it is of the form $8n_1 + 1$. This shows that all prime divisors of N are of the form $8n_1 + 1$. This implies that N is of the form

$8n_1 + 1$. This is contradiction. Hence, there are infinitely many primers of the form $8k - 1$.

Solved Examples

Example 1 : Evaluate $\left(\frac{504}{23}\right)$.

Solution : We have

$$\left(\frac{504}{23}\right) = \left(\frac{6^2 \times 14}{23}\right) = \left(\frac{6^2}{23}\right).\left(\frac{14}{23}\right) = \left(\frac{14}{23}\right) \qquad [\because (6, 23) = 1]$$

$$= -1. \qquad [\because 14 \text{ is a quadratic non-residue of } 23]. \qquad \textbf{Ans.}$$

Example 2 : Evaluate $\left(\frac{168}{11}\right)$.

Solution : We have

$$168 = 2^3.3.7.$$

$$\therefore \quad \left(\frac{168}{11}\right) = \left(\frac{2^3.3.7}{11}\right) = \left(\frac{2}{11}\right)^3.\left(\frac{3}{11}\right).\left(\frac{7}{11}\right)$$

$$= -(1)^3.(1).(-1).$$

[∵ 2 and 7 are quadratic non-residues of 11 and 3 is a quadratic residue of 11]

$$= 1. \qquad \textbf{Ans.}$$

Example 3 : Evaluate $\left(\frac{1372}{29}\right)$.

Solution : We have

$$1372 = 7 \times 14^2$$

$$\therefore \quad \left(\frac{1372}{29}\right) = \left(\frac{4 \times (14)^2}{29}\right) = \left(\frac{7}{29}\right).\left(\frac{14}{29}\right)^2$$

$$= \left(\frac{7}{29}\right) \qquad [\because (14, 29) = 1]$$

$$= 1. \qquad [\because 7 \text{ is a quadratic residue of } 29]. \textbf{ Ans.}$$

Example 4 : Evaluate $\left(\frac{-23}{59}\right)$.

Solution : We have

$$\left(\frac{-23}{59}\right)=\left(\frac{-1\times 23}{59}\right)=\left(-\frac{1}{59}\right)\cdot\left(\frac{23}{59}\right)$$

$$=-1.\left(\frac{23}{59}\right) \qquad [\because\ 59=4\times 14+3]$$

$$=-\left(\frac{23}{59}\right)$$

$$=-1. \qquad [\because\ 23 \text{ is a quadratic residue of } 59].$$ **Ans.**

Example 5 : Evaluate *n* of Gauss Lemma for $\left(\frac{5}{19}\right)$.

Solution : Here, $a = 5$ and $p = 19$. Therefore, $\frac{p-1}{2}=\frac{19-1}{2}=9$. So,

$$S = \{5, 10, 15, 20, 25, 30, 35, 40, 45\}.$$

With respect to modulo 19 the members of S will become

5, 10, 15, 1, 6, 11, 16, 2, 7.

Four of these numbers are greater than $\frac{p}{2}=\frac{19}{2}$. Therefore, $n = 4$. **Ans.**

Example 6 : Evaluate *n* of Gauss Lemma for $\left(\frac{11}{23}\right)$.

Solution : Here, $a = 11$ and $p = 23$. Therefore, $\frac{p-1}{2}=\frac{23-1}{2}=11$. So,

$$S = \{11, 22, 33, 44, 55, 66, 77, 88, 99, 110, 121\}$$

With respect to modulo 23 the members of S will become

11, 22, 10, 21, 9, 20, 8, 19, 7, 18, 6

Five of these numbers are greater than $\frac{p}{2}=\frac{23}{2}$. Therefore, $n = 5$

8.6 Quadratic Reciprocity Law

Theorem : If p and q are distinct odd primes than

$$\left(\frac{p}{q}\right)\left(\frac{q}{p}\right)=(-1)^{\left(\frac{p-1}{2}\right)\cdot\left(\frac{q-1}{2}\right)}.$$ **(C.C.S.U. 2001, 2003)**

Proof : We consider a rectangular region R (excluding the boundaries) with vertices $(0, 0)$, $\left(\frac{p}{2}, 0\right)$, $\left(0, \frac{q}{2}\right)$ and $\left(\frac{p}{2}, \frac{q}{2}\right)$.

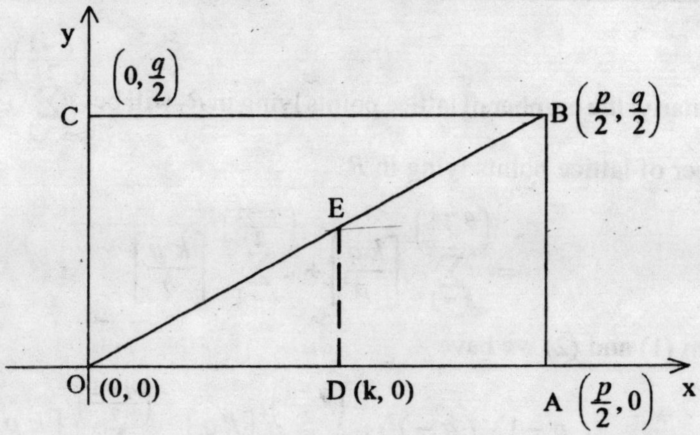

A lattice point (whose coordinates are integers) (m, n) inside the boundary $OABC$ satisfies

$$1 \leqslant m \leqslant \frac{p-1}{2} \quad \text{and} \quad 1 \leqslant n \leqslant \frac{q-1}{2}.$$

We will count these lattice points. Since p and q are odd integers, the number of such points will be

$$\left(\frac{p-1}{2}\right) \cdot \left(\frac{q-1}{2}\right). \qquad \text{.......(1)}$$

Now the equation of diagonal OB is given by, $y = \frac{q}{p} x$.

We will show that no lattice point lies on the diagonal OB.

Suppose if (m, n) lies on OB then

$$n = \frac{q}{p} m \quad \Rightarrow \quad pn = qm \quad \Rightarrow \quad p | qm$$

$$\Rightarrow \quad p \mid m. \qquad [\because (p, q) = 1]$$

This is not possible because $m \leqslant \frac{p-1}{2}$. Therefore no lattice point lies on the diagonal OB. Let R_1 be the portion of R below OB and R_2 the portion of R above OB. We will count the lattice points inside these two regions. We consider a point $D(k, 0)$ on OA. Let the perpendicular on D meets the diagonal on E. The number of lattice points lying on DE will be $\left[\frac{kq}{p}\right]$. Therefore, the number of lattice points lying in R_1 will be

$$\sum_{k=1}^{\left(\frac{p-1}{2}\right)} \left[\frac{kq}{p}\right].$$

Similarly, the number of lattice points lying in R_2 will be $\sum_{k=1}^{\left(\frac{q-1}{2}\right)} \left[\frac{kp}{q}\right]$. Thus, the total number of lattice points lying in R

$$= \sum_{k=1}^{\left(\frac{q-1}{2}\right)} \left[\frac{kq}{p}\right] + \sum_{k=1}^{\left(\frac{q-1}{2}\right)} \left[\frac{kp}{q}\right]. \quad \text{.......(2)}$$

From (1) and (2) we have

$$\left(\frac{p-1}{2}\right).\left(\frac{q-1}{2}\right) = \sum_{k=1}^{\left(\frac{q-1}{2}\right)} \left[\frac{kq}{p}\right] + \sum_{k=1}^{\left(\frac{q-1}{2}\right)} \left[\frac{kp}{q}\right]. \quad \text{.......(3)}$$

By Gauss lemma we have

$$\left(\frac{p}{q}\right).\left(\frac{q}{p}\right) = (-1)^{\sum_{k=1}^{\left(\frac{q-1}{2}\right)} \left[\frac{kq}{p}\right]} . (-1)^{\sum_{k=1}^{\left(\frac{q-1}{2}\right)} \left[\frac{kp}{q}\right]}$$

$$= (-1)^{\sum_{k=1}^{\left(\frac{q-1}{2}\right)} \left[\frac{kq}{p}\right] + \sum_{k=1}^{\left(\frac{q-1}{2}\right)} \left[\frac{kp}{q}\right]}$$

$$= (-1)^{\left(\frac{p-1}{2}\right).\left(\frac{q-1}{2}\right)}.$$

Proved.

Corollary 1 : If p and q are distinct odd primes then

$$\left(\frac{p}{q}\right)\left(\frac{q}{p}\right) = \begin{cases} 1 \text{ if } p \equiv 1 \pmod 4 \text{ or } q \equiv 1 \pmod 4 \\ -1 \text{ if } p \equiv q \equiv 3 \pmod 4 \end{cases}$$

Proof : We have

$$\left(\frac{p}{q}\right)\left(\frac{q}{p}\right) = (-1)^{\left(\frac{p-1}{2}\right).\left(\frac{q-1}{2}\right)}$$

$$= \begin{cases} 1 \text{ if } \left(\frac{p-1}{2}\right).\left(\frac{q-1}{2}\right) \text{ is even} \\ -1 \text{ if } \left(\frac{p-1}{2}\right).\left(\frac{q-1}{2}\right) \text{ is odd} \end{cases}$$

$$= \begin{cases} 1 \text{ if at least one of } p \text{ and } q = 4k+1 \\ -1 \text{ if both } p \text{ and } q = 4k+3 \end{cases}$$

$$= \begin{cases} 1 \text{ if } p \equiv 1 (\text{mod } 4) \text{ or } q \equiv 1 (\text{mod } 4) \\ -1 \text{ if } p \equiv q \equiv 3 (\text{mod } 4). \end{cases}$$

Proved

Another Form : If p and q are distinct odd primes then

$$\frac{p}{q} = \begin{cases} \left(\frac{q}{p}\right) \text{ if } p \equiv 1 (\text{mod } 4) \text{ or } q \equiv 1 (\text{mod } 4) \\ -\left(\frac{q}{p}\right) \text{ if } p \equiv q \equiv 3 (\text{mod } 4). \end{cases}$$

Example 1 : Show that, $\left(\frac{113}{43}\right) = \left(\frac{43}{113}\right)$.

Solution : Here 43 and 113 are both odd primes and 113 is of the form $4k + 1$ and 43 is of the form $4k + 3$.

$$\therefore \quad \left(\frac{113}{43}\right) = \left(\frac{43}{113}\right).$$

Example 2 : Show that, $\left(\frac{43}{23}\right) = -\left(\frac{23}{43}\right)$.

Solution : Here, we have that 23 and 43 both are odd primes and both

$$23 = 4 \times 5 + 3$$
$$43 = 4 \times 10 + 3$$

are of the form $4k + 3$. Therefore,

$$\left(\frac{43}{23}\right) = -\left(\frac{23}{43}\right).$$

Example 3 : Evaluate $\left(\frac{59}{131}\right)$.

Solution : Here 59 and 131 both are odd primes and

$$59 = 4 \times 14 + 3$$
$$131 = 4 \times 32 + 3$$

are of the form $4k + 3$. Therefore,

$$\left(\frac{59}{131}\right) = -\left(\frac{131}{59}\right) = -\left(\frac{13}{59}\right)$$

$$= -\left(\frac{59}{13}\right) \qquad [\because 13 \equiv 1 \ (\text{mod } 4)]$$

$$= -\left(\frac{7}{13}\right) = -\left(\frac{13}{7}\right) = -\left(-\frac{1}{7}\right)$$
$$= -(-1)$$
$$= 1$$ **Ans.**

Example 4 : Evaluate $\left(\frac{71}{73}\right)$.

Solution : We have

$$\left(\frac{71}{73}\right) = \left(\frac{73}{71}\right) \qquad [\because 73 = 4 \times 18 + 1]$$
$$= \left(\frac{2}{71}\right)$$
$$= 1. \qquad [\because 71 \text{ is an odd prime and } 71 \equiv 7 \pmod 8].$$ **Ans.**

8.7 Quadratic Congruences with Composite Module

Theorem 1 : If p is an odd prime and a is any integer such that $(a, p) = 1$ then the congruence

$$x^2 \equiv a \pmod{p^n}, \quad n \geqslant 1$$

has a solution if $\left(\frac{a}{p}\right) = 1$.

Proof : Suppose the given congruence has a solution x_0. Then

$$x_0^2 \equiv a \pmod{p^n}$$
$$\Rightarrow p^n \mid (x_0^2 - a)$$
$$\Rightarrow p \mid (x_0^2 - a)$$
$$\Rightarrow x^2 \equiv a \pmod p \text{ has a solution.}$$

Therefore by Euler's criterion $\left(\frac{a}{p}\right) = 1$.

Conversely, suppose $\left(\frac{a}{p}\right) = 1$. Then by Euler's criterion $x^2 \equiv a \pmod p$.

This shows that the given statement is true for $n = 1$.

Now we assume that $x^2 \equiv a \pmod{p^m}$ has a solution. We shall show that $x^2 \equiv a \pmod{p^{m+1}}$ also has a solution. Let x_0 be the solution of $x^2 \equiv a \pmod{p^m}$. Then $x_0^2 \equiv a + tp^m$ for some integer t. Obviously $(x_0, p) = 1$. Therefore the linear congruence

$$x_0 y \equiv 1 \pmod p$$

has a solution say y_0. Thus

$$x_0 y_0 = 1 + t_1 p \text{ for some integer } t_1.$$

Let $x_1 = x_0 - t y_0 p^m \cdot \left(\frac{p+1}{2}\right)$. Then

$$x_1^2 = x_0^2 - 2t\, x_0\, y_0 \left(\frac{p+1}{2}\right) p^m + t^2 y_0^2 \left(\frac{p+1}{2}\right)^2 p^{2m}$$

$$= x_0^2 - 2t(1 + t_1 p)\left(\frac{p+1}{2}\right) p^m + t^2 y_0^2 \left(\frac{p+1}{2}\right)^2 p^{2m}$$

$$= a + tp^m - tp^m + p^{m+1}, \text{ (some integer)}$$

$$= a + p^{m+1}. \text{ (some integer)}$$

$$\equiv a \pmod{p^{m+1}}.$$

This shows that x_1 is a solution of $x^2 \equiv a \pmod{p^{m+1}}$. Hence, by mathematical induction we have that

$$x^2 \equiv a \pmod{p^n}$$

has a solution for $n \geqslant 1$. **Proved.**

Theorem 2 : If a is an odd integer then

(i) $x^2 \equiv a \pmod 2$ **always has a solution**

(ii) $x^2 \equiv a \pmod 4$ **has a solution iff** $a \equiv 1 \pmod 4$

(iii) $x^2 \equiv a \pmod{2^n}$, $n \geqslant 3$ **has a solution iff** $a \equiv 1 \pmod 8$.

Proof :

(i) We have

$$a \equiv 1 \pmod 2. \qquad [\because a \text{ is an odd integer}]$$

Therefore 1 is the solution of $x^2 \equiv a \pmod 2$.

(ii) Since a is an odd integer we have

$$a \equiv 1 \text{ or } 3 \pmod 4.$$

Also, $b^2 \equiv 1 \pmod 4$, where b is an odd integer.

Now the congruence $x^2 \equiv a \pmod 4$ has a solution b if $a \equiv 1 \pmod 4$

Also, if $a \equiv 1 \pmod 4$, then 1 and 3 both satisfy $x^2 \equiv 1 \pmod 4$.

(iii) Suppose $a \equiv 1 \pmod 8$ then we have to show that $x^2 \equiv a \pmod{2^n}$, $n \geqslant 3$ has a solution.

For $n = 3$ we have $x^2 \equiv 1 \pmod 8$.

Obviously 1, 3, 5, 7 satisfy this congruence. Thus, the given congruence has a solution for $n = 3$. Suppose the congruence

$$x^2 \equiv 1 \pmod{2^n} \text{ has a solution } x_0 \text{ for } n \geqslant 3.$$

Then, $x_0^2 = 1 + t.2^n$ for some integer t.

Also, $x_0 y \equiv 1 \pmod 2$ has a unique solution y_0 so that $x_0 y_0 = 1 + 2t_1$ for some integer t_1.

Then $x_1 \equiv x_0 - 2^{n-1}\, t\, y_0$ is the solution of $x^2 \equiv 1 \pmod{2^{n+1}}$, because

$$x_1^2 = x_0^2 - 2^n\, t y_0 x_0 + 2^{2n-2}\, t^2 y_0^2$$

$$= 1 + 2^n t - 2^n t\,[1 + 2t_1] + 2^{n+2}.2^{n-3}\, t^2 y_0^2$$

$$\equiv 1 + \pmod{2^{n+1}}.$$

Hence, by mathematical induction we see that

$$x^2 \equiv 1 \pmod{2^n}$$

has a solution for $n \geqslant 3$.

Conversely, suppose $x^2 \equiv a \pmod{2^n}$ has a solution x_0 for each $n \geqslant 3$ then we have

$$x_0^2 \equiv a \pmod{2^n}$$

$$\Rightarrow \quad x_0^2 \equiv a \pmod 8.$$

As a is odd, x_0 will also be odd. We have

$$x_0 \equiv 1, 3, 5, 7 \pmod 8$$

or $$a \equiv x_0^2 \equiv 1 \pmod 8.$$

Example 1 : Show that the congruence

$$x^2 \equiv 3 \pmod{88}$$

has no solution.

Solution : We have, $x^2 \equiv 3 \pmod{88}$

$$\equiv 3 \pmod{8 \times 11}.$$

This shows that the given congruence is solvable if the congruences

$$x^2 \equiv 3 \pmod 8 \text{ and } x^2 \equiv 3 \pmod{13} \text{ are solvable.}$$

But, $x^2 \equiv 3 \pmod 8$ has no solution, because $3 \not\equiv 1 \pmod 8$.

Therefore, the given congruence has no solution.

Example 2 : Show that the congruence

$$x^2 \equiv 9 \pmod{40}$$

is solvable.

Solution : We have, $x^2 \equiv 9 \pmod{40}$

which is equivalent to the following simultaneous quadratic congruences

$$x^2 \equiv 9 \pmod 8$$

and $$x^2 \equiv 9 \pmod 5.$$

Now $9 \equiv 1 \pmod 8$ therefore, $x^2 \equiv 9 \pmod 8$ has a solution.

Also $\left(\frac{9}{5}\right)=\left(\frac{3^2}{5}\right)$

$= 1$

Therefore, $x^2 \equiv 9 \pmod 5$ has a solution. Hence, the given quadratic congruence has a solution.

Example 3 : Show that the congruence

$$x^2 \equiv 105 \pmod{199}$$

has no solution.

Solution : Here 199 is a prime. We have

$$\left(\frac{105}{199}\right)=\left(\frac{3\times5\times7}{199}\right)=\left(\frac{3}{199}\right).\left(\frac{5}{199}\right).\left(\frac{7}{199}\right)$$

$$=(-1)\left(\frac{199}{3}\right).\left(\frac{199}{5}\right).(-1)\left(\frac{199}{7}\right)$$

$[\because\ 199 \equiv 4\times49+3,\ 3=4\times0+3,\ 5=4\times1+1 \text{ and } 7=4\times1+3]$

$$=\left(\frac{1}{3}\right).\left(\frac{4}{5}\right).\left(\frac{3}{7}\right)=1.1.(-1).\left(\frac{7}{3}\right)$$

$$=(-1)\left(\frac{1}{3}\right)$$

$$=-1.1$$

$$=-1.$$

Therefore, the given congruence has no solution.

Example 4 : Show that the congruence

$$x^2 \equiv 608 \pmod{743}$$

is solvable.

Solution : Here 743 is a prime. We have

$$\left(\frac{608}{743}\right)=\left(\frac{4^2\times2\times19}{743}\right)=\left(\frac{4^2}{743}\right).\left(\frac{2}{743}\right).\left(\frac{19}{743}\right)$$

$$=1.(-1)^{\left(\frac{744}{4}\right)}.(-1).\left(\frac{743}{19}\right) \qquad [\because\ 19=4\times4+3]$$

$$=(-1)^{186}(-1).\left(\frac{2}{19}\right)=(-1).(-1)^{\left(\frac{20}{4}\right)}$$

$$=(-1).(-1)^5=1.$$

Hence, the given congruence is solvable.

Example 5 : Solve the congruence

$$x^2 \equiv 91 \pmod{27}$$

Solution : We have

$$x^2 \equiv 91 \pmod{27}$$
$$\equiv 91 \pmod{3^3}.$$

Now $\left(\frac{91}{3}\right) = \left(\frac{1}{3}\right) = 1$. Therefore, $x^2 \equiv 91 \pmod{3^3}$ has a solution.

We know that any solution of $x^2 \equiv 91 \pmod{3^3}$ is also a solution of $x^2 \equiv 91 \pmod 3$.

Now

$$x^2 \equiv 91 \pmod 3$$
$$\Rightarrow \quad x^2 = 1 \pmod 3$$

Obviously 1 is a solution of this congruence. Let $x_0 = 1$. Then, $x_0 y \equiv 1 \pmod 3$ has a solution $y_0 \equiv 1 \pmod 3$.

Now, $\quad x_0^2 = 1 = 91 - 90$

$$= 91 + 3(-30).$$

$$\therefore \quad x_0 = 1 - (-30).1.\left(\frac{3+1}{2}\right).3$$

$$= 181$$

is a solution of $x^2 \equiv 91 \pmod{3^2}$.

Further, $\quad 181y \equiv 1 \pmod 3$

$$\Rightarrow \quad y \equiv 1 \pmod 3.$$

Obviously $y_1 = 1$ is a solution of $y \equiv 1 \pmod 3$

Then

$$x_1^2 = 181^2 = 91 + 3^2.(-3430),\ x_1 = 1$$

$$x_2 = 181 - (-3430).1.\left(\frac{3+1}{2}\right) = 61921$$

is the solution of the congruence

$$x^2 \equiv 91 \pmod{3^3}$$
$$\equiv 91 \pmod{27}.$$

8.8 Jacobi Symbol

If $p > 1$ is an odd integer and $p = p_1 p_2 \ldots p_r$ is its prime factorization. Then for an integer a the Jacobi symbol denoted by $\left(\frac{a}{p}\right)$ is defined as

$$\left(\frac{a}{p}\right) = \left(\frac{a}{p_1}\right) \cdot \left(\frac{a}{p_2}\right) \cdots \left(\frac{a}{p_r}\right).$$

The symbols on the right hand side are Legendre symbols.

Theorem 1 : If $a \equiv b \pmod{p}$. Then, $\left(\frac{a}{p}\right) = \left(\frac{b}{p}\right)$.

Proof : Let $p = p_1 p_2 \ldots p_k$. Then

$$a \equiv b \pmod{p} \quad \Rightarrow a \equiv b \pmod{p_i},\ i = 1, 2, \ldots k.$$

Therefore, $\left(\frac{a}{p_i}\right) = \left(\frac{b}{p_i}\right)$. Hence

$$\left(\frac{a}{p}\right) = \left(\frac{a}{p_1}\right)\left(\frac{a}{p_2}\right) \cdots \left(\frac{a}{p_k}\right)$$

$$= \left(\frac{b}{p_1}\right)\left(\frac{b}{p_2}\right) \cdots \left(\frac{b}{p_k}\right)$$

$$= \left(\frac{b}{p}\right).$$

Proved

Theorem 2 : Show that

$$\left(\frac{a}{P}\right)\left(\frac{a}{Q}\right) = \left(\frac{a}{PQ}\right)$$

where Q is an odd integer.

Proof : Let $Q = q_1, q_2, \ldots, q_k$ where $q_1, q_2, \ldots, q_l$ are odd primes. Then

$$\left(\frac{a}{P}\right)\left(\frac{a}{Q}\right) = \left(\frac{a}{p_1}\right)\left(\frac{a}{p_2}\right) \cdots \left(\frac{a}{p_k}\right)\left(\frac{a}{q_1}\right) \cdots \left(\frac{a}{q_l}\right)$$

$$= \left(\frac{a}{p_1 p_2 \cdots p_k q_1 q_2 \cdots q_l}\right)$$

$$= \left(\frac{a}{PQ}\right).$$

Proved.

Theorem 3 : Show that,

$$\left(\frac{a}{P}\right) \cdot \left(\frac{b}{P}\right) = \left(\frac{ab}{P}\right).$$

Proof : We have

$$\text{R.H.S.} = \left(\frac{ab}{P}\right)$$

$$= \left(\frac{ab}{p_1}\right)\left(\frac{ab}{p_2}\right)\cdots\left(\frac{ab}{p_k}\right)$$

$$= \left(\frac{a}{p_1}\right)\cdot\left(\frac{b}{p_1}\right)\cdot\left(\frac{a}{p_2}\right)\cdot\left(\frac{b}{p_2}\right)\cdots\left(\frac{a}{p_k}\right)\cdot\left(\frac{b}{p_k}\right)$$

$$= \left(\frac{a}{p_1}\right)\cdot\left(\frac{a}{p_2}\right)\cdots\left(\frac{a}{p_k}\right)\cdot\left(\frac{b}{p_1}\right)\cdot\left(\frac{b}{p_2}\right)\cdots\left(\frac{b}{p_k}\right)$$

$$= \left(\frac{a}{P}\right)\cdot\left(\frac{b}{P}\right)$$

$$= \text{L.H.S.}$$

Proved

Theorem 4 : Show that

$$\left(-\frac{1}{P}\right) = (-1)^{\left(\frac{P-1}{2}\right)}.$$

Proof : We have

$$\text{L.H.S.} = \left(-\frac{1}{P}\right)$$

$$= \left(-\frac{1}{p_1}\right)\cdot\left(-\frac{1}{p_2}\right)\cdots\left(-\frac{1}{p_k}\right)$$

$$= (-1)^{\frac{p_1-1}{2}}\cdot(-1)^{\frac{p_2-1}{2}}\cdots(-1)^{\frac{p_k-1}{2}}$$

$$= (-1)^{\frac{p_1-1}{2}+\frac{p_2-1}{2}+\cdots+\frac{p_k-1}{2}}$$

$$= (-1)^{\frac{P-1}{2}}$$

$$= \text{R.H.S.}$$

Proved

Theorem 5 : Show that

$$\left(\frac{2}{P}\right) = (-1)^{\frac{P^2-1}{8}} = (-1)^{\left[\frac{P+1}{4}\right]}$$

Proof : Since p_i is an odd integer for $i = 1, 2, ..., k$, $p_i - 1$ is divisible by 8. Therefore, the product of two or more terms of the form $p_i^2 - 1$ is divisible by 64.

$$P^2 = p_1^2 p_2^2 \dots p_k^2.$$
$$= (1 + p_1^2 - 1)(1 + p_2^2 - 1) \dots (1 + p_k^2 - 1)$$
$$= 1 + (p_1^2 - 1) + (p_2^2 - 1) + \dots (p_k^2 - 1)$$
$$+ \text{ terms divisible by 64.}$$

$$\therefore \quad P^2 - 1 \equiv (p_1^2 - 1) + (p_2^2 - 1) + \dots + (p_k^2 - 1) \bmod (64).$$

This, implies

$$\frac{P^2-1}{8} \equiv \frac{p_1^2-1}{8} + \frac{p_2^2-1}{8} + \dots + \frac{p_k^2-1}{8} \pmod 8. \qquad \dots\dots(1)$$

Now

$$\left(\frac{2}{P}\right) = \left(\frac{2}{p_1}\right)\cdot\left(\frac{2}{p_2}\right)\dots\left(\frac{2}{p_k}\right)$$

$$= (-1)^{\frac{p_1^2-1}{8} + \frac{p_2^2-1}{8} + \dots + \frac{p_k^2-1}{8}}$$

$$= (-1)^{\frac{P^2-1}{8} + 8t} \qquad \text{for some integer } t \text{ (using (1)]}$$

$$= (-1)^{\frac{P^2-1}{8}}$$

$$= (-1)^{\left[\frac{P^2+1}{4}\right]}.$$

Theorem 6 : If P and Q are relatively prime odd positive integers. Then

$$\left(\frac{Q}{P}\right) = (-1)^{\frac{P-1}{2}\cdot\frac{Q-1}{2}}\cdot\left(\frac{P}{Q}\right).$$

Proof : We have

$$\left(\frac{Q}{P}\right) = \left(\frac{Q}{p_1}\right)\cdot\left(\frac{Q}{p_2}\right)\dots\left(\frac{Q}{p_k}\right)$$

$$= (-1)^{\frac{p_1-1}{2}\cdot\frac{Q-1}{2}}\left(\frac{p_1}{Q}\right)\cdot(-1)^{\frac{p_2-1}{2}\cdot\frac{Q-1}{2}}\left(\frac{p_2}{Q}\right)\dots$$
$$\dots(-1)^{\frac{p_k-1}{2}\cdot\frac{Q-1}{2}}\left(\frac{p_k}{Q}\right)$$

$$= (-1)^{\frac{Q-1}{2}\left(\frac{p_1-1}{2} + \frac{p_2-1}{2} + \dots + \frac{p_k-1}{2}\right)}\left(\frac{P}{Q}\right).$$

$$= (-1)^{\frac{Q-1}{2}\left(\frac{P-1}{2}+2t\right)} \left(\frac{P}{Q}\right)$$

$$= (-1)^{\frac{Q-1}{2}\cdot\frac{P-1}{2}} \left(\frac{P}{Q}\right).$$

This is generalized quadratic reciprocity law.

Corollary 1 : If P and Q are relatively prime odd integers then

$$\left(\frac{Q}{P}\right)\left(\frac{P}{Q}\right) = (-1)^{\frac{P-1}{2}\cdot\frac{Q-1}{2}}.$$

Proof : We have

$$\left(\frac{Q}{P}\right) = (-1)^{\frac{P-1}{2}\cdot\frac{Q-1}{2}} \left(\frac{P}{Q}\right)$$

$$\Rightarrow \left(\frac{Q}{P}\right)\cdot\left(\frac{P}{Q}\right) = (-1)^{\frac{P-1}{2}\cdot\frac{Q-1}{2}} \left(\frac{P}{Q}\right)\cdot\left(\frac{P}{Q}\right)$$

$$= (-1)^{\frac{P-1}{2}\cdot\frac{Q-1}{2}} \left(\frac{P^2}{Q}\right)$$

$$= (-1)^{\frac{P-1}{2}\cdot\frac{Q-1}{2}}.$$

Example 1 : Find the value of the Jacobi symbol $\left(\frac{32}{15}\right)$.

Solution : We have

$$\left(\frac{32}{15}\right) = \left(\frac{32}{3\times 5}\right)$$

$$= \left(\frac{32}{3}\right)\cdot\left(\frac{32}{5}\right)$$

$$= \left(\frac{2}{3}\right)\cdot\left(\frac{2}{5}\right)$$

$$= (-1)^{\left[\frac{3+1}{4}\right]} \times (-1)^{\left[\frac{5+1}{4}\right]}$$

$$= (-1)^1 \times (-1)^1$$

$$= 1.$$

Ans

Example 2 : Find the value of Jacobi symbol $\left(\frac{22}{105}\right)$.

Solution : We have

$$\left(\frac{22}{105}\right) = \left(\frac{22}{3\times5\times7}\right)$$

$$= \left(\frac{22}{3}\right)\cdot\left(\frac{22}{5}\right)\cdot\left(\frac{22}{7}\right)$$

$$= \left(\frac{1}{3}\right)\cdot\left(\frac{2}{5}\right)\cdot\left(\frac{1}{7}\right)$$

$$= 1.(-1)^{\left[\frac{5+1}{4}\right]}$$

$$= -1.$$

EXERCISE

1. Solve the quadratic congruence
$$x^2 + 3x + 11 = 0 \pmod{13}.$$
(Ans. 6, 7)
2. Show that the Diophantine equation $x^2 = 3y^2 - 1$ has no solution.
3. Solve the quadratic congruence
$$x^2 \equiv 52 \pmod{101}$$
(Ans. 31, 70)
4. Show that the congruence
$$x^2 \equiv 18 \pmod{79} \text{ is solvable.}$$
5. Solve $x^{78} \equiv 1 \pmod{13}$. **(Ans. 1, 3, 4, 9, 10, 12)**
6. Prove that if p is an odd prime then
$$\sum_{r=1}^{p-1} \left(\frac{r}{p}\right) = 0.$$
7. Show that, $x^2 \equiv 2 \pmod{13}$ has no solution.
8. Prove that if p is an odd prime then
$$\sum_{r=1}^{p-2} \left(\frac{r(r+1)}{p}\right) = -1.$$
9. Solve the quadratic congruence
$$x^2 \equiv 91 \pmod{94}.$$
10. Solve the quadratic congruence
$$x^2 \equiv 145 \pmod{256}.$$
(Ans. 41, 215 (mod 2^8)]
11. Solve the quadratic congruence
$$x^2 + 5x + 6 \equiv 0 \pmod{5^3}.$$
[Ans. 122, 123 (mod 5^3)]
12. Evaluate the Legendre symbol $\left(\frac{461}{773}\right)$. **(Ans. – 1)**
13. Solve $x^2 \equiv 2 \pmod{7^3}$. **[Ans. x = 108, 135 (mod 7^3)]**
14. Solve the congruence
$$x^2 \equiv 9 \pmod{2^3.3.5^2}.$$
[Ans. 3, 147, 453, 597 (mod $2^3.3.5^2$)]

❑

CHAPTER 9 PERFECT NUMBERS

9.1 Introduction

In this chapter, we shall discuss some special numbers called perfect numbers. The name perfect number was given by Pythagorous.

Perfect numbers carried mystical and religious significance also besides their mathematical properties. Saint Augustine thought that God took six days to create the world as the perfection of the work is symbolized by the perfect number 6. Some commentators on the old Testament argued that the perfection of universe took 28 days.

Perfect numbers were also considered essential for numerical speculations substituted for scientific explanations of natural phenomena.

9.2 Perfect Numbers [C.C.S. (B.P.) 2006]

A positive integer n is called a perfect number if the sum of its proper divisors is equal to n. Thus, a positive integer n is a perfect number if $\sigma(n) = 2n$

For example, 6 is a perfect number because

$$6 = 1 + 2 + 3$$

Also $$\sigma(6) = 1 + 2 + 3 + 6 = 12 = 2.6$$

Similarly for $n = 496$ we have

$$496 = 2^4 \times 31$$

$$\therefore \quad \sigma(496) = \sigma(2^4 \times 31)$$

$$= \sigma(2^4).\sigma(31)$$

$$= \left(\frac{2^5 - 1}{2 - 1}\right).(31 + 1)$$

$$= 31.32$$

$$= 2.496$$

Hence, 296 is a perfect number.

Theorem 1 : (Euclid) : If $2^k - 1$ is a prime ($k > 1$) then $2^{k-1}(2^k - 1)$ is a perfect number.

Proof : Let $p = 2^k - 1$ be a prime. Let $n = 2^{k-1}(2^k - 1)$. We have to show that n is a perfect number. We have

$$\begin{aligned}\sigma(n) &= \sigma[2^{k-1}(2^k - 1)] \\ &= \sigma(2^{k-1}p) \\ &= \sigma(2^{k-1})\sigma(p) \qquad \text{[by multiplicativity of } \sigma] \\ &= (2^k - 1)(p + 1) \\ &= (2^k - 1)2^k \\ &= 2.2^{k-1}(2^k - 1) \\ &= 2n.\end{aligned}$$

This shows that $n = 2^{k-1}(2^k - 1)$ is a perfect number.

Euclid Type Number : A number of the form $2^{k-1}(2^k - 1)$ is called Euclid type number.

Theorem 2 : (Eulers) : Every even perfect number is of the form $2^{k-1}(2^k - 1)$ where $2^k - 1$ is a prime.

Proof : Let n be an even perfect number. Therefore $n = 2^{k-1} \times a$ for some $k > 1$ and for some odd integer a. Since $(2^{k-1}, a) = 1$ we have

$$\begin{aligned}\sigma(n) &= \sigma[2^{k-1} \times a] \\ &= \sigma(2^{k-1})\sigma(a) \\ &= (2^k - 1)\,\sigma(a). \qquad \text{.......(1)}\end{aligned}$$

Also n is a perfect number. Therefore.

$$\sigma(n) = 2n$$

$$\Rightarrow \quad (2^k - 1)\,\sigma(a) = 2^k \times a \qquad \text{.......(2)}$$

$$\Rightarrow \quad 2^k \mid \sigma(a) \qquad [\because (2^k - 1, 2^k) = 1]$$

$$\Rightarrow \quad \sigma(a) = 2^k \times q \quad \text{for some integer } q. \qquad \text{.......(3)}$$

Using this in (2) we have

$$(2^k - 1)\,2^k \times q = 2^k \times a$$

$$\Rightarrow \quad a = (2^k - 1)q. \qquad \text{.......(4)}$$

Now if $q > 1$ then a has at least four factors $1, 2^k - 1, q$ and $(2^k - 1)q$. Therefore

$$\begin{aligned}\sigma(a) &\geqslant 1 + 2^k - 1 + q + (2^k - 1)q \\ &> 2^k[1 + q]. \qquad \text{.......(5)}\end{aligned}$$

This contracticts (3). So $q = 1$ and therefore $a = 2^k - 1$. Hence,

$$n = 2^{k-1}a = 2^{k-1}(2^k - 1).$$

We have still to show that $2^k - 1$ is a prime. We have $a = 2^k - 1$ and $\sigma(a) = 2^k$. Therefore, $2^k - 1$ will have only two divisions 1 and $2^k - 1$. Hence, $a = 2^k - 1$ is a prime.

Proved

Theorem 3 : If $a^k - 1$ is a prime ($a > 0, k \geqslant 2$) then $a = 2$ and k is a prime.

Proof : We have

$$a^k - 1 = (a-1)(a^{k-1} + a^{k-2} + \ldots + a + 1).$$

Since $a > 0$ we have $a \geqslant 1$ and therefore

$$a^{k-1} + a^{k-2} + \ldots + a + 1 \geqslant a + 1 \geqslant 2.$$

By hypothesis $a^k - 1$ is a prime. Therefore, the other factor

$$a - 1 = 1$$

or $$a = 2.$$

Suppose if possible k is a composite number.

Then $k = rt$ with $r, t > 1$. Thus,

$$\begin{aligned} a^k - 1 &= a^{rt} - 1 \\ &= (a^r)^t - 1 \\ &= (a^r - 1)(a^{r(t-1)} + a^{r(t-2)} + \ldots + a^r + 1). \end{aligned}$$

Each factor on the right hand side is greater than 1 which is not possible because $a^k - 1$ is a prime. Thus, we have a contradiction. Hence, k must be a prime.

Proved.

Theorem 4 : Every even perfect number has the last digit either 6 or 8.

(C.C.S.U. 2004)

Proof : Let n be an even perfect number. It is of the form $2^{k-1}(2^k - 1)$ for some prime k which is of the form $4q + 1$ or $4q + 3$. If $k = 4q + 1$ then $n = 2^{4q}[2^{4q+1} - 1]$ $= 16^q[2.16^q - 1]$. The last digit of 16^q is 6 and that of $(2.16^q - 1)$ is 1. Therefore, the last digit of n in this case is 6.

If $k = 4q + 3$ then $n = 2^{4q+3-1}[2^{4q+3} - 1]$

$$= 4.16^q[8.16^q - 1].$$

The last digit of 4.16^q is 4 and that of $8.16^q - 1$ is 7. Therefore, the last digit of n is 8.

Proved

Theorem 5 : Every even perfect number $n = 2^{k-1}[2^k - 1]$ is the sum of first $2^{(k-1)/2}$ odd cubes.

Proof : Since n is a perfect number k is an odd prime and consequently $\frac{k-1}{2} = a$ (say) is an integer. Now the sum of first a odd cubes

$$= 1^3 + 3^3 + \ldots + (2a-1)^3.$$

$$= \sum_{r=1}^{a} (2r-1)^3$$

$$= \sum_{r=1}^{a} [8r^3 - 12r^2 + 6r - 1]$$

$$= 8\sum_{r=1}^{a} r^3 - 12\sum_{r=1}^{a} r^2 + 6\sum_{r=1}^{a} r - \sum_{r=1}^{a} 1$$

$$= 8\frac{a^2(a+1)^2}{4} - \frac{12a(a+1)(2a+1)}{6} + \frac{6a(a+1)}{2} - a$$

$$= a^2[2a^2 - 1]$$

$$= 2^{k-1}[2^k - 1]$$

$$= n.$$ **Proved.**

List of perfect numbers known so far :

Perfect Number	Number of digits
$2[2^2 - 1] = 6$	1
$2^2[2^3 - 1] = 28$	2
$2^4[2^5 - 1] = 496$	3
$2^6[2^7 - 1] = 8126$	4
$2^{12}[2^{13} - 1] = 33550336$	8
$2^{16}[2^{17} - 1]$	10
$2^{18}[2^{19} - 1]$	12
$2^{30}[2^{31} - 1]$	19
$2^{60}[2^{61} - 1]$	37
$2^{88}[2^{89} - 1]$	54
$2^{106}[2^{107} - 1]$	65
$2^{126}[2^{127} - 1]$	77
$2^{520}[2^{521} - 1]$	314
$2^{605}[2^{606} - 1]$	366
$2^{1278}[2^{1279} - 1]$	770
$2^{2202}[2^{2203} - 1]$	1327
$2^{2280}[2^{2281} - 1]$	1373
$2^{3216}[2^{3217} - 1]$	1937
$2^{4252}[2^{4253} - 1]$	2561
$2^{4422}[2^{4423} - 1]$	2663
$2^{9688}[2^{9689} - 1]$	5834
$2^{9940}[2^{9941} - 1]$	5985

$2^{11212}[2^{11213} - 1]$	6751
$2^{19936}[2^{19937} - 1]$	12003
$2^{21700}[2^{21701} - 1]$	13066
$2^{23208}[2^{23209} - 1]$	13973
$2^{44496}[2^{44497} - 1]$	26790
$2^{86242}[2^{86243} - 1]$	51924
$2^{110502}[2^{110503} - 1]$	66530
$2^{132048}[^{132049} - 1]$	79502
$2^{216090}[2^{216091} - 1]$	130100
$2^{756838}[2^{756839} - 1]$	455663

Example 1 : Show that the integer $n = 2^{10}(2^{11} - 1)$ is not a perfect number.

Solution : We have

$$\sigma(n) = \sigma[2^{10}(2^{11} - 1)]$$

$$= \sigma[2^{10}.23.89] \qquad [\because \quad 2^{11} - 1 = 23.89]$$

$$= \sigma[2^{10}]\sigma(23)\ \sigma(89)$$

$$= [2^{11} - 1].24.90$$

$$\neq 2^{10}(2^{11} - 1)$$

$$= n.$$

Therefore $n = 2^{10}(2^{11} - 1)$ is not a perfect number.

Example 2 . If n is an even perfect number then prove that $\sum_{d|n} \frac{1}{d} = 2$.

Solution : We have

$$\sum_{d|n} \frac{1}{d} = \sum_{d|n} \left(\frac{d}{n}\right)$$

$$= \frac{1}{n} \sum_{d|n} d$$

$$= \frac{\sigma(n)}{n}$$

$$= \frac{2n}{n} \qquad [\because n \text{ is a perfect number}]$$

$$= 2.$$

Example 3 : Let $n = 2^{k-1}(2^k - 1), k \geqslant 2$ be any even perfect number. Then show that

$$\prod_{d|n} d = n^k$$

Solution : Let $n = 2^{k-1}(2^k - 1), k \geqslant 2$ be any even perfect number. We know that

$$\prod_{d|n} d = n^{\frac{\tau(n)}{2}} \quad ....(1)$$

Now $$\tau(n) = \tau[2^{k-1}(2^k - 1)]$$
$$= k.2$$
$$= 2k.$$

Substituting the value of $\tau(n)$ in (1) we get

$$\prod_{d|n} d = n^{\frac{2k}{2}}$$
$$= n^k.$$

Proved

Example 4 : Find the last two digits of the perfect number
$$n = 2^{19936}[2^{19937} - 1].$$

Solution : We have

$$n = 2^{19936}[2^{19937} - 1]$$
$$= (2^4)^{4984}[2(2^4)^{4984} - 1]$$
$$= 16^{4984}(2.16^{4984} - 1).$$

Now $$2^{19936} = 16^{4984} \equiv 36 \pmod{100}$$
$$2^{19937} - 1 = 2.2^{19936} - 1 \equiv 71 \pmod{100}.$$

Hence, $n = 36.71 \pmod{100} = 56 \pmod{100}$.

9.3 Mersenne Primes

[C.C.S. (B.P.) 2006]

The numbers $M_n = 2^n - 1, n > 1$ are called *Mersenne numbers*. A Mersenne number which is a prime is called a *Mersenne prime*.

Thus, if M_k is a Mersenne number then $2^{k-1} M_k$ is a perfect number. There is one-one correspondence between the Mersenne primes and even perfect numbers. M_2, M_3, M_5, M_7 are few Mersenne primes, 32 Mersenne primes in all are known so far . The last and the largest Mersenne prime was discovered by British scientists in 1992 on a Honey Well Computer. It is still not decided whether Mersenne numbers are finite or infinite.

Theorem 1 : (Fermat) : If $p > 2$ is a prime then any prime divisor of M_p must be of the form $2kp + 1$ for $k = 1, 2, 3, ...$

Proof : Let q be a prime divisor of M_p. Then $q \mid (2^p - 1)$ obviously q is an odd integer. By Fermat's theorem we have $2^{q-1} \equiv 1 \pmod{q}$ *i.e.*, $q \mid (2^{q-1} - 1)$. If $d = (p, q - 1)$ then $d \mid p$ and $d \mid (q - 1)$. Since p is a prime we have $d = p$ or $d = 1$. If $d = p$ and $q = dt + 1$ then t must be even (as p and q both are odd). Therefore, $q = 2pk + 1$ for some $k = 1, 2, ...$

If $d = 1$ then

$$(2^p - 1, 2^{q-1} - 1) = 2^{(p,\, q-1)} - 1$$
$$= 2 - 1 = 1$$

This is false because q divides $2^p - 1$ and $2^{q-1} - 1$. So $d \neq 1$.

Theorem 2 : If $q = 2m + 1$ is prime then $q \mid M_m$ provided $q \equiv 1 \pmod 8$ or $q \equiv 7 \pmod 8$.

Proof : We know that

$$\left(\frac{2}{q}\right) = 1$$

when $q \equiv 1 \pmod 8$ or $q \equiv 7 \pmod 8$.

This gives

$$2^m \equiv 1 \pmod q$$

or $\quad 2^{\left(\frac{q-1}{2}\right)} \equiv 1 \pmod q$

$\Rightarrow \quad q \mid M_m$.

Thus, we see that $q \mid M_m$ when $q \equiv 1 \pmod 8$

or $\quad q \equiv 7 \pmod 8$.

Theorem 3 : For $p > 2$ every prime divisor of M_p is of the form $8k \pm 1$.

Proof : Since M_p is an odd number, any prime divisor q of it is also odd.

Let, $q = 2m + 1$

If $a = 2^{(p+1)/2}$ then

$$a^2 - 2 = 2^{p+1} - 2$$
$$= 2M_p$$
$$\equiv 0 \pmod q \qquad [\because q \mid M_p \Rightarrow q \mid 2M_p]$$

$\Rightarrow \quad a^2 \equiv 2 \pmod q$

$\Rightarrow \quad a^{2m} \equiv 2^m \pmod q$

$\Rightarrow \quad a^{q-1} \equiv 2^m \pmod q$. ....(1)

Since q is an odd integer, we have

$$(a, q) = 1$$

Therefore, $\quad a^{q-1} \equiv 1 \pmod q$. ....(2)

From (1) and (2) we have

$$2^m \equiv 1 \pmod q$$

$$\Rightarrow \quad q \mid M_m$$

Hence, $q \equiv \pm 1 \pmod 8$ or $q = 8k \pm 1$

Theorem 4 : If p and $q = 2p + 1$ ar both odd primes and $p \equiv 3 \pmod 4$ then $q \mid M_p$

Proof : Since p is an odd prime it is either of the form $4k + 1$ or $4k + 3$.

If $p = 4k + 1$ then $q = 8k + 7$. Hence, by theorem 2 $q \mid M_p$

Theorem 5 : (Euler) : If n is an odd perfect number then

$$n = p_1^{a_1} p_2^{2a_2} p_3^{2a_3} \ldots p_r^{2a_r}$$

where p_i are distinct odd primes and $p_1 \equiv a_1 \equiv 1 \pmod 4$.

Proof : Let, $n = p_1^{a_1} p_2^{a_2} \ldots p_r^{a_r}$ be the prime factorization of n. Since n is a perfect number, we have

$$2n = \sigma(n)$$
$$= \sigma(p_1^{a_1} p_2^{a_2} \ldots p_r^{a_r}]$$
$$= \sigma(p_1^{a_1})\, \sigma(p_2^{a_2}) \ldots \sigma(p_r^{a_r}).$$

Since n is an odd number we have

$$n \equiv 1 \pmod 4 \quad \text{or} \quad n \equiv 3 \pmod 4$$

$$\Rightarrow \quad 2n \equiv 2 \pmod 4.$$

This shows that $\sigma(n) = 2n$ is divisible by 2 but not by 4. This implies that one of the $\sigma(p_i^{a_i})$ [say $\sigma(p_1^{a_1})$] must be an even integer (not divisible by 4) and the remaining $\sigma(p_i^{a_i})$ are odd integer.

Now for a given p_i, we have

$$p_i \equiv 1 \pmod 4 \quad \text{and} \quad p_i \equiv 3 \pmod 4$$
$$\equiv -1 \pmod 4.$$

Therefore,

$$\sigma(p_i^{a_i}) = 1 + p_i + p_i^2 + \ldots p_i^{a_i}$$
$$= 1 - 1 + (-1)^2 + \ldots (-1)^{a_i} \pmod 4$$
$$= \begin{cases} 0 \pmod 4 & \text{when } a_i \text{ is odd} \\ 1 \pmod 4 & \text{when } a_i \text{ is even} \end{cases}$$

Since $\sigma(p_1^{a_1}) \equiv 2 \pmod 4$, we have $p_1 \not\equiv 3 \pmod 4$ *i.e.*, $p_1 \equiv 1 \pmod 4$.

Also the congruence $\sigma(p_i^{a_i}) \equiv 0 \pmod 4$ implies that $4 \mid \sigma(p_i^{a_i})$. This is not possible. This gives that if $p_i \equiv 3 \pmod 4$ for $i = 2, \ldots r$ then a_i is an even integer.

If $p_i \equiv 1 \pmod 4$ then

$$\sigma(p_i^{a_i}) = 1 + p_i + p_i^2 + ... p_i^{a_i}$$
$$= 1 + 1 + 1^2 + ... 1^{a_r} \pmod 4$$
$$= a_i + 1 \pmod 4$$

Now $\sigma(p_i^{a_i}) \equiv 2 \pmod 4$ gives $a_i \equiv 1 \pmod 4$

For $\sigma(p_i^{a_i}) \equiv 1$ or $3 \pmod 4$ we have

$a_i \equiv 0$ or $2 \pmod 4$. Therefore a_i is even.

Thus, in any case a_i is even.

Corollary : If n is an odd perfect number then it is of the form

$$n = p^a m^2$$

where p is a prime, $p \nmid m$ and $p \equiv a \equiv 1 \pmod 4$.

Example 1 : Show that the Mersenne number M_{19} is a prime.

Solution : Let a prime p divides M_{19}. Then p is of the form

$$p = 2 \times 19 \times k + 1$$
$$= 38k + 1 \quad ....(1)$$

for some k.

Also we have

$$724 < \sqrt{(M_{19})} \quad ....(2)$$

From (1) we can show that primes less than 724 are 191, 229, 457 and 647. None of these primes divides M_{19}. Therefore M_{19} is a prime.

Example 2 : Show that M_{29} is a composite number.

Solution : Let a prime p divides M_{29}. Then p is of the form

$$p = 2 \times 29k + 1$$
$$= 58k + 1 \quad ....(1)$$

for some k. Putting $k = 1, 2, 3, 4, 5$ in (1) we get $p = 59, 117, 175, 233, 291$ respectively. Out of these values of p, 59 and 233 are prime. By actual division we can see that 233 divides M_{29}. Hence, M_{29} is a composite number.

Example 3 : Find the smallest divisor of M_{11}.

Solution : Let a prime p divides M_{11}. Then p is of the form

$$p = 2 \times 11k + 1$$
$$= 22k + 1$$

For $k = 1, p = 23$ is a prime. We can see that 23 divides M_{11}. Therefore 23 is the smallest divisor of M_{11}.

9.4 Fermat Number

[C.C.S. (B.P.) 2006

An integer of the form

$$F_m = 2^{2^m} + 1, m \geqslant 0$$

is called Fermat number.

If F_m is a prime, it is called a Fermat prime. $F_0 = 3$, $F_1 = 5$, $F_2 = 17$, $F_3 = 25$ $F_4 = 65, 537$ are the only Fermat prime known so far. Euler in 1732 found th $F_5 = 4, 294, 967, 297$ is divisible by 641. Thus, F_5 is a composite number.

Theorem 1 : The Fermat number F_5 is divisible by 641.

Proof : If we take $a = 2^7$ and $b = 5$ then

$$\begin{aligned} 1 + ab &= 1 + 2^7.5 \\ &= 1 + 640 \\ &= 641 \end{aligned}$$

Also

$$\begin{aligned} 1 + ab - b^4 &= 1 + (a - b^3)\,b \\ &= 1 + (2^7 - 5^3)5 \\ &= 1 + (128 - 125)5 \\ &= 1 + 3.5 \\ &= 1 + 15 \\ &= 16 \\ &= 2^4 \end{aligned}$$

Now

$$\begin{aligned} F_5 &= 2^{2^5} + 1 \\ &= 2^{32} + 1 \\ &= 2^4.2^{28} + 1 \\ &= 2^4.(2^7)^4 + 1 \\ &= 2^4\,a^4 + 1 \\ &= (1 + ab - b^4)\,a^4 + 1 \\ &= (1 + ab)a^4 + 1 - a^4 b^4 \\ &= (1 + ab)\,[a^4 + (1 - ab)(1 + a^2b^2)] \\ &= 641[a^4 + (1 - ab)(1 + a^2b^2)] \end{aligned}$$

This shows that $641 \mid F_5$. **Prov**

Theorem 2 : For integers $m > n \geqslant 0$. $(F_m, F_n) = 1$ *i.e.*, Fermat numbers a relatively prime. (C.C.S.U. 200

Proof : Let $d = (F_m, F_n)$ and $m > n \geqslant 0$. Then d is odd as F_m and F_n are odd intege

Let, $x = 2^n$ and $r = 2^{m-n}$ then

$$\frac{F_m - 2}{F_n} = \frac{2^{2^m} + 1 - 2}{2^{2^n} + 1}$$

$$= \frac{(2^{2^n})^{2^{m-n}} - 1}{2^{2^n} + 1}$$

$$= \frac{x^r - 1}{x + 1}$$

$$= x^{r-1} - x^{r-2} + \ldots - 1.$$

This shows that $F_n \mid (F_m - 2)$.

Further $d \mid F_n$ impels $d \mid (F_m - 2)$. Also $d \mid F_m$. Therefore $d \mid 2$. But d is an odd nteger so $d = 1$. Thus we have $(F_m, F_n) = 1$ **Proved.**

heorem 3 : For each $m > 0$ show that,

$$F_{m+1} = F_0 F_1 F_2 \ldots F_m + 2.$$

roof : We shall prove this result by mathematical induction.

For $m = 1$ we have

$$\text{R.H.S.} = F_0 F_1 + 2$$

$$= (2^{2^0} + 1)(2^{2^1} + 1) + 2$$

$$= (2 + 1)(4 + 1) + 2$$

$$= 17$$

$$= (2^{2^2} + 1)$$

$$= F_2$$

$$= \text{L.H.S.}$$

This shows that the result is true for $m = 1$.

Let, $$F_k = F_0 F_1 \ldots F_{k-1} + 2. \quad \ldots\ldots(1)$$

Then $$F_{k+1} = 2^{2^{k+1}} + 1$$

$$= (2^{2^k})^2 + 1$$

$$= (F_k - 1)^2 + 1$$

$$= F_k^2 - 2F_k + 1 + 1$$

$$= F_k[F_k - 2] + 2$$

$$= F_k(F_0 F_1 \ldots F_{k-1}) + 2$$

$$= F_0F_1 \ldots F_k + 2.$$

This shows that the result is true for $m = k$ when it is true for $m = k - 1$. Hence, by mathematical induction the given result is true for all integral values of m.

Theorem 4 : (Pepin) : For $m \geqslant 1$ the Fermat number $F_m = 2^{2^m} + 1$ is prime iff $3^{(F_m - 1)/2} \equiv -1 \pmod{F_m}$

Proof : First we assume that F_m, $m \geqslant 1$ is a prime. Then by quadratic reciprocity law, we have

$$\left(\frac{3}{F_m}\right) = \left(\frac{F_m}{3}\right) = \left(\frac{2}{3}\right) = -1.$$

We have

$$F_n \equiv (-1)^{2^n} + 1 = 2 \pmod 3.$$

Applying Euler's criterion, we have

$$3^{(F_n - 1)/2} \equiv -1 \pmod{F_n}.$$

Conversely suppose

$$3^{(F_m - 1)/2} \equiv -1 \pmod{F_m}. \quad \ldots\ldots(1)$$

Then $$3^{F_m - 1} \equiv 1 \pmod{F_m}.$$

Also for any prime p divisor of F_m we

$$3^{F_m - 1} \equiv \pmod p.$$

Let r be the order of 3 modulo p. Then $r \mid F_m - 1 \Rightarrow r \mid 2^{2^m}$. Therefore order of r should be 2.

Now $$3^r \equiv 1 \pmod p$$

$$\Rightarrow \quad 3^{2^{2^n - 1}} \equiv 1 \pmod p \quad \text{[By repeated squaring}$$

or $$3^{(F_m - 1)/2} \equiv 1 \pmod p. \quad \ldots\ldots(2$$

From (1) and (2) we have

$$1 \equiv -p \pmod p$$

$$\Rightarrow \quad p = 2$$

which is a contradiction.

Therefore the only possibility is that

$$r = 2^{2^m} = F_m - 1$$

By Fermats theorem we have

$$r \leqslant p - 1$$

which implies

$$F_m = k + 1 \leqslant p.$$

Since $p \mid F_m$ we have $F_m \geqslant p$

Thus, we have -

$$F_m = p$$

Therefore, F_m is a prime.

Theorem 5 : Any prime divisor p of the Fermat number $F_m = 2^{2^m} + 1, m \geqslant 0$ is of the form $p = k.2^{m+2} + 1$.

Proof : Since p is a prime divisor of F_m, we have

$$2^{2^m} \equiv -1 \pmod{p}$$

$$\Rightarrow \quad 2^{2^{m+1}} \equiv 1 \pmod{p}. \qquad \text{[On squaring]}$$

Let a be the order of 2 modulo p. then

$$a \mid 2^{m+1}$$

Now a cannot be of the form

$$a = 2^r, \quad 1 \leqslant r \leqslant m$$

otherwise

$$2^{2^m} \equiv 1 \pmod{p}.$$

This provides a contradiction that $p = 2$. This gives that

$$a = 2^{m+1}.$$

We know that the order of 2 modulo p divides $\phi(p) = p - 1$.

Therefore $2^{m+1} \mid p - 1$ and consequently for $m \geqslant 2$, $p \equiv 1 \pmod{8}$ and $(2/p) = 1$

By the application of Euler's criterion, we have

$$2^{(p-1)/2} \equiv (2/p) = 1 \pmod{p}$$

Hence, $\quad a \mid (p-1)/2 \quad$ or $\quad 2^{m+1} \mid (p-1)/2$

$$\Rightarrow \quad 2^{m+2} \mid (p-1)$$

$$\Rightarrow \quad p \equiv k.2^{m+2} + 1$$

where k is an integer.

Theorem 6 : There are infinitely many primes. **(C.C.S.U. 2005)**

Proof : Every pair of Fermat numbers are relatively prime and for each Fermat number F_n there corresponds a prime p_n which divides. F_n and does not divide other Fermat number. Thus, corresponding to any Fermat number there is a prime that divides that

Fermat number. Since Fermat numbers are infinite, the corresponding primes are also infinite.

F-number : A composite number n is called an F-number if for each a relatively prime to n.

$$a^{n-1} \equiv 1 \pmod{n}$$

R. D. Carmichael first showed the existence of such numbers. The smallest F-number is 561.

Example 1 : Prove that the last digit of F_n, $n \geqslant 3$ is 7.

Solution : For $n = 3$ we have

$$F_3 = 2^{2^3} + 1$$
$$= 256 + 1 = 257$$

Thus, for $n = 3$ the last digit of F_3 is 7. Let for $n = m$ the last digit is 7. *i.e.*, For $F_m = 2^{2^m} + 1$. The last digit is 7.

Then $$F_{m+1} = 2^{2^{m+1}} + 1$$
$$= 2^{2^m.2} + 1$$

$\Rightarrow$ the last digit of 2^{2^m} is 6.

Now $$F_{m+1} = 2^{2^{m+1}} + 1$$
$$= 2^{2^m.2} + 1$$
$$= (2^{2^m})^2 + 1.$$

Since the last digit of 2^{2^m} is 6, the last digit of $(2^{2^m})^2$ will be 6 and consequently the last digit of $F_{m+1} = (2^{2^m})^2 + 1$ will be 7. Hence by mathematical induction the last digit of F_n, $n \geqslant 3$ is 7

Example 2 : From the congruence

$$\mathbf{5.2^7 \equiv -1 \pmod{641}}$$

deduce that $2^{32} + 1 \equiv 0 \pmod{641}$. Hence, $641 \mid F_5$.

Solution : We have

$$5.2^7 \equiv -1 \pmod{641}$$

On squaring, we get

$$25.2^{14} \equiv 1 \pmod{641}$$

Again squaring we get

$$625.2^{28} \equiv 1 \pmod{641}$$

or $$2^{28} \equiv \frac{1}{625} \pmod{641}$$

or $$2^{28} \times 2^4 \equiv \frac{2^4}{625} \pmod{641}$$

$$\text{or} \qquad 2^{32} \equiv \frac{16}{625} \pmod{641}$$

$$\equiv \frac{16 - 641 \times 1}{625} \pmod{641}$$

$$\equiv -1 \pmod{641}$$

$$\Rightarrow \quad 2^{32} + 1 \equiv 0 \pmod{641}$$

$$\Rightarrow \quad 641 \mid (2^{32} + 1)$$

$$\Rightarrow \quad 641 \mid F_5.$$

Example 3 : Find the last two digits of the perfect number

$$n = 2^{19936}[2^{19937} - 1]$$

Solution :

$$n = 2^{19936}[2^{19937} - 1]$$

$$= (2^4)^{4984}[2.(2^4)^{4984} - 1]$$

$$= 16^{4984}[2.16^{4984} - 1].$$

Now $\quad 16^{4984} \equiv 36 \pmod{100}$

and $\quad 2.16^{4984} - 1 \equiv 71 \pmod{100}.$

Therefore, $\quad n \equiv 36.71 \pmod{100}$

$$\equiv 56 \pmod{100}.$$

Thus, last two digits of the given perfect number are 56.

9.5 Pythagorean Triples

A **Pythagorean triple** is a set of three integers x, y and z, such that

$$x^2 + y^2 = z^2$$

The triple is said to be **primitive** if $(x, y, z) = 1$. For example 3, 4, 5 and 5, 12, 13 are Pythagorean triples.

Note : If x, y, z is a Pythagorean triple and $d = (x, y, z)$ then $x_1 = dx$, $y_1 = dy$ and $z_1 = dz$ is also a Pythagorean triples and it is primitive Pythagorean triple.

Lemma 1 : If x, y, z is a primitive Pythagorean triple then one of x or y is even and the other is odd.

Proof : Suppose x and y are both even, then $2 \mid x$ and $2 \mid y \Rightarrow 4 \mid x^2 + y^2 \Rightarrow 4 \mid z^2 \Rightarrow 2 \mid z$. This is not possible because $(x, y, z) = 1$. Similarly, if x and y are both odd then $x^2 \equiv 1 \pmod 4$ and $y^2 \equiv 1 \pmod 4$

$$\Rightarrow x^2 + y^2 = z^2 \equiv 2 \pmod 4$$

This is impossible because square of any integer is either congruent to 0 or 1 modulo 4. Hence, either x or y is even and the other is odd.

Lemma 2 : If $ab = c^2$ and $(a, b) = 1$ then a and b are also squares.

Proof : Let $a > 1$, $b > 1$ and

$$a = p_1^{r_1}.p_2^{r_2}....\ p_l^{r_l} \quad \text{and} \quad b = q_1^{s_1}.q_2^{s_2}\ ....\ q_k^{s_k}$$

be the prime factorizations of a and b. Since $(a, b) = 1$, all p_i and q_j are distinct primes and integers r_i and s_j are $\geqslant 1$.

Now $ab = p_1^{r_1}.p_2^{r_2}\ ....\ p_l^{r_l}.q_1^{s_1}.q_2^{s_2}\ ....\ q_k^{s_k} = c^2$ is a square. Therefore, each r_i and s_j must be even integers. This shows that a and b both are squares.

Theorem 1 : All solutions of Pythagorean equations

$$x^2 + y^2 = z^2 \qquad ....(1)$$

satisfying the conditions

$$(x, y, z) = 1,\ 2 \mid x,\ x > 0,\ y > 0,\ z > 0$$

are given by

$$x = 2rs,\ y = r^2 - s^2,\ z = r^2 + s^2.$$

For integers $r > s > 0$ such that $(r, s) = 1$ and $r \equiv s \pmod 2$.

(C.C.S. 2004)

Proof : Let x, y, z be a primitive Pythagorean triple. Then one of x and y is even and the other is odd. Let x be even. Then y and z both are odd. This gives that $z - y$ and $z + y$ both are even *i.e.* $\frac{z-y}{2}$ and $\frac{z+y}{2}$ are integers

Now $\qquad x^2 + y^2 = z^2$

$$\Rightarrow \quad x^2 = z^2 - y^2$$

$$\Rightarrow \quad \frac{x^2}{4} = \frac{(z-y)(z+y)}{4}$$

$$\Rightarrow \quad \left(\frac{x}{2}\right)^2 = \frac{(z-y)}{2}.\frac{(z+y)}{2}$$

If $\qquad d = \left(\frac{z-y}{2}, \frac{z+y}{2}\right)$

then $\quad d \left| \frac{z-y}{2}, d \right| \frac{z+y}{2}$

$$\Rightarrow \quad d \left| \frac{z-y}{2} + \frac{z+y}{2}, d \right| \frac{z+y}{2} - \frac{z-y}{2}$$

$$\Rightarrow d \mid z,\ d \mid y.$$

But $(x, y, z) = 1 \Rightarrow (y, z) = 1$.

Therefore, $\quad d = 1$.

By lemma 2, $\frac{z-y}{2}$ and $\frac{z+y}{2}$ are perfect square. Let $\frac{z+y}{2} = r^2$ and $\frac{z-y}{2} = s^2$. for some positive integers r and s. Obviously

$$(r, s) = 1, (r > s > 0 \text{ and}$$
$$x = 2rs$$
$$y = r^2 - s^2$$
and $$z = r^2 + s^2.$$

Since z is odd, one of r and s is even and the other is odd.

Conversely let, r and s be any two integers satisfying the conditions. Then

$$\begin{aligned} x^2 + y^2 &= (2rs)^2 + (r^2 - s^2)^2 \\ &= 4r^2s^2 + r^4 + s^4 - 2r^2s^2 \\ &= r^4 + s^4 + 2r^2s^2 \\ &= (r^2 + s^2)^2 \\ &= z^2. \end{aligned}$$

If $d = (x, y, z)$ then

$$\begin{aligned} d \mid x, y, z &\Rightarrow d \mid 2rs, r^2 - s^2, r^2 + s^2 \\ &\Rightarrow d \mid r^2 - s^2 + r^2 + s^2 \\ &\Rightarrow d \mid 2r^2 \end{aligned}$$

and $$d \mid (r^2 + s^2) - (r^2 - s^2)$$
$$\Rightarrow d \mid 2s^2.$$

Thus, $$d \mid 2r^2, 2rs, 2s^2.$$

If p is a prime divisor of d then

$$p \mid 2r^2, 2rs, 2s^2$$
$$\Rightarrow \quad p \mid 2 \text{ or } p \mid r^2 \text{ and } p \mid s^2$$
$$\Rightarrow \quad p \mid 2 \text{ or } p \mid r \text{ and } p \mid s.$$

Now $p \neq 2$ because y or z are odd. If $p \mid r$ (and $p \mid s$). Then it is a contradiction because $(r, s) = 1$. Thus, we have $d = 1$. Therefore, $x = 2rs$, $y = r^2 - s^2$ and $z = r^2 + s^2$ is a primitive solution of (1).

Theorem 2 : If x, y, z is a solution of $x^2 + y^2 = z^2$ and $(x, y, z) = 1$ then one of x, y is a multiple of 3 and the other a multiple of 4. Also one of x, y, z is a multiple of 5. Hence, xyz is a multiple of 60.

Proof : Suppose if possible both x, y are not multiple of 3. Also an integer not a multiple of 3 is of the form $3n \pm 1$. Now

$$(3n \pm 1)^2 = 9n^2 \pm 6n + 1$$
$$= 3(3n^2 \pm 2n) + 1$$
$$= 3m + 1.$$

Therefore

$x^2 + y^2$ is of the form $3m - 1$ which is not a square. This is contradiction because $x^2 + y^2 = z^2$. Hence one of x, y is a multiple of 3.

Further, suppose if possible both x, y are not a multiple of 4. We know that an integer not a multiple of 4 can be written as un ± 1 or ± 2. Now

$$(4n \pm 1)^2 = 16n^2 \pm 8n + 1$$
$$= 8(2n^2 \pm n) + 1$$
$$= 8m + 1$$

and
$$(4n \pm 2)^2 = 16n^2 \pm 16n + 4$$
$$= 8(2n^2 \pm 2n) + 4$$
$$= 8m + 4.$$

Therefore, if x, y are $4n \pm 1$ or $4n \pm 2$ then $x^2 + y^2$ is of the form $8m + 2$ or $8m + 5$ which are not square. Hence one of x, y must be a multiple of 4.

Finally, if none of x, y, z is a multiple of 5, then they must have the forms $5n \pm 1$, $5n \pm 2$. Now

$$(5n \pm 1)^2 = 25n^2 \pm 10n + 1$$
$$= 5(5n^2 \pm 2n) + 1$$
$$= 5m + 1$$

and
$$(5n \pm 2)^2 = 25n^2 \pm 20n + 4$$
$$= 5(5n^2 \pm 4n + 1) - 1$$
$$= 5m - 1.$$

Thus, $x^2 + y^2$ is of the form $5k + 2$, $5k - 1$, $5k$. In the first two cases $x^2 + y^2$ is not a square. In the third case z is a multiple of 5. These contradicts the assumption and therefore one of x, y, z must be a multiple of 5.

Theorem 3 : The general solution of the equation

$x^2 + y^2 + z^2 = w^2$, $(x, y, z, w) = 1$ is given by

$x = a^2 - b^2 + c^2 - d^2$, $y = 2ab + 2cd$,

$z = 2ad - 2bc$ and $w = a^2 + b^2 + c^2 + d^2$.

Proof : Let y and z are both even and x and w both are odd. Let $\left(\frac{y}{2}, \frac{z}{2}\right) = r$, $(x, w) = s$, $y = 2ry$, $z = 2sz_1$, $x = sx_1$ and $w = sw_1$. Since x_1 and w_1 are odd, the given equation reduces to

$$r^2({y_1}^2 + {z_1}^2) = s^2 \left(\frac{w_1^2 - x_1^2}{2}\right)$$

$$= s^2\left(\frac{w_1 + x_1}{2}\right)\left(\frac{w_1 - x_1}{2}\right).$$

Also $(r, s) = 1$,

$$\left(\frac{w_1 + x_1}{2}, \frac{w_1 - x_1}{2}\right) = (w_1, x_1) = 1.$$

Therefore, $r = r_1.r_2,\ (r_1, r_2) = 1.$

$$\Rightarrow \quad r_1^2 \left| \left(\frac{w_1 + x_1}{2}\right),\ r_2^2 \right| \left(\frac{w_1 - x_1}{2}\right).$$

Further

$$y_1^2 + z_1^2 = s^2\left(\frac{w_1 + x_1}{2r_1^2}\right)\left(\frac{w_1 - x_1}{2r_2^2}\right).$$

Since odd prime factor of $y_1^2 + z_1^2$ are of the form $4k + 1$ which can be expressed as the sum of two squares numbers. So there exist integers a_1, b_1, c_1 and d_1 such that

$$\frac{w_1 + x_1}{2r_1^2} = a_1^2 + b_1^2 = c_1^2 + d_1^2$$

$\therefore$ $$y_1^2 + z_1^2 = (a_1^2 + b_1^2)(c_1^2 + d_1^2).$$

But $$y^2 + z_1^2 = [y_1^2 - \{\sqrt{(-1)}\, z_1\}^2]$$
$$= [y_1 + \sqrt{(-1)}\, z_1]\,[y_1 - \sqrt{(-1)}\, z_1]$$

Thus, we have

$$y_1 + (-1)\, z_1 = [a_1 + \sqrt{(-1)}\, z_1]$$

9.6 Other Diophantine Equation

Example 1 : Show that the positive integral solution of $x^{-1} + y^{-1} = z^{-1}$, (x, y, z) is of the form

$$x = a(a + b,\ y = b(a + b),\ z = ab.$$

Solution : Let (x, y, z) be the solution of the given equation and let $x = ca$, $y = cb$, $(a, b) = 1$

Then $$z^{-1} = x^{-1} + y^{-1}$$
$$= \frac{1}{ca} + \frac{1}{cb}$$
$$= \frac{a + b}{cab}.$$

This gives $$z = \frac{cab}{a + b}.$$

Since $(a, b) = 1$, we have $(ab, a + b) = 1$. So $(a + b) \mid c$. Let $c = c_1(a + b)$, then $z = c_1 ab$.

Now $(x, y, z) = 1$

$\Rightarrow \quad (ca, cb, c_1ab) = 1$

$\Rightarrow \quad [c_1a(a + b), ab(a + b), c_1ab) = 1$

$\Rightarrow \quad c_1 = 1$

$\therefore \quad c = c_1(a + b)$

$= (a + b).$

Thus, $x = a(a + b)$, $y = b(a + b)$ and $z = ab$.

Example 2 : Show that the positive integer solution of the equation $x^{-2} + y^{-2} = z^{-2}$, $(x, y, z) = 1$ is given by

$$x = a^4 - b^4, y = 2ab(a^2 + b^2), z = 2ab(a^2 - b^2).$$

where $a > b > 0$, $(a, b) = 1$, one of a, b is even and the other is odd.

Solution : Since $(x, y, z) = 1$, we have $(x^2, y^2 + z^2) = 1$.

Therefore,

$$x^2 = a_1(a_1 + b_1), y^2 = b_1(a_1 + b_1) \text{ and } z^2 = a_1b_1$$

where $a_1, b_1 > 0$, $(a_1, b_1) = 1$

Since, $z^2 = a_1b_1$, we have a_1 and b_1 both are square numbers. Similarly, from $x^2 = a_1(a_1 + b_1)$ we have $a_1 + b_1$ is also a square number. Let $a_1 = a_2^2$, $b_1 = b_2^2$ and $a_1 + b_1 = c_2^2$.

Therefore, $a_2^2 + b_2^2 = c_2^2$.

Now using theorem 1 of Pythagorean triples, we have

$$a_2 = a^2 - b^2, b_2 = 2ab \text{ and } c_2 = a^2 + b^2.$$

where $a > b > 0$, $(a, b) = 1$ and one of a and b is odd and the other is even.

Therefore, $x = a_2 c_2$

$= (a^2 - b^2)(a^2 + b^2)$

$= a^4 - b^4$

$y = b_2 c_2$

$= 2ab(a^2 + b^2)$

and $z = a_2b_2$

$= 2ab(a^2 - b^2).$

Example 1 : Find all Pythagorean triples where terms are in A.P.

Solution : Let $x - d$, x, $x + d$ be the required Pythagorean triples. Then

$$(x + d)^2 = x^2 + (x - d)^2$$

or $x^2 + 2xd + d^2 = x^2 + x^2 - 2xd + d^2$

or $x^2 - 4xd = 0$

or $\qquad x[x - 4d] = 0$

This gives $\qquad x - 4d = 0$

or $\qquad x = 4d$

Therefore, the required triple is

$$3d, 4d, 5d$$

where $d = 1, 2, ...$

Example 2 : Show that the radius of the inscribed circle of Pythagorean triangle is always an integer.

Solution : Pythagorean triangle is a right angle triangle whose sides are of integral length. Let x, y, z be the lengths of a Pythagorean triangle such that

$$x^2 + y^2 = z^2.$$

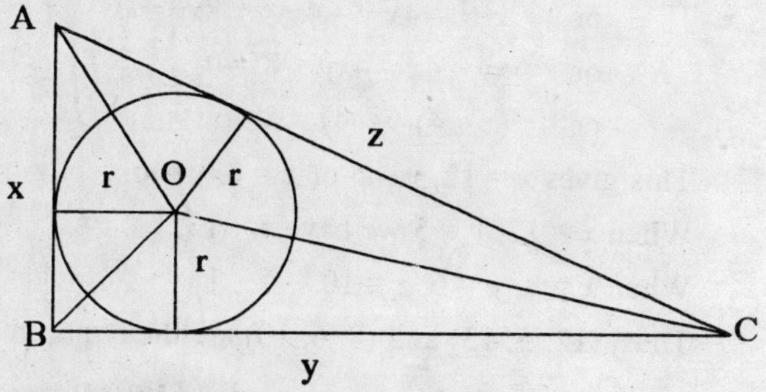

Let r be the length of the radius of the in circle.

The area of ΔABC

$$= \text{area of } \Delta ABO + \text{area of } \Delta BOC + \text{area of } \Delta AOC$$

or $\qquad \frac{1}{2}xy = \frac{1}{2}xr + \frac{1}{2}yr + \frac{1}{2}zr.$

$$= \frac{1}{2}r[x + y + z] \quad \text{or} \quad xy = r[x + y + z]. \qquad ....(1)$$

Now the positive integral solution of the equation $x^2 + y^2 = z^2$ are given by

$$x = 2uvt,\ y = (u^2 - v^2)t,\ z = (u^2 + v^2)t$$

for appropriate choice of positive integers u, v and t.

Putting these values of x, y and z in (1), we get

$$2uvt\,(u^2 - v^2)t = r[2uvt + (u^2 - v^2)t + (u^2 + v^2)t]$$

or $\qquad r = \dfrac{2uv[u^2 - v^2]t^2}{(2uv + 2u^2)t} = \dfrac{v\,|\,u^2 - v^2\,|\,t}{u + v}$

$$= v[u - v]\,t.$$

This is an integer. **Proved.**

Example 3 : Find all Pythagorean triangles whose areas are equal to their perimeters.

Solution : Let ABC be a Pythagorean triangle whose sides are x, y and z respectively. Then we have

$$x^2 + y^2 = z^2 \qquad \text{.......(1)}$$

and $$x + y + z = \frac{1}{2}xy \qquad \text{.......(2)}$$

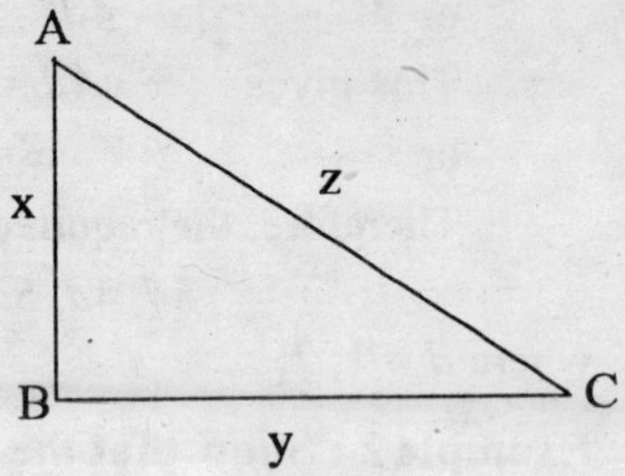

Eliminating z from (1) and (2) we have

$$x^2 + y^2 = (\tfrac{1}{2}xy - x - y)^2$$

$$= \frac{1}{4}x^2y^2 + x^2 + y^2 + z(-\frac{1}{2}x\frac{1}{4} - \frac{1}{2}xy^2 + xy)$$

or $\quad x^2y^2 - 4x^2y - 4xy^2 + 8xy = 0$

or $\quad xy - 4x - 4xy + 8 = 0$

or $\quad (x - 4)(y - 4) = 8.$

This gives $x = 12$, $y = 5$ or $x = 8$, $y = 6$.

When $x = 12$, $y = 5$ we have $z = 13$.

When $x = 8$, $y = 6$, $z = 10$.

Thus, (12, 5, 13) and (8, 6, 10) are the required Pythagorean triangles.

Example 4 : Show that if x, y, z is a primitive Pythagorean triples in which x an.l z are consecutive positive integers then

$$\mathbf{x = 2s(s + 1)}$$
$$\mathbf{y = 2s + 1}$$
$$\mathbf{z = 2s(s + 1) + 1.}$$

Solution : We know that if x, y, z is a primitive Pythagorean triple then

$$\left.\begin{aligned} x &= 2rs \\ y &= r^2 - s^2 \\ \text{and} \quad z &= r^2 + s^2 \end{aligned}\right\} \qquad \text{.......(1)}$$

Since x and z are consecutive integers, we have, $z = x + 1$

$$\Rightarrow \quad r^2 + s^2 = 2rs + 1$$
$$\Rightarrow \quad (r - s)^2 = 1$$
$$\Rightarrow \quad r - s = 1$$
$$\Rightarrow \quad r = s + 1.$$

Putting the value of r in (1), we get

$$x = 2(s + 1)s$$
$$y = (s + 1)^2 - s^2$$
$$= s^2 + 2s + 1 - s^2$$
$$= 2s + 1$$

and $$z = (s+1)^2 + s^2$$
$$= s^2 + 2s + 1 + s^2$$
$$= 2s^2 + 2s + 1$$
$$= 2s(s+1) + 1$$

Thus, we have

$$x = 2s(s+1)$$
$$y = 2s + 1$$

and $$z = 2s(s+1) + 1.$$

9.7 Fermat's Last Theorem

Fermat stated in the margin of his copy of Diophantus Arithmetician :

"It is impossible to write a cube as a sum of two cubes, a fourth power as a sum of two fourth powers and in general any power beyond the second as a sum of two similar powers. For this I have discovered a wonderful proof but the margin is too small to contain it". This theorem can be stated as :

The diaphantive equation

$$x^n + y^n = z^n$$

has no integral solution for $n > 2$ other than the trivial solution in which x or y is zero.

This theorem is known as Fermat's last theorem. This theorem remained a challenge for mathematical community for a long time. In June 1993 a mathematician Andrew Wales of Princton University claimed to prove this theorem. The whole mathematics world is excited today because this theorem defied the best minds of several generations of mathematicians. It is one of the important theorems. For the recognition of its importance, a German mathematician established a prize of 100000 DM in 1908 for offering a correct published proof.

∎

EXERCISE

1. Show that the integer $n = 2^{10}(2^{11} - 1)$ is not a perfect number.
2. A number n such that $\sigma(\sigma(n)) = 2n$ is called super perfect number. Show that $n = 2^k$ with $2^{k+1} - 1$ a prime, is super perfect.
3. Show that 64 is super perfect.
4. A number n such that $\sigma(n) > 2n$ is called abundant. If $\sigma(n) < 2n$ then n is called deficient. Show that 24 is abudent and 14 is deficient.
5. Show that 945 is an abundent number.
6. Show that every multiple of a perfect number is an abundent number.
7. A pair of numbers m, n is said to be amicable if the sum of the proper divisors of m equals n and the sum of proper divisors of n equals to m. Show that 220, 284 are amicable.
8. Show that $12 \mid xy$ for any primitive Pythagorean triple x, y, z.
9. Show that $60 \mid xyz$ for any primitive Pythagorean triple x, y, z.

❑

CHAPTER 10

SUM OF SQUARES OF INTEGERS

10.1 Introduction

In this chapter, we shall discuss the problems of representing numbers as sum of squares of two or more integers.

10.2 Sum of Two Squares

We have,

$$2 = 1^2 + 1^2 \quad \text{and}$$

$$5 = 2^2 + 1^2.$$

Thus, 2 and 5 can be expressed as sum of two squares. But

$$3 = 1^2 + 1^2 + 1^2 \quad \text{and}$$

$$6 = 2^2 + 1^2 + 1^2.$$

This shows that 3 and 6 are not sum of two squares. They are sum of three squares. Thus, integers cannot be expressed as sum of two squares.

Theorem 1 : If m and n are each sum of two squares. Then their product mn is also a sum of two squares.

Proof : Let $m = a_1^2 + b_1^2$ and $n = a_2^2 + b_2^2$ where a_1, b_1, a_2 and b_2 are integers. Then

$$mn = (a_1^2 + b_1^2)(a_2^2 + b_2^2)$$

$$= a_1^2a_2^2 + a_1^2b_2^2 + b_1^2a_2^2 + b_1^2b_2^2$$

$$= a_1^2a_2^2 + a_1^2b_2^2 + b_1^2a_2^2 + b_1^2b_2^2 + 2a_1a_2b_1b_2 - 2a_1b_2\, a_2b_1)$$

$$= (a_1a_2 + b_1b_2)^2 + (a_1b_2 - a_2b_1)^2.$$

This shows that the product mn can be expressed as sum of two squares.

Corollary : If $m_1, m_2, \ldots, m_r$ are integers such that $m_i = a_i^2 + b_i^2$, $1 \leqslant i \leqslant r$ then

$m_1m_2 \ldots m_r = a^2 + b^2$ for some integers a and b.

Theorem 2 : Any integer of the form $4k + 3$ cannot be expressed as sum of two squares. **(C.C.S.U. 2001, 2003)**

Proof : Any integer n can be written as

$$n = 4k + r$$

where $r = 0, 1, 2, 3$

Therefore,

$$n \equiv 0, 1, 2, 3, \pmod 4$$

$$\Rightarrow \quad n^2 \equiv 0, 1 \pmod 4.$$

Suppose $n = 4k + 3$ and if possible

$$n = a^2 + b^2$$

$$\equiv (a^2 + b^2) \pmod 4$$

$$\therefore \quad 3 \equiv (a^2 + b^2) \pmod 4.$$

Now $a^2 + b^2$ is either 0, 1 or 2 (mod 4). It will never be 3

$$\therefore \quad a^2 + b^2 \equiv 3 \pmod 4 \text{ never holds.}$$

So $\quad n \neq a^2 + b^2.$ **Proved**

Theorem 3 : If p is a prime and $(a, p) = 1$ then the linear congruence

$$ax \equiv y \pmod p$$

has a solution (x_0, y_0), where $0 < |x_0| < \sqrt{p}$ and $0 < |y_0| < \sqrt{p}$.

Proof : Let $m = 1 + [\sqrt{p}]$. Then $m^2 > p$. The set of integer

$$S = \{(ax - y) : 0 \leqslant x < m - 1, 0 \leqslant y \leqslant m - 1\}$$

contains m^2 elements. Since $ax = y$ can take atmost p values, there exists integers (x_1, y_1) and (x_2, y_2) such that

$$(ax_1 - y_1) \equiv (ax_2 - y_2) \pmod p$$

where $x_1 \neq x_2$ or $y_1 \neq y_2$

or $$a[x_1 - x_2] \equiv (y_1 - y_2) \pmod p$$

Setting $x_0 = x_1 - x_2$ and $y_0 = y_1 - y_2$ we see that (x_0, y_0) satisfies the given congruence and

$$0 < |x_0| = |x_1 - x_2| \leqslant m - 1 = [\sqrt{p}] < \sqrt{p}$$

and $$0 < |y_0| = |y_1 - y_2| \leqslant m - 1 = [\sqrt{p}] < \sqrt{p}.$$

Thus (x_0, y_0) is the required solution.

Theorem 4. (Fermat) : An odd prime p is expressible as a sum of two squares iff $p \equiv 1 \pmod 4$. **(C.C.S. 2004)**

Proof : Suppose p is expressible as a sum of two square. Since p is an odd prime, we have $p \equiv 1 \pmod 4$ or $p \equiv 3 \pmod 4$. If $p \equiv 3 \pmod 4$ then by theorem 1, it cannot be expressed as sum of two squares. Therefore, the only possibility is $p \equiv 1 \pmod 4$.

Conversely, suppose $p \equiv 1 \pmod 4$. Then the congruence

$$x^2 \equiv -1 \pmod p$$

has a solution a (say). This gives

$$a^2 \equiv -1 \pmod{p}$$
$$\Rightarrow (a, p) = 1.$$

Therefore, the linear congruence

$$ax \equiv y \pmod{p}$$

has a solution (x_0, y_0) such that $0 < |x_0| < \sqrt{p}$ and $0 < |y_0| < \sqrt{(p)}$.

Now $$a^2 \equiv -1 \pmod{p}$$
$$\Rightarrow \quad a^2x_0^2 \equiv -x_0^2 \pmod{p}$$
$$\Rightarrow \quad y_0^2 \equiv -x_0^2 \pmod{p}$$
$$\Rightarrow \quad x_0^2 + y_0^2 \equiv 0 \pmod{p}$$

This gives that there exists an integer $k > 0$ such that

$$x_0^2 + y_0^2 = kp$$

Now $$kp = x_0^2 + y_0^2$$
$$< (\sqrt{p})^2 + (\sqrt{p})^2$$
$$= 2p$$

Thus, we have

$$0 < kp < 2p$$
$$\Rightarrow \quad 0 < k < 2.$$

This gives $k = 1$.

Hence, $$x_0^2 + y_0^2 = p.$$

Thus, p is expressible as sum of two squares.

Corollary : Any prime p of the form $4k + 1$ can be represented as sum of two squares uniquely.

Proof : Suppose if possible

$$p = a^2 + b^2 = c^2 + d^2$$

where a, b, c and d are positive integers. Then

$$a^2d^2 - b^2c^2 = p(d^2 - c^2) \equiv 0 \pmod{p}$$
$$\Rightarrow \quad ad \equiv bc \pmod{p} \quad \text{or} \quad ad \equiv -bc \pmod{p}$$

Since a, b, c and d are less than $\sqrt{p}$, we have

$$ad - bc = 0 \quad \text{or} \quad ad + bc = p.$$

Now $$p^2 = (a^2 + b^2)(c^2 + d^2) = (ad + bc)^2 + (ac - bd)^2$$
$$= p^2 + (ac - bd)^2.$$

This gives $ac - bd = 0$. Thus we have $ad = bc$ or $ac = bd$

If $ad = bc$ then $a \mid bc \Rightarrow a \mid c$ as $(a, b) = 1$.

So $c = ka$. Putting this value of c in $ad = bc$ we have $d = bk$.

Now $p = c^2 + d^2 = k^2(a^2 + b^2)$. This implies $k = 1$. Thus $a = c$ and $b = d$.

Similarly from the condition $ac = bd$ we can show that $a = d$ and $b = c$.

Hence, the representation of p as a sum of two squares is unique.

Theorem 5 : **(Euler) : If an integer n can be expressed as the sum of two squares in two different ways then n is composite.**

Proof : Let n be an odd integer and

$$n = a_1^2 + b_1^2 = a_2^2 + b_2^2 \qquad ....(1)$$

where a_1, b_1, a_2 and b_2 are integers and one of a_1 and b_1 is odd and one of a_2 and b_2 is odd.

Let a_1 and a_2 be odd and b_1 and b_2 be even. From (1) we have

$$a_1^2 - a_2^2 = b_2^2 - b_1^2$$

$$\Rightarrow \quad (a_1 - a_2)(a_1 + a_2) = (b_2 - b_1)(b_2 + b_1). \qquad ....(2)$$

Let, $(a_1 - a_2, b_2 - b_1) = d$. Since $a_1 - a_2$ and $b_2 - b_1$ both are even integers, we have d is an even integer.

Let,
$$a_1 - a_2 = rd$$
$$b_2 - b_1 = sd \qquad ....(3)$$

for some integers r and s. Obviously $(r, s) = 1$. From (2) and (3) we have

$$r(a_1 + a_2) = s(b_2 + b_1) \qquad ....(4)$$

From (4) we see that $s \mid a_1 + a_2$ and $r \mid b_2 + b_1$.

Therefore,
$$a_1 + a_2 = st \qquad ....(5)$$

for some integer t. Then from (4) we have

$$b_2 + b_1 = rt. \qquad ....(6)$$

Since $(r, s) = 1$ we see from (5) and (6) that $t = (a_1 + a_2, b_2 + b_1)$.

Since $a_1 + a_2$, $b_2 + b_1$ both are even, t is even.

Therefore,

$$\begin{aligned} 4n &= 2a_1^2 + 2b_1^2 + 2a_2^2 + 2b_2^2 \\ &= (a_1 - a_2)^2 + (a_1 + a_2)^2 + (b_2 - b_1)^2 + (b_2 + b_1)^2 \\ &= r^2d^2 + s^2t^2 + s^2d^2 + r^2t^2 \\ &= (r^2 + s^2)(d^2 + t^2). \end{aligned}$$

Hence, $n = (r^2 + s^2)\left[\left(\frac{d}{2}\right)^2 + \left(\frac{t}{2}\right)^2\right].$

This shows that n is a composite number.

Theorem 6 : **A positive integer $n > 1$ can be written as the sum of two squares iff either it has no prime factor congruent to 3 (mod 4) or if it has a prime factor congruent to 3 (mod 4) then it occurs to an even power in the prime factorization of n.**

Proof : Suppose n has the prime factorization

$$n = 2^r p_1^{r_1} p_2^{r_2} \;....\; p_l^{r_l} q_1^{s_1} q_2^{s_2} \;....\; q_m^{s_m} \qquad ....(1)$$

where $p_i \equiv 1 \pmod 4$ $(1 \leqslant i \leqslant l)$ and $q_j \equiv 3 \pmod 4$ $(1 \leqslant j \leqslant m)$.

Suppose $$n = x^2 + y^2. \qquad \text{.......(2)}$$

We will show that either each $s_j = 0$ or if some $s_j \neq 0$ then it is an even integer.

If all $s_j = 0$ then we have nothing to prove. If at least one s_j say $s_1 \neq 0$ then we have to show that s_1 is even. Suppose if possible s_1 is odd. Let $d = (x, y)$. Then we have $x = x_0 d$, $y = y_0 d$, $(x_0, y_0) = 1$

Now, $$n = x^2 + y^2$$
$$= (x_0^2 + y_0^2)d^2$$
$$\Rightarrow \quad \frac{n}{d^2} = x_0^2 + y_0^2. \qquad \text{.......(3)}$$

Since s_1 is odd, q_1 divides $x_0^2 + y_0^2$ to an odd power.

Further $(x_0, q_1) = (y_0, q_1) = 1$

Let, $$y_0 t \equiv x_0 \pmod{q_1} \qquad \text{.......(4)}$$

Obviously it has a unique solution
$$t = t_1 \pmod{q_1}.$$

Therefore,
$$\frac{n}{d^2} = x_0^2 + y_0^2$$
$$= y_0^2 t_1^2 + y_0^2 \pmod{q_1}$$

This gives $y_0^2(1 + t_1^2) = 0 \pmod{q_1}$.

$\Rightarrow$ $(1 + t_1^2) \equiv 0 \pmod{q_1}$ $\qquad [\because (y_0, q_1) = 1]$

$\Rightarrow$ $x^2 \equiv -1 \pmod{q_1}$ has a solution t_1.

Then $q_1 \equiv 3 \pmod 4$ which is not possible.

So s_1 cannot be odd. Hence, s_1 is even. Conversely suppose each s_j, $1 \leqslant j \leqslant m$ is an even integer in the expression (1) we have
$$2 = 1 + 1 = 1^2 + 1^2$$
$$\Rightarrow \quad 2^r = a^2 + b^2.$$

If $p_i = a_i^2 + b_i^2$ then $p_i^{r_i} = c_i^2 + d_i^2$. Therefore,
$$n = 2^r p_1^{r_1} \ldots\ldots p_l^{r_l} q_1^{s_1} \ldots\ldots q_m^{r_m}$$
$$= (a^2 + b^2)(c_1^2 + d_1^2) \ldots\ldots (c_l^2 + d_l^2)(q_1^{s_1/2})^2 \ldots\ldots (q_m^{s_m/2})^2.$$
$$= c^2 + d^2.$$

Proved.

Method for expression of a prime $p = 4k + 1$ as sum of two squares

We use the continued fraction method to express $p = 4k + 1$ as sum of two squares. The method is as follows.
$$\alpha_1 = \sqrt{p} = P_1 + \sqrt{p} - P_1$$
where $$P_1 = [\sqrt{p}]$$

$$\alpha_2 = \frac{\sqrt{p} + P_1}{Q_1}, \quad Q_1 = (p - P_1)$$

$$\alpha_3 = \frac{\sqrt{p} + P_2}{Q_2}, \quad Q_2 = (p - P_2)$$

$$\vdots \qquad\qquad \vdots$$

$$\alpha_{n+1} = \frac{\sqrt{p} + P_n}{Q_n}, \quad Q_n = (p - P_n)$$

If $Q_r = Q_{n+1}$ then

$$p = P^2_{r+1} + Q^2_{r+1}$$

Theorem 7 : A positive integer n can be expressed as the difference of two squares iff n is not of the form $4k + 2$.

Proof : We know that $a^2 \equiv 0$ or 1 (mod 4) for all integer a. Therefore $a^2 - b^2 \equiv 0, 1$ or 3 (mod 4). Hence if $n \equiv 2$ (mod 4) we cannot have

$n = a^2 - b^2$ for any integers a and b.

If n is not of the form $4k + 2$ then $n \equiv 0, 1$ or 3 (mod 4).

If $n = 1$ or 3 (mod 4) then $(n + 1)$ and $(n - 1)$ are even integers such that

$$n = \left(\frac{n+1}{2}\right)^2 - \left(\frac{n-1}{2}\right)^2$$

which is a difference of two squares.

If $n = 0$ (mod 4) then we have

$$n = \left(\frac{n}{4} + 1\right)^2 - \left(\frac{n}{4} - 1\right)^2$$

which is again a difference of two square.

Corollary : A odd prime is the difference of two succession squares.

Example 1 : Express 113 and 229 as sum of two squares. (C.C.S.U. 2003, 2004)

Solution : We have

$$113 = 4.28 + 1$$
$$229 = 4.57 + 1$$

Both are of the form $4k + 1$.

Therefore 113 and 229 can be expressed as sum of two squares.

Now

$$113 = 8^2 + 7^2$$
$$229 = 15^2 + 2^2$$

Example 2 : Express 153 as sum of two squares. **[C.C.S.(B.P.) 2006]**

Solution : We have

$$153 = 3^2.\ 17$$
$$= 3^2.[4^2 + 1^2]$$
$$= 12^2 + 3^2$$

Example 3 : Express 1225 as the sum of two squares.

Solution : We have

$$1225 = 5^2.49$$
$$= 5^2.7^2$$
$$= (4^2 + 3^2).7^2$$
$$= 28^2 + 21^2.$$

Example 4 : Express 1613 as the sum of two squares.

Solution : We have

$$1613 = 4.403 + 1$$

which is of the form $4k + 1$. Therefore it can be expressed as sum of two squares. We adopt the process of converting $\sqrt{1613}$ into a continued fraction till we get

$$Q_r = Q_{r+1} \text{ for some } r.$$

Now

$$\alpha_1 = \sqrt{1613} = 40 + \frac{\sqrt{1613} - 40}{1} \qquad [\because 40 < \sqrt{1613}]$$

$$\alpha_2 = \frac{\sqrt{1613} + 40}{1613 - 40^2}$$

$$= \frac{\sqrt{1613} + 40}{13} = 6 + \frac{\sqrt{1613} - 38}{13}$$

$$\alpha_3 = \frac{\sqrt{1613} + 38}{\frac{1613 - 38^2}{13}} = \frac{\sqrt{1613} + 38}{13}$$

Thus, we have $Q_2 = Q_3 = 13$. Here $P_3 = 38$

Now $$1613 = P_3^2 + Q_3^2$$
$$= 38^2 + 13^2.$$

Example 5 : Express 3185 as sum of two squares.

Solution : We have

$$3185 = 5.7^2.13$$

This prime factorization contains no odd power of a prime congruent to 3 modulo4. Therefore, the given number can be expressed as sum of two squares.

Now

$$\begin{aligned}3185 &= 5.7^2.13\\ &= (2^2+1^2).(7^2+0^2)(3^2+2^2)\\ &= (14^2+7^2).(3^2+2^2)\\ &= (14.3+7.2)^2+(14.2-7.3)^2\\ &= 56^2+7^2.\end{aligned}$$

Example 6 : Express 333 as the sum of two squares.

Solution : We have

$$333 = 3^2.37$$

This prime factorization contains no odd power of a prime congruent to 3 modulo 4. Therefore, it can be expressed as sum of two squares.

Now

$$\begin{aligned}333 &= 3^2.37\\ &= 3^2.(6^2+1^2)\\ &= 18^2+3^2.\end{aligned}$$

Example 7 : Express 317 as sum of two squares.

Solution : We have

$$317 = 4.79 + 1$$

which is of the form $4k + 1$. Therefore, the given prime number can be expressed as sum of two squares.

Now

$$\alpha_1 = \sqrt{317} = 17 + \sqrt{317} - 17 \qquad [\because\ 17 < \sqrt{317}]$$

$$\alpha_2 = \frac{\sqrt{317}+17}{317-17^2} = \frac{\sqrt{317}+17}{28} = 1 + \frac{\sqrt{317}-11}{28}$$

$$\alpha_3 = \frac{\sqrt{317}+11}{\frac{317-11^2}{28}} = \frac{\sqrt{317}+11}{7} = 4 + \frac{\sqrt{317}-17}{7}$$

$$\alpha_4 = \frac{\sqrt{317}+17}{\frac{317-17^2}{7}} = \frac{\sqrt{317}+17}{4} = 8 + \frac{\sqrt{317}-15}{4}$$

$$\alpha_5 = \frac{\sqrt{317}+15}{\frac{317-15^2}{4}} = \frac{\sqrt{317}+15}{23} = 1 + \frac{\sqrt{317}-8}{23}$$

$$\alpha_6 = \frac{\sqrt{317}+8}{\frac{317-8^2}{23}} = \frac{\sqrt{317}+8}{11} = 2 + \frac{\sqrt{317}-14}{11}$$

$$\alpha_7 = \frac{\sqrt{317}+14}{\frac{317-14^2}{11}} = \frac{\sqrt{317}+14}{11}$$

Thus $Q_6 = Q_7$. Here $P_7 = 14$. Therefore,

$$317 = P_7^2 + Q_7^2$$
$$= 14^2 + 11^2.$$

Example 8 : Express 153 as the difference of two squares.

Solution : We have

$$153 \equiv 1 \pmod 4$$

Therefore,

$$n = \left(\frac{n+1}{2}\right)^2 - \left(\frac{n-1}{2}\right)^2 = \left(\frac{153+1}{2}\right)^2 - \left(\frac{153-1}{2}\right)^2$$
$$= 77^2 - 76^2.$$

10.3 Sum of More Than Two Squares

Theorem 1 : If n is of the form $8q+7$ then n is not expressible as the sum of three squares.

Proof : Suppose $n = 8q + 7$ and if possible n is the sum of three squares, *i.e.*,

$$n \equiv a^2 + b^2 + c^2 \qquad ....(1)$$

for some integers a, b and c. Then we have

$$a^2 + b^2 + c^2 \equiv 7 \pmod 8 \qquad ....(2)$$

Now $\quad a^2 \equiv 1 \pmod 8$ if a is odd

$\equiv 0$ or $4 \pmod 8$ if a is even.

Similar, behaviour is that of b^2 and c^2. Therefore, $a^2 + b^2 + c^2$ will be congruent (mod 8) to one of the integers 0, 1, 2, 3, 4, 5, 6 and not to 7. This contradicts (2). Hence, $n = 8q + 7$ is not expressible as sum of three squares.

Theorem 2 : Any integer of the form $n = 4^m(8q+7)$ for integers m and $q \geqslant 0$ is not a sum of three squares.

Proof : For $m = 0$ the statement reduces to theorem 1.

Suppose if possible

$$n = 4^m(8q + 7) = a^2 + b^2 + c^2 \qquad ....(1)$$

for $m \geqslant 1$ and integers a, b, c.

Therefore,

$$a^2 + b^2 + c^2 \equiv 0 \pmod 4. \qquad ....(2)$$

Now

$$a^2 \equiv 1 \pmod 4 \text{ if } a \text{ is odd}$$
$$\equiv 0 \pmod 4 \text{ if } a \text{ is even}.$$

It is obvious that a, b, c all are even integers. Therefore, from (1) we have

$$\left(\frac{a}{2}\right)^2 + \left(\frac{b}{2}\right)^2 + \left(\frac{c}{2}\right)^2 = 4^{m-1}(8q+7)$$

Thus, we see that if $4^m(8q + 7)$ is the sum of three squares then $4^{m-1}(8q + 7)$ is also a sum of three squares. Repeating the same procedure we see that $4^{m-2}(8q + 7)$, ..., $4^0(8q + 7)$ is the sum of three squares. But $4^0(8q + 7)$ is not the sum of three squares. Thus, we have a contradiction. Hence, $n = 4^m(8q + 7)$ is not expressible as the sum of three squares.

Proved

Theorem 3 : (Euler) : If the integers *m* and *n* are each the sum of four squares then *mn* is also the sum of four squares.

Proof : If $m = a_1^2 + b_1^2 + c_1^2 + d_1^2$

and $n = a_2^2 + b_2^2 + c_2^2 + d_2^2$

then

$$mn = (a_1^2 + b_1^2 + c_1^2 + d_1^2)(a_2^2 + b_2^2 + c_2^2 + d_2^2)$$
$$= (a_1a_2 + b_1b_2 + c_1c_2 + d_1d_2)^2 + (a_1b_2 - a_2b_1 + c_1d_2 - c_2d_1)^2$$
$$+ (a_1c_2 - a_2c_1 + b_1d_2 - b_2d_1)^2 + (a_1d_2 - a_2d_1 + b_1c_2 - b_2c_1)^2$$

This shows that mn is the sum of four squares.

Theorem 4 : If *p* is an odd prime, then there exists integers *a*, *b* and *h* such that $a^2 + b^2 + 1 = hp$ where $0 \leqslant a < p/2$, $0 \leqslant b < p/2$ and $0 < h < p$.

(C.C.S.U. 2005)

Proof : Let

$$S_1 = \left\{0, 1^2, 2^2, ..., \left(\frac{p-1}{2}\right)^2\right\}$$

$$S_2 = \left\{-1, -1, -1^2, -1, -2^2, ..., -1, \left(\frac{p-1}{2}\right)^2\right\}$$

Then the integers of S_1 and S_2 are all incongruent (mod p). The total numbers of integers in $S_1 \cup S_2$ is $p + 1$. Therefore, there will be at least two integers among these $p + 1$ integers which are congruent to each other (mod p). So at least one number of S_1 say a^2 is congruent (mod p) to some number say $-1- b^2$ of S_2 such that $0 \leqslant a < \frac{p}{2}$ and $0 \leqslant b < \frac{p}{2}$. Thus, we have

$$a^2 \equiv -1 - b^2 \pmod{p}$$
$$\Rightarrow a^2 + b^2 + 1 = hp \text{ for some positive integer } h. \text{ Also}$$

$$h = \frac{1}{p}\,[a^2 + b^2 + 1]$$

$$< \frac{1}{p}\left[\frac{p^2}{4} + \frac{p^2}{4} + 1\right]$$

$$< p.$$

Theorem 5 : A prime p can be expressed as the sum of four squares.

Proof : If $p = 2$ then we have

$$2 = 1^2 + 1^2 + 0^2 + 0^2$$

For an odd prime p let h be the smallest positive integer such that hp is the sum of four squares *i.e.*,

$$hp = a^2 + b^2 + c^2 + d^2.$$

We shall show that $h = 1$. First we shall show that h is odd. Suppose if possible h is even. Then a, b, c and d are all even an all odd or two are even and two are odd. These numbers may be arranged as

$$a \equiv b \pmod 2 \quad \text{and} \quad c \equiv d \pmod 2$$

This gives that $\frac{1}{2}(a - b)$, $\frac{1}{2}(a + b)$, $\frac{1}{2}(c - d)$ and $\frac{1}{2}(c + d)$ are all integers.

Also $\frac{1}{2}(hp) = \left(\frac{a-b}{2}\right)^2 + \left(\frac{a+b}{2}\right)^2 + \left(\frac{c-d}{2}\right)^2 + \left(\frac{c+d}{2}\right)^2$ a representation of $\left(\frac{h}{2}\right)p$ as a sum of four squares. This is contradiction as we have assumed that h is the smallest such integer. Therefore, h is odd. For showing $h = 1$ we assume that $h \neq 1$ then least value of h is 3. We may choose integers a_1, b_1, c_1 and d_1 such that

$$a_1 \equiv a \pmod h,\ b_1 \equiv b \pmod h$$

$$c_1 \equiv c \pmod h,\ d_1 \equiv d \pmod h$$

and $\quad a_1, b_1, c_1, d_1 < \frac{h}{2}$

For obtaining the value of a_1 we find the remainder r when a is divided by h. We put $a_1 = r$ or $a_1 = r - h$ according as $r < \frac{h}{2}$ or $r > \frac{h}{2}$ respectively.

Then

$$a_1^2 + b_1^2 + c_1^2 + d_1^2 \equiv a^2 + b^2 + c^2 + d^2$$

$$\equiv 0 \pmod h$$

$$\Rightarrow \quad a_1^2 + b_1^2 + c_1^2 + d_1^2 = nh$$

for some non-negative integer n.

Thus, we have,

$$0 \leqslant nh = a_1^2 + b_1^2 + c_1^2 + d_1^2 < 4.\left(\frac{h}{2}\right)^2 = h^2.$$

Now, n cannot be zero otherwise, $a_1 = b_1 = c_1 = d_1$ and consequently $k \mid p$ which is not possible because

$$1 < k < p$$

Also $\quad nh < h^2 \Rightarrow n < h$

Thus, we have

$$\begin{aligned} h^2np &= (hp)(nh) \\ &= (a^2 + b^2 + c^2 + d^2).(a_1{}^2 + b_1{}^2 + c_1{}^2 + d_1{}^2) \\ &= r^2 + s^2 + t^2 + u^2 \end{aligned}$$

where $r = aa_1 + bb_1 + cc_1 + dd_1$

$s = ab_1 - ba_1 + cd_1 - c_1d$

$t = ac_1 - a_1c + bd_1 - b_1d$

$u = ad_1 - a_1d + bc_1 - b_1c$

Now

$$\begin{aligned} r &= aa_1 + bb_1 + cc_1 + dd_1 \\ &\equiv a_1{}^2 + b_1{}^2 + c_1{}^2 + d_1{}^2 \equiv 0 \pmod{h} \end{aligned}$$

Similarly,

$$s \equiv t \equiv u \equiv 0 \pmod{h}$$

So

$$np = \left(\frac{r}{h}\right)^2 + \left(\frac{s}{h}\right)^2 + \left(\frac{t}{h}\right)^2 + \left(\frac{u}{h}\right)^2$$

where $\frac{r}{h}, \frac{s}{h}, \frac{t}{h}, \frac{u}{h}$ are all integers. Since $0 < n < h$, we have a contradiction.

Therefore, $\quad h = 1$

Theorem 6 : (Lagrange) : Any positive integer n can be expressed as a sum of four squares.

Proof : If $n = 1$ then

$$n = 1^2 + 0^2 + 0^2 + 0^2$$

which is a sum of four squares.

For $n > 1$ we take

$$n = p_1p_2 \dots p_r.$$

as prime factorization. Since each prime can be expressed as the sum of four squares, there product which is equal to n will also be expressed as sum of four squares.

Example 1 : Express 459 as sum of four squares.

Solution : We have

$$\begin{aligned} 459 &= 3^3.17 \\ &= 3^2.3.17 \end{aligned}$$

$= 3^2[1^2 + 1^2 + 1^2 + 0^2].[4^2 + 1^2 + 0^2 + 0^2]$
$= 3^2[(4 + 1 + 0 + 0)^2 + (1 - 4 + 0 - 0)^2 + (0 - 0 - 4 + 0)^2 + (0 + 0 - 1 - 0)^2]$
$= 3^2[5^2 + 3^2 + 4^2 + 1^2]$
$= 15^2 + 9^2 + 12^2 + 3^2.$

Example 2 : Find the relation $a^2 + b^2 + 1 = hp$ for $p = 19$ and hence show that $3 \times 19 = 4^2 + 4^2 + 4^2 + 3^2$.

Solution : We have $\frac{p-1}{2} = \frac{19-1}{2} = 9$

Therefore, $S_1 = \{0^2, 1^2, 2^2, ..., 9^2\}$

$S_2 = \{-1, 0, -1 - 1^2, -1 - 2^2, ... -1 - 9^2\}$

Now we will find the integers of S_1 which are congruent (mod 19) to the integers of S_2. We have

$$1^2 \equiv -1 - 6^2 \pmod{19}$$
$$3^2 \equiv -1 - 3^2 \pmod{19}$$
$$8^2 \equiv -1 - 7^2 \pmod{19}$$

Therefore,
$$6^2 + 1^2 + 1 = 2 \times 19$$
$$3^2 + 3^2 + 1 = 1 \times 19$$
$$8^2 + 7^2 + 1 = 6 \times 19$$

These are the required relations.

Since $6 \times 19 = 8^2 + 7^2 + 1^2 + 0^2$ we have

$$3 \times 19 = \left(\frac{8+0}{2}\right)^2 + \left(\frac{8-0}{2}\right)^2 + \left(\frac{7+1}{2}\right)^2 + \left(\frac{7-1}{2}\right)^2$$
$$= 4^2 + 4^2 + 4^2 + 3^2$$

10.4 Waring's Problem

Waring, E in 1770 stated that every positive integer can be written as the sum of four squares, nine cubes, nineteen fourth powers and so on.

When we say that every number is expressible as the sum of four squares we mean that four is such a least number. It may also be more than four.

For example, $36 = 3^2 + 4^2 + 5^2 + 6^2$

Similarly, waring's assertion regarding cubes we mean that 9 is the least number of positive integers. Whose sum of cubes is the given positive integer.

Waring's assertion can be stated as follow :

For any given positive integer k there exists a smallest integer $N(k)$ depending only on k such that every positive integer can be represented as the sum of $N(k)$ kth powers.

Thus, waring conjectured that $N(2) = 4$, $N(3) = 9$ and $N(4) = 19$.

EXERCISE

1. Express 7250 as sum of two squares. [**Ans.** $71^2 + 47^2$]
2. Express 541 as sum of two squares. [**Ans.** $21^2 + 10^2$]
3. Express 315 as sum of two squares. [**Ans.** Not possible]
4. Express 13572 as sum of two squares. [**Ans.** $114^2 + 24^2$, $66^2 + 36^2$]
   [C.C.S. (B.P.) 2006]
5. Express 454 as sum of three squares. [**Ans.** $15^2 + 15^2 + 3^2$]
6. Express 2109 as sum of four squares. [**Ans.** $18^2 + 22^2 + 25^2 + 26^2$]
7. Express 47 as sum of four squares. [**Ans.** $3^2 + 2^2 + 3^2 + 5^2$]

❑

CHAPTER 11 ADDITIONAL TOPICS

11.1 Introduction

In this chapter we shall discuss types of number theory, the Tchebychef's theorem concerning the distribution of prime numbers, Bertrand's conjecture, Gaussian integers prime number theorem and partitions.

11.2 Types of Number Theory

Number theory can be divided into four classes :

1. Classical number theory (or elementary number theory).
2. Analytic number theory
3. Algebraic number theory
4. Geometric number theory

Now we give brief introduction of these classes of number theory.

1. Classical Number Theory

Classical number theory is the basic number theory which deals with the divisibility, congruences, diophantine equations etc., by means of four fundamental operations (addition, subtraction, multiplication and division).

2. Analytic Number Theory

In analytic number theory we study the analytic methods i.e., the mathematical analysis and the method of the theory of functions. First of all Euler used the analytic methods to study the number theory. Dirichlet, G. L. and Riemaun developed this branch.

3. Algebraic Number Theory

A number α is called an algebraic number if it is a root of the algebraic equation

$$f(x) = a_0 x^n + a_1 x^{n-1} + ... + a_n = 0$$

where a_i are integers. The number α is called an algebraic number of degree n if $f(x)$ is an irreducible polynomial of degree n. If $a_0 = 1$ then α is called an algebraic integer. In algebraic number theory the algebraic integers or algebraic integral ring are studied. Natural numbers are algebraic integers of degree 1. The non-algebraic numbers are called transcendental numbers.

4. Geometric Number Theory

A point (x, y), in a plane orthogonal coordinate system, is called a lattice point or an integral point if x and y are integers. The study of these lattice points is called geometric number theory.

There is a very famous and difficult unsolved problem in geometric number theory known as Gauss's integral point problem. How many integral points are there inside the circle with centre origin and radius r ?

If $A(r)$ is the number of integral points inside and on the boundary of the circle then Gauss's problem is to find a relationship between $A(r)$ and r.

11.3 Theta Function

If x is a positive real number and $p_1, p_2, \ldots p_r$ are primes not exceeding x then theta function is defined as

$$\theta(x) = \sum_{p \leqslant x} \log p$$

Examples :

$$\theta(1) = 0 \qquad [\because \text{ There is no prime exceeding } 1]$$

$$\theta\left(4\frac{1}{4}\right) = \log 2 + \log 3 = \log 6$$

$$\theta(8) = \log 2 + \log 3 + \log 5 + \log 7$$
$$= \log 210.$$

11.4 ψ Function

If x is a positive real number and $p_1, p_2, \ldots p_r$ are primes not exceeding x then ψ-function is defined as

$$\psi(x) = \sum_{p^a \leqslant x} \log p$$

where p^a ranges over all the powers of $p_1, p_2, \ldots. p_r$ not exceeding x.

Examples :

$$\psi(1) = 0$$

$$\psi\left(4\frac{1}{4}\right) = \log 2 + \log 3 = \log 6$$

$$\psi(8) = 3\log 2 + \log 3 + \log 5 + \log 7.$$

11.5 π-Functions

If x is a positive real number. Then π-function is defined as

$$\pi(x) = \text{number of primes not exceeding } x$$
$$= \sum_{p \leqslant x} 1$$

Theorem 1 : **(Tchebychef) : If $x \geqslant 2$ is a real number then there exist two positive real numbers a_1 and a_2 such that**

$$a_1 < \frac{\theta(x)}{x} < a_r$$

Proof : Let $x \geqslant 2$. First we shall show that

$$\theta(x) < 2x \log 2.$$

We have

$$\theta(1) = 0 < 2\log 2$$
$$\theta(2) = \log 2 < 4 \log 2 = 2.2 \log 2$$
$$\theta(3) = \log 2 \ \psi \log 3 < 6 \log 2 = 2.3 \log 2.$$

Similarly, we can show that

$$\theta(n) < 2n \log 2$$

If $n < x < n + 1$ for some $n > 0$ then

$$\theta(x) = \theta(n) < 2n \log 2 < 2x \log 2.$$

This gives

$$\frac{\theta(x)}{x} < 2 \log 2 = a_2 \text{ (say)} \qquad ....(1)$$

Further it can be shown that for $x \geqslant 2$.

$$\theta(x) < \psi(x) - x^{1/2} (\log x)^2. \qquad ....(2)$$

Also it can be shown that

$$\psi(x) > \frac{1}{3} x \log 2. \qquad ....(3)$$

From (2) and (3) we have

$$\theta(x) > \frac{1}{3} x \log 2 - x^{1/2} (\log x)^2$$

$$\Rightarrow \quad \frac{\theta(x)}{x} > \frac{1}{3} \log 2 - \frac{(\log x)^2}{x^{1/2}}. \qquad ....(4)$$

We know that

$$\lim_{x \to \infty} \frac{(\log x)^2}{x^{1/2}} = 0.$$

Therefore, there exists a real number x_0 such that

$$\frac{(\log x)^2}{x^{1/2}} < \frac{1}{12} \log 2 \quad \text{for } x \geqslant x_0.$$

Here $\frac{1}{12} \log 2$ is a suitable number less than $\frac{1}{3} \log 2$.

Therefore,

$$\frac{\theta(x)}{x} > \frac{1}{3} \log 2 - \frac{1}{12} \log 2$$

or $$\frac{\theta(x)}{x} > \frac{1}{4} \log 2 \quad \text{for} x \geqslant x_0$$

Let δ be the least value of $\dfrac{\theta(x)}{x}$ for $2 \leqslant x < x_0$ and $a_1 = \min(\delta, \frac{1}{4}\log 2)$.

Then we have

$$\frac{\theta(x)}{x} > a_1 \qquad \text{.......(5)}$$

From (1) and (5) we have

$$a_1 < \frac{\theta(x)}{x} < a_2$$

Theorem 2 : (Tchebychef) : There exist two positive real number b_1 and b_2 such that

$$b_1 < \frac{\pi(x)\log x}{x} < b_2 \text{ for all } x \geqslant 2.$$

Proof : If can be shown that for $x \geqslant 2$.

$$\theta(x) \leqslant \pi(x)\log x$$

$$\Rightarrow \quad \frac{\pi(x)\log x}{x} \geqslant \frac{\theta(x)}{x} > a_1. \qquad \text{[By theorem (1)]}$$

Taking $b_1 = a_1$ we have

$$b_1 < \frac{\pi(x)\log x}{x}. \qquad \text{.......(1)}$$

Further we have

$$\theta(x) = \sum_{p \leqslant x} \log p$$

$$> \sum_{x^{1/2} < p \leqslant x} \log p$$

$$\geqslant \sum_{x^{1/2} < p \leqslant x} \log x^{1/2}$$

$$= \frac{1}{2}\log x \sum_{x^{1/2} < p \leqslant x} 1$$

$$= \frac{1}{2}\log x \left[\sum_{p \leqslant x} 1 - \sum_{p \leqslant x^{1/2}} 1\right]$$

$$= \frac{1}{2}\log x \left[\pi(x) - \pi(x^{1/2})\right]$$

$$\geqslant \frac{1}{2}\log x\,[\pi(x) - x^{1/2}]. \qquad [\because \pi(x^{1/2}) < x^{1/2}]$$

This gives

$$\pi(x)\log x \leqslant 2\theta(x) + x^{1/2}\log x$$

or $$\frac{\pi(x)\log x}{x} \leqslant \frac{2\theta(x)}{x} + \frac{\log x}{x^{1/2}}$$

$$< 2a_2 + \frac{\log x}{x^{1/2}}.$$

Now $\lim_{x\to\infty} \frac{\log x}{x^{1/2}} = 0$. Therefore, $\frac{\log x}{x^{1/2}} < a$ constant say a_3 for $x \geqslant 2$.

So $$\frac{\pi(x)\log x}{x} < 2a_2 + a_3$$

$$= b_2. \qquad ....(2)$$

From (1) and (2) we have

$$b_1 < \frac{\pi(x)\log x}{x} < b_2 \quad \text{for } x \geqslant 2.$$

11.6 Elementary Properties of $\pi(x)$

Thereom 1 : $\lim_{x\to\infty} \pi(x) = \infty$ *i.e.*, there are infinitely many primes.

Proof : Suppose there are only finite number of primes $p_1, p_2, ..., p_n$. Let

$$M = p_1 p_2 .... p_n + 1$$

If we divide M by $p_1, p_2, ... p_n$ then the remainder is 1. This shows that M has no prime factorization. This is contradiction of the fundamental theorem of arithmetic. Hence, there are infinitely many primes *i.e.*,

$$\lim_{x\to\infty} \pi(s) = \infty$$

Theorem 2 : If k is any positive integer

$$\frac{\pi(x)}{x} \leqslant \frac{\theta(k)}{k} + \frac{2k}{x}.$$

Proof : For any real number x, we have

$[x] = kl + r$, $0 \leqslant r < k$, $[x]$ is the largest integer not exceeding x.

This is division of integers of $[1, x]$ into l sets of k consecutive integers and remaining set of r integers.

Among the integers 1, 2, 3, ..., k there are at most k primes. Among the integers $k+1, k+2, ..., 2k$ there are at most $\phi(k)$ primes as any integer not relatively prime to k has a prime factor in common with k. Similarly in each of the remaining s sets of k consecutive integers there are $\phi(k)$ primes. On the remaining set of r integers there are at most r primes. Therefore,

$$\pi(x) = k + (l-1)\,\phi(k) + r$$

$$= k + \left[\frac{[x]-r}{k}\right]\phi(k) + r$$

$$< 2k + \frac{x}{k}\phi(k). \qquad \left[\because r < k, \frac{[x]-r}{k} < \frac{x}{k}\right]$$

Therefore,

$$\frac{\pi(x)}{x} < \frac{2k}{x} + \frac{\phi(k)}{k}.$$ **Proved**

Theorem 3 : If $m > 1$ and $p_1, p_2, ..., p_r$ are all primes in $A = \{1, 2, ..., M\}$ then

$$\sum_{n=1}^{M} \frac{1}{n} < \frac{1}{\left(1-\frac{1}{p_1}\right)\left(1-\frac{1}{p_2}\right)....\left(1-\frac{1}{p_r}\right)}$$ (C.C.S.U. 2001)

Proof : For each i, $1 \leqslant i \leqslant r$ we have

$$\frac{1}{1-\frac{1}{p_i}} = \left(1-\frac{1}{p_i}\right)^{-1}$$

$$= 1 + \frac{1}{p_i} + \frac{1}{p_i^2} + \frac{1}{p_i^3} + ...$$

Therefore,

$$\frac{1}{\left(1-\frac{1}{p_1}\right)\left(1-\frac{1}{p_2}\right)....\left(1-\frac{1}{p_r}\right)} = \left(1+\frac{1}{p_1}+\frac{1}{p_1^2}+....\right)\left(1+\frac{1}{p_2}+\frac{1}{p_2^2}+....\right)$$

$$....\left(1+\frac{1}{p_r}+\frac{1}{p_r^2}+....\right)$$

$$= \sum_{n\in A} \frac{1}{n} > \sum_{n=1}^{M} \frac{1}{n}.$$

where A is the set of all integers each of whose prime factors are at most M. The terms on the right hand side are of the form.

$$\frac{1}{p_1^{a_1} \cdot p_2^{a_2} \dots p_r^{a_r}}, \; p_i \leqslant M$$

Theorem 4 : Show that $\lim_{x\to\infty} \frac{\pi(x)}{x} = 0$.

Proof : For $x > 0$ we have $\frac{\pi(x)}{x} > 0$. Therefore, we have to show that $\frac{\pi(x)}{x}$ can be made arbitrarily small by taking x sufficiently large. By theorem 2 we have

$$\frac{\pi(x)}{x} \leqslant \frac{\phi(k)}{k} + \frac{2k}{x}.$$

for each positive integer k.

Let M be a large integer and $p_1, p_2, ..., p_r$ all are primes $\leqslant M$. Then for

$$k = p_1 p_2 .... p_r$$

We have

$$\frac{\phi(k)}{k} = \frac{\phi(p_1)\phi(p_2)....\phi(p_r)}{p_1 p_2 .... p_r}$$

$$= \left(1 - \frac{1}{p_1}\right)\left(1 - \frac{1}{p_2}\right)....\left(1 - \frac{1}{p_r}\right)$$

$$< \left(\sum_{n=1}^{M} \frac{1}{n}\right)^{-1}.$$

Thus,

$$\frac{\pi(x)}{x} < \left(\sum_{n=1}^{M} \frac{1}{n}\right)^{-1} + \frac{2 p_1 p_2 ..... p_r}{x}.$$

Since $\sum \frac{1}{n}$ is a divergent series, for each arbitrary small number $t > 0$ there exist an integer M_0, such that

$$\sum_{n=1}^{M_0} \frac{1}{n} > \frac{2}{\in}$$

We choose $M = M_0$. Then for each

$$x > \frac{4 p_1 p_2 .... p_r}{\in}$$

We have

$$\frac{\pi(x)}{x} < \frac{\in}{2} + \frac{2 p_1 p_2 .... p_r \in}{4 p_1 p_2 .... p_r}$$

$$= \in$$

Therefore,

$$\lim_{x \to \infty} \frac{\pi(x)}{x} = 0.$$

Proved.

Theorem 5 : (Prime Number Theorem)

The celebrated prime number theorem predicts in gross sense about the distribution of primes. It states that if the number is n then there are about $n \mid \log n$ primes before n. Thus, prime number theorem tells us about the coverage (probable) distribution of primes.

The prime number theorem asserts that

(a) $$\lim_{x \to \infty} \frac{\pi(x)}{(x/\log x)} = 1$$

where log x is the natural logarithm of x

(b) $$\pi(x) = \frac{x}{\log x} + 0\left(\frac{x}{\log x}\right)$$

where $0\left(\frac{x}{\log x}\right)$ is a function $h(x)$ such that

$$\lim_{x \to \infty} \frac{h(x)}{(x/\log x)} = 1$$

which is equivalently.

(c) $$\pi(x) = L_i(x) + 0\left(\frac{x}{\log x}\right)$$

where $L_i(x) = \int_2^x \frac{dy}{\log y}$.

Legendre, *A.M.* asserted that $\pi(x)$ is of the form $\frac{x}{A \log x + B}$ where *A, B* are constants. Later on he refined this result in the form

$$\pi(x) = \frac{x}{\log x + A(x)}$$

where $A(x)$ is approximately 1.08366

Gauss conjectured that

$$\pi(x) \sim \frac{x}{\log x}.$$

This is known as prime number theorem. Tchebychef's proved that these exist positive constants a and b, $a < 1 < b$ such that

$$a\left(\frac{x}{\log x}\right) < \pi(x) < b\left(\frac{x}{\log x}\right).$$

He further showed that

$$\lim_{x \to \infty} \frac{\pi(x)}{(x \mid \log x)} = 1.$$

There was an opinion among mathematicians that the prime number theorem could not be proved without the application of xeta function without the use of complex function theory. In 1949 the Norwegian mathematician Atle Selberg discovered a purely arithmetical proof. His research paper 'An elementary proof of the prime number theorem' is elementary in technical sense without any modern complicated analysis. Selberg was awarded a Fields medal in the International Congress of Mathematicals for his work in this area in 1950.

11.7 Bertrand's Conjecture

If $n \geqslant 2^6$ then $\theta(2n) - \theta(n) > 0$

11.8 Gaussian Integer

The complex number $a + ib$, where a and b are integers, is called a Gaussian Integer.

For example $2 + 3i$, $7 - 5i$, $-6 + 7i$ are Gaussian integers.

The set of Gaussian integers is denoted by $Z(i)$.

11.9 Properties of Gaussian Integers

(*i*) The sum and product of two Gaussian integers is a Gaussian integer, *i.e.*,

$$(a_1 + ib_1) + (a_2 + ib_2) = (a_1 + a_2) + i(b_1 + b_2)$$

$$(a_1 + ib_1).(a_2 + ib_2) = (a_1a_2 - b_1b_2) + i(a_1b_2 + a_2b_1)$$

(*ii*) If α and β are two Gaussian integers then α is said to divide β if there exists a Gaussian integer γ, such that $\alpha = \beta\gamma$.

(*iii*) If α divides β and β divides γ then α divides γ.

(*iv*) If $\alpha = a + ib$, is a Gaussian integer then $\alpha = a - ib$ is called conjugate of α.

If $\alpha = a + ib$ is or Gaussian integer then $a^2 + b^2$ is called norm of α. It is denoted by $N(\alpha)$

$$N(\alpha) = \alpha\alpha'$$

$$N(\alpha\beta) = N(\alpha).N(\beta)$$

11.10 Partition

A partition of a positive integer n is a representation of n as a sum of positive integer. Two partition are considered same if they differ in the order of their summoned. The partition function $p(n)$ is defined as the number of partitions of n. It is defined that $p(0) = 1$.

Example 1 : Find $p(3)$.

Solution : We have $3 = 3$

$= 2 + 1$

$= 1 + 1 + 1$

These are the partitions of 3. Thus, $p(3) = 3$.

Example 2 : Find *p* (5).

Solution : We have

$$\begin{aligned} 5 &= 5 \\ &= 4 + 1 \\ &= 3 + 2 \\ &= 3 + 1 + 1 \\ &= 2 + 2 + 1 \\ &= 2 + 1 + 1 + 1 \\ &= 1 + 1 + 1 + 1 + 1. \end{aligned}$$

These are the partitions of 5. Thus, $p(5) = 7$.

Example 3 : Find *p* (7)

Solution : We have

$$\begin{aligned} 7 &= 7 \\ &= 6 + 1 \\ &= 5 + 2 \\ &= 5 + 1 + 1 \\ &= 4 + 3 \\ &= 4 + 2 + 1 \\ &= 4 + 1 + 1 + 1 \\ &= 3 + 3 + 1 \\ &= 3 + 2 + 2 \\ &= 3 + 2 + 1 + 1 \\ &= 3 + 1 + 1 + 1 + 1 \\ &= 2 + 2 + 2 + 1 \\ &= 2 + 2 + 1 + 1 + 1 \\ &= 2 + 1 + 1 + 1 + 1 + 1 \\ &= 1 + 1 + 1 + 1 + 1 + 1 + 1. \end{aligned}$$

These are the partitions of 7. Thus, $p(7) = 15$.

11.11 Graphical Representation of Partition

Some partition problems can be solved by graphical representation. In this representation a partition is represented by horizontal rows of dots.

Example 1 : The graphical representation for 5 + 4 + 1, a partition of 10 is given by

• • • • •
• • • •
•

The left hand dots of each row lie on a vertical line and the dots are equidistant. If we read the above graphical representation of 10 columnwise then we have

$$3 + 2 + 2 + 2 + 1 = 10.$$

This partition of 10 is called the conjugate of the given partition of 10.

11.12 Conjugate Partition

The conjugate partition of a given partition is obtained by reading the dots columnwise in the graphical representation of the given partition.

Example 1 : The graphical representation of for 6 + 3 + 3 + 2 + 1

• • • • • •
• • •
• • •
• •
•

The corresponding conjugate partition is given by

$$15 = 5 + 4 + 3 + 1 + 1 + 1.$$

Some Notations

(*i*) $p(n)$ denotes the total number of partitions .

(*ii*) $p_m(n)$ denotes the number of partitions of n in which each summoned is atmost m.

(*iii*) $p^0(n)$ ($p^e(n)$) denotes the number of partitions of n with odd (even) summands.

(*iv*) $p_d(n)$ the number of partition of n with distinct summands.

(*v*) $\pi_m(n)$ denotes the number of partitions of n with number of summands not exceeding m.

Theorem 1 : Show that

$$p_m(n) = \pi_m(n).$$

Proof : We consider a partition of n in which at most m parts appear. The conjugate partition of such a partition has no part larger than m. Thus, there is a one-one correspondence between the two partitions. Therefore, there must be the same number of each type, *i.e.*,

$$p_m(n) = \pi_m(n).$$

Note : $p_m(n) = p_{m-1}(n) + p_{mn}(n - m)$.

Example 1 : For $n = 5$ and $m = 4$ we have

$p_m(n)$	$\pi_m(n)$
4 + 1	2 + 2 + 1
3 + 1 + 1	2 + 1 + 1 + 1
3 + 2	2 + 2
2 + 1 + 1 + 1	3 + 1 + 1
2 + 2 + 1	4 + 1
1 + 1 + 1 + 1 + 1	5

Thus, $p_4(5) = 6$ and $\pi_4(5) = 6$.

Therefore, $p_4(5) = \pi_4(5)$. **Proved**

Theorem 2 : (Euler's Partition Theorem)

For any positive integer n, $p^0(n) = p_d(n)$ *i.e.*, the number of partitions of a positive integer n in which all parts are odd is equal to the number of partitions of n in which all parts are distinct.

Proof : We consider a partition of n having odd parts only in which 1 repeats n_1 times, 3 repeats n_3 times, 5 repeats n_5 times and so on $2M - 1$ repeats n_{2M-1} times. Thus, we have

$$n = \underbrace{1 + 1 + \ldots + 1}_{n_1 \text{ times}} + \underbrace{3 + 3 + \ldots + 3}_{n_3 \text{ times}} + \underbrace{5 + 5 + \ldots + 5}_{n_5 \text{ times}} + \underbrace{(2M-1) + (2M-1) + \ldots + (2M-1)}_{(2M-1) - \text{times}}$$

$$= 1.n_1 + 3.n_3 + 5.n_5 + \ldots. + (2M-1).n_{2M-1}$$

By the basis representation theorem each n_i can be represented uniquely as a sum of distinct powers of 2. Thus, we have

$$n_1 = 2^{a_1} + 2^{a_2} + \ldots. + 2^{a_r}, \; a_1 > a_2 > \ldots. > a_r$$

$$n_3 = 2^{b_1} + 2^{b_2} + \ldots. + 2^{b_s}, \; b_1 > b_2 > \ldots. > b_s$$

$$\vdots$$

$$n_{2M-1} = 2^{c_1} + 2^{c_2} + \ldots. + 2^{c_t}, \; c_1 > c_2 > \ldots. > c_t.$$

Therefore,

$$n = (2^{a_1} + 2^{a_2} + \ldots. + 2^{a_r}) + 3(2^{b_1} + 2^{b_2} + \ldots. + 2^{b_s}) + (2M-1)(2^{c_1} + 2^{c_2} + \ldots. + 2^{c_t})$$

$$= 2^{a_1} + 2^{a_2} + \ldots. + 2^{a_r} + 3.2^{b_1} + 3.2^{b_2} + \ldots. + 3.2^{b_s} + (2M-1)2^{c_1} + (2M-1)2^{c_2} + \ldots. + (2M-1)2^{c_t}.$$

This expression is a partition of n into distinct parts.

Now we will establish a one-to-one correspondence between the partition of n with odd parts and these with distinct parts. Suppose we start with a partition of n into distinct parts. We can write each part as the product of an odd number and a power 2. Let

$$n = m_1(2^{r_1} + 2^{r_2} + \ldots. + 2^{r_i}) + m_3(2^{s_1} + 2^{s_2} + \ldots. + 2^{s_j}) + \ldots. m_{2r-1}(2^{t_1} + 2^{t_2} + \ldots. + 2^{t_k})$$

where $m_1 > m_3 > \ldots. > m_{2r-1}$ and all m_i are odd integers. This is a partition of n into odd parts.

Thus, there is one to one correspondence between the partition of n in $p^0(n)$ and the partition in $p_d(n)$. Therefore $p^0(n) = p_d(n)$.

Example 1 : For $n = 9$ we have

$p^0(n)$	$p_d(n)$	
9	9	
7 + 1 + 1	7 + 2	[∵ 7 + 1 + 1 = 7 + 2.1]
5 + 3 + 1	5 + 3 + 1	
5 + 1 + 1 + 1 + 1	5 + 4	[∵ 5 + 1 + 1 + 1 + 1 = 5 + 4.1]
3 + 3 + 3	6 + 3	[∵ 3 + 3 + 3 + 3.3 = 3.(2 + 1)]
3 + 3 + 1 + 1 + 1	6 + 2 + 1	[∵ 3 + 3 + 1 + 1 + 1 = 2.3 + 3. 1]
3 + 1 + 1 + 1 + 1 + 1 + 1	3 + 4 + 2	[∵ 3 + 1 + 1 + 1 + 1 + 1 + 1 = 3 + (4 + 2).1]
1+1+1+1+1+1+1+1+1	8 + 1	[1 + 1 + 1 + 1 + 1 + 1 + 1 + 1 + 1 = 9.1 = (8 + 1).1]

Thus,

$$p^0(n) = p_d(n) = 8$$

11.13 Generating Function

If $\{a_n\}$ is a sequence of real numbers then the function

$$F(x) = \sum a_n x^n$$

is called the generating function for the sequence $\{a_n\}$. The function $F(x)$ is defined for all values of x for which the series $\sum a_n x^n$ converges.

For example the function

$$F(x) = -\log(1-x), \ |x| < 1$$

is the generating function of the sequence $\{1/n\}$.

The Generating Function for $\pi_m(n)$

Theorem 1 : Show that

$$\sum_{n=0}^{\infty} p_m(n) x^n = \prod_{r=1}^{m} \frac{1}{1-x^r} = F_m(x), \ |x| < 1.$$

Proof : We know that

$$\frac{1}{1-x} = 1 + x + x^2 + \ldots. \text{ for } |x| < 1$$

Therefore,

$$\prod_{r=1}^{m} \frac{1}{1-x^r} = \frac{1}{1-x} \cdot \frac{1}{1-x^2} \cdots \frac{1}{1-x^m}$$

$$= (1 + x + x^2 + \ldots.)(1 + x^2 + x^4 + \ldots.) \ldots. (1 + x^m + x^{2m} + \ldots.)$$

$$= 1 + x^1 + (x^2 + x^2) + (x^{3.1} + x^{2+1} + x^3) + (x^{4.1} + x^{2+2.1} + x^{2.2} + x^{3+1} + x^4) + \ldots.$$

The exponents of Vth term are

$$4.1(= 1 + 1 + 1 + 1),\ 2 + 2.1(= 2 + 1 + 1),\ 2.2(= 2 + 2),\ 3 + 1 \text{ and } 4.$$

These are the partition of 4. In general the expression for each exponent of sum n contains $p_m(n)$ terms which is the partition of n into parts each not exceeding m. Thus, we have

$$\prod_{r=1}^{m} \frac{1}{1 - x^r} = \sum_{n=0}^{\infty} p_m(n) x^n = F_m(x). \qquad \textbf{Proved.}$$

The Generating Function For $p(n)$

Theorem 2 : Show that

$$\prod_{r=1}^{\infty} (1 - x^r)^{-1} = \sum_{n=0}^{\infty} p_m(n) x^n = F(x).$$

Proof : We know that $p_m(n) \leqslant p(n)$ for each $n \geqslant 0$ and if $m \geqslant n, p_m(n) = p(n)$. Therefore,

$$F_m(x) = \sum_{n=0}^{\infty} p_m(n) x^n$$

$$= \sum_{n=0}^{m} p_m(n) x^n + \sum_{n=m+1}^{\infty} p_m(n) x^n$$

$$= \sum_{n=0}^{m} p(n) x^n + \sum_{n=m+1}^{\infty} p_m(n) x^n.$$

Also $\quad p_m(n) \leqslant (n + 1)^m$

$$\Rightarrow \quad \sum_{n=0}^{m} p_m(n) x^n \leqslant \sum_{n=0}^{\infty} (n + 1)^m x^n.$$

The series on the right hand side converges for $|x| < 1$. Therefore, the series $\sum_{n=0}^{\infty} p_m(n) x^n$ converges and $\Sigma p_m(n) x^n \to 0$ as $m \to \infty$.

Hence,

$$\lim_{m \to \infty} F_m(x)^n = \lim_{m \to \infty} \sum_{n=0}^{\infty} p(n) x^n$$

$$= \lim_{m \to \infty} \sum_{n=0}^{\infty} p(n) x^n.$$

This gives

$$\prod_{r=1}^{\infty}(1-x^r)^{-1}=\sum_{n=0}^{\infty}p(n)x^n=F(x)$$

Similarly, we have

(*i*) $\sum_{n=0}^{\infty}p_d(n)x^n=\prod_{r=1}^{\infty}(1-x^r),\ |x|<1$

(*ii*) $\sum_{n=0}^{\infty}p^0(n)x^n=\prod_{r=1}^{\infty}(1-x^{2r-1})^{-1}$

(*iii*) $\sum_{n=0}^{\infty}p^e(n)x^n=\prod_{r=1}^{\infty}(1-x^{2r})^{-1}$

(*iv*) $\sum_{n=0}^{\infty}p_d^0(n)x^n=\prod_{r=1}^{\infty}(1-x^{2r-1})$

Theorem 3 : (Euler) : Show that $p_d(n)=p^0(n)$ for each n.

Proof : We have

$$\sum_{n=0}^{\infty}p_d(n)x^n=\prod_{r=1}^{\infty}(1-x^r),\ |x|<1$$

$$=(1+x)(1+x^2)\ ....$$

$$=\frac{(1-x^2)}{(1-x)}\cdot\frac{(1-x^4)}{(1-x^2)}\ ....$$

$$=\prod_{r=1}^{\infty}(1-x^{2r-1})^{-1}$$

$$=\sum_{n=0}^{\infty}p^0(n)\,x^n$$

Now since both series converges absolutely for $|x|<1$ we have $p_d(n)=p^0(n)$ for each n.

❑

Some Important Tables

Table 1 : List of prime numbers less than 10000

2	151	359	587	821	1051	1301
3	157	367	593	823	1061	1303
5	163	373	599	827	1063	1307
7	167	379	601	829	1069	1319
11	173	383	607	839	1087	1321
13	179	389	613	853	1091	1327
17	181	397	617	857	1093	1361
19	191	401	619	859	1097	1367
23	193	409	631	863	1103	1373
29	197	419	641	877	1109	1381
31	199	421	643	881	1117	1399
37	211	431	647	883	1123	1404
41	223	433	653	887	1129	1423
43	227	439	659	907	1151	1427
47	229	443	661	911	1153	1429
53	233	449	673	919	1163	1433
59	239	457	677	929	1171	1439
61	241	461	683	937	1181	1447
67	251	463	691	941	1187	1451
71	257	467	701	947	1193	1453
73	263	479	709	953	1201	1459
79	269	487	719	967	1213	1471
83	271	491	727	971	1217	1481
89	277	499	733	977	1223	1483
97	281	503	739	983	1229	1487
101	283	509	743	991	1231	1489
103	293	521	751	997	1237	1493
107	311	523	757	1009	1249	1499
109	313	541	761	1013	1259	1511
113	317	547	769	1019	1277	1523
127	331	557	773	1021	1279	1531
131	337	563	787	1031	1283	1543
137	347	569	797	1033	1289	1549
139	349	571	809	1039	1291	1553
149	353	577	811	1049	1297	1559

1567	1873	2179	2477	2801	3167	3451
1561	1877	2203	2503	2803	3169	3499
1579	1879	2207	2521	2819	3181	3511
1583	1889	2213	2531	2833	3187	3517
1597	1901	2221	2539	2837	3191	3527
1601	1907	2237	2543	2843	3103	3529
1607	1913	2239	2549	2851	3203	3533
1609	1931	2243	2551	2857	3217	3539
1613	1933	2251	2557	2861	3221	3541
1619	1949	2267	2579	2879	3229	3547
1621	1951	2269	2591	2887	3251	3557
1627	1973	2273	2593	2897	3253	3559
1637	1979	2281	2609	2903	3257	3571
1657	1987	2287	2617	2909	3259	3581
1663	1993	2293	2633	2917	3271	3583
1667	1997	2297	2647	2927	3299	3593
1669	1999	2309	2657	2939	3301	3607
1693	2003	2311	2659	2953	3307	3613
1697	2011	2333	2663	2957	3313	3617
1699	2017	2339	2671	2963	3319	3623
1709	2027	2341	2677	2969	3323	3631
1721	2029	2347	2683	2971	3329	3637
1723	2039	2351	2687	2999	3331	3643
1733	2053	2357	2689	3001	3343	3659
1741	2063	2371	2693	3011	3347	3671
1747	2069	2377	2699	3019	3359	3673
1753	2081	2381	2707	3023	3361	3679
1759	2083	2383	2711	3037	3371	3691
1777	2087	2389	2713	3041	3373	3697
1783	2084	2393	2719	3049	3389	3701
1787	2099	2399	2729	3061	3391	3709
1789	2111	2411	2731	3067	3407	3719
1801	2113	2417	2741	3079	3413	3727
1811	2129	2423	2749	3083	3433	3733
1823	2131	2437	2753	3089	3449	3739
1831	2137	2441	2767	3109	3457	3761
1847	2141	2447	2777	3119	3461	3767
1861	2143	2459	2789	3121	3463	3769
1867	2153	2467	2791	3137	3467	3779
1871	2161	2473	2797	3163	3469	3793

3797	4129	4481	4813	5167	5507	5849
3803	4133	4483	4817	5171	5519	5851
3821	4139	4493	4831	5179	5521	5857
3823	4153	4507	4861	5189	5527	5861
3833	4157	4513	4871	5197	5531	5867
3847	4159	4517	4877	5209	5557	5869
3851	4177	4519	4889	5227	5563	5879
3853	4201	4523	4903	5231	5569	5881
3863	4211	4547	4909	5233	5573	5891
3877	4217	4549	4919	5237	5581	5903
3881	4219	4561	4931	5261	5591	5923
3889	4229	4567	4933	5273	5623	5927
3907	4231	4583	4937	5279	5639	5939
3911	4241	4591	4943	5281	5641	5953
3917	4243	4597	4951	5297	5647	5981
3919	4253	4603	4957	5303	5651	5987
3923	4259	4621	4967	5309	5653	6007
3929	4261	4637	4969	5323	5657	6011
3931	4271	4639	4973	5333	5659	6029
3943	4273	4643	4987	5347	5669	6037
3947	4283	4649	4993	5351	5683	6043
3967	4289	4651	4999	5381	5689	6047
3989	4297	4657	5003	5387	5693	6053
4001	4327	4663	5009	5393	5701	6067
4003	4337	4673	5011	5399	5711	6073
4007	4339	4679	5021	5407	5717	6079
4013	4349	4691	5023	5413	5737	6089
4019	4357	4703	5039	5417	5741	6091
4021	4363	4721	5051	5419	5743	6101
4027	4373	4723	5059	5431	5749	6113
4049	4391	4729	5077	5437	5779	6121
4051	4397	4733	5081	5441	5783	6131
4057	4409	4751	5087	5443	5791	6133
4073	4421	4759	5099	5449	5801	6143
4079	4423	4783	5101	5471	5807	6151
4091	4441	4787	5107	5477	5813	6163
4093	4447	4789	5113	5479	5821	6173
4099	4451	4793	5119	5483	5827	6197
4111	4457	4799	5147	5501	5839	6199
4127	4463	4801	5153	5503	5843	6203

6211	6563	6907	7253	7621	8009	8369
6217	6569	6911	7283	7639	8011	8377
6221	6571	6917	7297	7643	8017	8387
6229	6577	6947	7307	7649	8039	8389
6247	6581	6949	7309	7669	8053	8419
6257	6599	6959	7321	7673	8059	8423
6263	6607	6961	7331	7681	8069	8429
6269	6619	6967	7333	7687	8081	8431
6271	6637	6971	7349	7691	8087	8443
6277	6653	6977	7351	7699	8089	8447
6287	6659	6983	7369	7703	8093	8461
6299	6661	6991	7393	7717	8101	8467
6301	6673	6997	7411	7723	8111	8501
6311	6679	7001	7417	7727	8117	8513
6317	6689	7013	7433	7741	8123	8521
6323	6691	7019	7451	7753	8147	8527
6329	6701	7027	7457	7757	8161	8537
6337	6703	7039	7459	7759	8167	8539
6343	6709	7043	7477	7789	8171	8543
6353	6719	7057	7481	7793	8179	8563
6359	6733	7069	7487	7817	8191	8573
6361	6737	7079	7489	7823	8209	8581
6367	6761	7103	7499	7829	8219	8597
6373	6763	7109	7507	7841	8221	8599
6379	6779	7121	7517	7853	8231	8609
6389	6781	7127	7523	7867	8233	8623
6397	6791	7129	7529	7873	8237	8627
6421	6793	7151	7537	7877	8243	8629
6427	6803	7159	7541	7879	8263	8641
6449	6823	7177	7547	7883	8269	8647
6451	6827	7187	7549	7901	8273	8663
6469	6829	7193	7559	7907	8287	8669
6473	6833	7207	7561	7919	8291	8677
6481	6841	7211	7573	7927	8293	8681
6491	6857	7213	7577	7933	8297	8689
6521	6863	7219	7583	7937	8311	8693
6529	6869	7229	7589	7949	8317	8699
6547	6871	7237	7591	7951	8329	8707
6551	6883	7243	7603	7963	8353	8713
6553	6899	7247	7697	7993	8363	8719

8731	8893	9091	9277	9433	9623	9803
8737	8923	9103	9281	9437	9629	9811
8741	8929	9109	9283	9439	9631	9817
8747	8833	9127	9293	9461	9643	9829
8753	8941	9133	9311	9463	9649	9833
8761	8951	9137	9319	9467	9661	9839
8779	8963	9151	9323	9473	9677	9851
8783	8969	9157	9337	9479	9679	9857
8803	8971	9161	9341	9491	9689	9859
8807	8999	9173	9343	9497	9697	9871
8819	9001	9181	9349	9511	9719	9883
8821	9007	9187	9371	9521	9721	9887
8831	9011	9199	9377	9533	9733	9901
8837	9013	9203	9391	9539	9739	9907
8839	9029	9209	9397	9547	9743	9923
8849	9041	9221	9403	9551	9749	9929
8861	9043	9227	9413	9587	9767	9931
8863	9049	9239	9419	9601	9769	9941
8867	9059	9241	9421	9613	9781	9949
8887	9067	9257	9431	9619	9787	9967
					9791	9973

Table 2 : Squares and Cubes of integers, n, where 1 ⩽ n ⩽ 200

n	n^2	n^3	n	n^2	n^3
1	1	1	37	1 369	50 653
2	4	8	38	1 444	54 872
3	9	27	39	1 521	59 319
4	16	64	40	1 600	64 000
5	25	125	41	1 681	68 921
6	36	216	42	1 764	74 088
7	49	343	43	1 849	79 507
8	64	512	44	1 936	85 184
9	81	729	45	2 025	91 125
10	100	1 000	46	2 116	97 336
11	121	1 331	47	2 209	103 823
12	144	1 728	48	2 304	110 592
13	169	2 197	49	2 401	117 649
14	196	2 744	50	2 500	125 000
15	225	3 375	51	2 601	132 651
16	256	4 096	52	2 704	140 608
17	289	4 913	53	2 809	148 877
18	324	5 832	54	2 916	157 464
19	361	6 859	55	3 025	166 375
20	400	8 000	56	3 136	175 616
21	441	9 261	57	3 249	185 193
22	484	10 648	58	3 364	195 112
23	529	12 167	59	3 481	205 379
24	576	13 824	60	3 600	216 000
25	625	15 625	61	3 721	226 981
26	676	17 576	62	3 844	238 328
27	729	19 683	63	3 969	250 047
28	784	21 952	64	4 096	262 144
29	841	24 389	65	4 225	274 625
30	900	27 000	66	4 356	287 496
31	961	29 791	67	4 489	300 763
32	1 024	32 768	68	4 624	314 432
33	1 089	35 937	69	4 761	328 509
34	1 156	39 304	70	4 900	343 000
35	1 225	42 875	71	5 041	357 911
36	1 296	46 656	72	5 184	373 248

n	n^2	n^3	n	n^2	n^3
73	5 329	389 017	111	12 321	1 367 631
74	5 476	405 224	112	12 544	1 404 928
75	5 625	421 875	113	12 769	1 442 897
76	5 776	438 976	114	12 996	1 481 544
77	5 929	456 533	115	13 225	1 520 875
78	6 084	474 552	116	13 456	1 560 896
79	6 241	493 039	117	13 689	1 601 613
80	6 400	512 000	118	13 924	1 643 032
81	6 561	531 441	119	14 161	1 685 159
82	6 724	551 368	120	14 400	1 728 000
83	6 889	571 787	121	14 641	1 771 561
84	7 056	592 704	122	14 884	1 815 848
85	7 225	614 125	123	15 129	1 860 867
86	7 396	636 056	124	15 376	1 906 624
87	7 569	658 503	125	15 625	1 953 125
88	7 744	681 472	126	15 876	2 000 376
89	7 921	704 969	127	16 129	2 048 383
90	8 100	729 000	128	16 384	2 097 152
91	8 281	753 571	129	16 641	2 146 689
92	8 464	778 688	130	16 900	2 197 000
93	8 649	804 357	131	17 161	2 248 091
94	8 836	830 584	132	17 424	2 299 968
95	9 025	857 375	133	17 689	2 352 637
96	9 216	884 736	134	17 956	2 406 104
97	9 409	912 673	135	18 225	2 460 375
98	9 604	941 192	136	18 496	2 515 456
99	9 801	970 299	137	18 769	2 571 353
100	10 000	1 000 000	138	19 044	2 628 072
101	10 201	1 030 301	139	19 321	2 685 619
102	10 404	1 061 208	140	19 600	2 744 000
103	10 609	1 092 727	141	19 881	2 803 221
104	10 816	1 124 864	142	20 164	2 862 388
105	11 025	1 157 625	143	29 449	2 924 207
106	11 236	1 191 916	144	20 736	2 985 984
107	11 449	1 225 043	145	21 025	3 048 625
108	11 664	1 259 712	146	21 316	3 112 136
109	11 881	1 295 029	147	21 609	3 176 523
110	12 100	1 331 000	148	21 904	3 241 792

n	n^2	n^3	n	n^2	n^3
149	22 201	3 307 949	175	30 625	5 359 375
150	22 500	3 375 000	176	30 976	5 451 776
151	22 801	3 442 951	177	31 329	5 545 233
152	23 104	3 511 808	178	31 684	5 639 752
153	23 409	3 581 577	179	32 041	5 735 339
154	23 716	3 652 264	180	32 400	5 832 000
155	24 025	3 723 875	181	32 761	5 929 741
156	24 336	3 796 416	182	33 124	6 028 568
157	24 649	3 869 893	183	33 489	6 128 487
158	24 964	3 944 312	184	33 856	6 229 504
159	25 281	4 019 679	185	34 225	6 331 625
160	25 600	4 096 000	186	34 596	6 434 856
161	25 921	4 173 281	187	34 969	6 539 203
162	26 244	4 251 528	188	35 344	6 644 672
163	26 569	4 330 747	189	35 721	6 751 269
164	26 896	4 410 944	190	36 100	6 859 000
165	27 225	4 492 125	191	36 481	6 967 871
166	27 556	4 574 296	192	36 864	7 077 888
167	27 889	4 657 463	193	37 249	7 189 057
168	28 224	4 741 632	194	37 636	7 301 384
19	28 561	4 826 809	195	38 025	7 414 875
170	28 900	4 913 000	196	38 416	7 529 536
171	29 241	5 000 211	197	38 809	7 645 373
172	29 584	5 088 448	198	39 204	7 762 392
173	29 929	5 117 717	199	39 601	7 880 599
174	30 276	5 268 024	200	40 000	8 000 000

Table 3 : Least primitive root r of each prime p, where 2 ⩽ p < 1000

p	r	p	r	p	r	p	r	p	r	p	r
2	1	127	3	283	3	467	2	661	2	877	2
3	2	131	2	293	2	479	13	673	5	881	3
5	2	137	3	307	5	487	3	677	2	883	2
7	3	139	2	311	17	491	2	683	5	887	5
11	2	149	2	313	10	499	7	691	3	907	2
13	2	151	6	317	2	503	5	701	2	911	17
17	3	157	5	331	3	509	2	709	2	919	7
19	2	163	2	337	10	521	3	719	11	929	3
23	5	167	5	347	2	523	2	727	5	937	5
29	2	173	2	349	2	541	2	733	6	941	2
31	3	179	2	353	3	547	2	739	3	947	2
37	2	181	2	359	7	557	2	743	5	953	3
41	6	191	19	367	6	563	2	751	3	967	5
43	3	193	5	373	2	569	3	757	2	971	6
47	5	197	2	379	2	571	3	761	6	977	3
53	2	199	3	383	5	577	5	769	11	983	5
59	2	211	2	389	2	587	2	773	2	991	6
61	2	223	3	397	5	593	3	787	2	997	7
67	2	227	2	401	3	599	7	797	2		
71	7	229	6	409	21	601	7	809	3		
73	5	233	3	419	2	607	3	811	3		
79	3	239	7	421	2	613	2	821	2		
83	2	241	7	431	7	617	3	823	3		
89	3	251	6	433	5	619	2	827	2		
97	5	257	3	439	15	631	3	829	2		
101	2	263	5	443	2	641	3	839	11		
103	5	269	2	449	3	643	11	853	2		
107	2	271	6	457	13	647	5	857	3		
109	6	277	5	461	2	653	2	859	2		
113	3	281	3	463	3	659	2	863	5		

Table 4 : $\tau(n)$, $\sigma(n)$, $\phi(n)$ and $\mu(n)$ where $1 \leqslant n \leqslant 100$

n	$\tau(n)$	$\sigma(n)$	$\phi(n)$	$\mu(n)$	n	$\tau(n)$	$\sigma(n)$	$\phi(n)$	$\mu(n)$
1	1	1	1	1	37	2	38	36	– 1
2	2	3	1	– 1	38	4	60	18	1
3	2	4	2	– 1	39	4	56	24	1
4	3	7	2	0	40	8	90	16	0
5	2	6	4	– 1	41	2	42	40	– 1
6	4	12	2	1	42	8	46	12	– 1
7	2	8	6	– 1	43	2	44	42	– 1
8	4	15	4	0	44	6	84	20	0
9	3	13	6	0	45	6	78	24	0
10	4	18	4	1	46	4	72	22	1
11	2	12	10	– 1	47	2	48	46	– 1
12	6	20	4	0	48	10	124	16	0
13	2	14	12	– 1	49	3	57	42	0
14	4	24	6	1	50	6	93	20	0
15	4	24	8	1	51	4	72	32	1
16	5	31	8	0	52	6	98	24	0
17	2	18	16	– 1	53	2	54	52	– 1
18	6	39	6	0	54	8	120	18	0
19	2	20	18	– 1	55	4	72	40	1
20	6	42	8	0	56	8	120	24	0
21	4	32	12	1	57	4	80	36	1
22	4	36	10	1	58	4	90	28	1
23	2	24	22	– 1	59	2	60	58	– 1
24	8	60	8	0	60	12	168	16	0
25	3	31	20	0	61	2	62	60	– 1
26	4	42	12	1	62	4	96	30	1
27	4	40	18	1	63	6	104	36	0
28	6	56	12	0	64	7	127	32	0
29	2	30	28	– 1	65	4	84	48	1
30	8	72	8	– 1	66	8	144	20	– 1
31	2	32	30	– 1	67	2	68	66	– 1
32	6	63	16	0	68	6	126	32	0
33	4	48	20	1	69	4	96	44	1
34	4	54	16	1	70	8	144	24	– 1
35	4	48	24	1	71	2	72	70	– 1
36	9	91	12	0	72	12	195	24	0

n	$\tau(n)$	$\sigma(n)$	$\phi(n)$	$\mu(n)$	n	$\tau(n)$	$\sigma(n)$	$\phi(n)$	$\mu(n)$
73	2	74	72	– 1	87	4	120	56	1
74	4	114	36	1	88	8	180	40	0
75	6	124	40	0	89	2	90	88	– 1
76	6	140	36	0	90	12	234	24	0
77	4	96	60	1	91	4	112	72	1
78	8	168	24	– 1	92	6	168	44	0
79	2	80	78	– 1	93	4	128	60	1
80	10	186	32	0	94	4	144	46	1
81	5	121	54	0	95	4	120	72	1
82	4	126	40	1	96	12	252	32	0
83	2	84	82	– 1	97	2	98	96	– 1
84	12	224	24	0	98	6	171	42	0
85	4	108	64	1	99	6	156	60	0
86	4	132	42	1	100	9	217	40	0

Notes

Notes